About the author

Cynthia Cockburn, a feminist researcher and writer, lives in London where she is Visiting Professor in the Department of Sociology at City University and active in the international antimilitarist network Women in Black. She is known for writings based on empirical social research, and for an approach that grounds theory in the practice of labour or political action.

She has contributed, over a quarter of a century, to the literature on gender and technology, labour process and trade unionism, and transformative change in and through organizations. Her books include *The Local State* (Pluto Press 1977), *Brothers* (Pluto Press 1983), *The Machinery of Dominance* (Pluto Press 1985), *In the Way of Women* (Macmillan 1991) and *Gender and Technology in the Making* (with Susan Ormrod, Sage Publications 1993).

Since 1995 her research has focused on gender in armed conflict and peace processes, particularly in Northern Ireland, Bosnia-Herzegovina, Israel/Palestine and Cyprus. Her most recent books are *The Space Between Us: Negotiating Gender and National Identities in Conflict* (Zed Books 1998); (co-edited with Dubravka Žarkov) *The Postwar Moment: Militaries, Masculinities and International Peacekeeping* (Lawrence and Wishart 2002); and *The Line: Women, Partition and the Gender Order in Cyprus* (Zed Books 2004).

About the book

Why do so many women organize against militarism and war? And why, very often, do they choose to do so in women-only groups? This original study, the product of 80,000 miles of travel by the author over a two-year period, examines women's activism against wars as far apart as Sierra Leone, Colombia and India. It shows women on different sides of conflicts in the former Yugoslavia and Israel, refusing racism, enmity and collective guilt, working together for peace with justice. It describes transnational networks of women opposing US and Western European militarism and the so-called 'war on terror' and its accompanying racism.

Women are often motivated by adverse experiences in the male-dominated anti-war movements, preferring to choose different methods of protest and remain in control of their own actions. But like the mainstream movements, women's groups differ. They debate pacifism – must justice come before peace? They differ on nationalism, some condemning it as a cause of war, others seeing it as a legitimate source of identity. Yet despite women's varied positionalities and perspectives on war, a coherent feminism emerges in this transnational campaigning, and it suggests to both theory and activism a radical analytical shift: we cannot understand war, nor can we effectively campaign against it, without reference to gender power and gendered violence.

Cynthia Cockburn

From where we stand: war, women's activism and feminist analysis

Zed Books
LONDON · NEW YORK

From where we stand: war, women's activism and feminist analysis was first published in 2007 by Zed Books Ltd, 7 Cynthia Street, London N1 9JF, UK and Room 400, 175 Fifth Avenue, New York, NY 10010, USA

<www.zedbooks.co.uk>

Photography by Cynthia Cockburn
Cover designed by Andrew Corbett
Set in Sabon and Gill Sans Heavy by Ewan Smith, London
Printed and bound in Malta by Gutenberg Press Ltd

Distributed in the USA exclusively by Palgrave Macmillan, a division of St Martin's Press, LLC, 175 Fifth Avenue, New York, NY 10010.

A catalogue record for this book is available from the British Library.
US CIP data are available from the Library of Congress.

ISBN 978 1 84277 820 3 hb
ISBN 978 1 84277 821 0 pb

Contents

Acknowledgements | vii

Introduction 1

Origins of the book | 2 Research approach | 3 Some concepts and theories | 5 The shape of the book | 8

1 **Different wars, women's responses** 13

'Violence came here yesterday': the women's movement against war in Colombia | 13 War against women: a feminist response to genocide in Gujarat | 23 Sierra Leone: women, civil society and the rebuilding of peace | 33

2 **Against imperialist wars: three transnational networks** . 48

Women in Black – for justice – against war | 51 Code Pink: Women for Peace | 62 East Asia–US–Puerto Rico Women's Network against Militarism | 67

3 **Disloyal to nation and state: antimilitarist women in Serbia** 79

The Federal Republic of Yugoslavia: the manipulation of national identity | 80 A feminist response to nationalism and war | 83 Feminist analysis and counter-information | 86 Addressing the deadly issues of identity and place | 88 The personal is international | 93 After war: from guilt to responsibility | 97

4 **A refusal of othering: Palestinian and Israeli women** . . . 106

The creation of Israel: 'independence' and 'catastrophe' | 106 'Facts on the ground': unilateral Israeli moves | 109 Israeli activism against the occupation | 110 Bat Shalom, the Jerusalem Center for Women and the Jerusalem Link | 112 Problems of dialogue: Palestinian perspectives | 116 Problems of dialogue: Israeli perspectives | 118 'Being women': a basis for dialogue? | 120 Within Israel: Palestinians in a Jewish state | 122 Moving beyond dialogue | 125

5 **Achievements and contradictions: WILPF and the UN** . . 132

The Women's International League for Peace and Freedom | 133 WILPF's organization and scope | 136 Carrying 'women, peace and security' into the UN | 138

Implementation: the hard road from rhetoric to practice | 143 Limitations of the institutional route | 147 A valuable lever for women anti-war activists | 152

6 **Methodology of women's protest** 156

Responsible process, minimal structure | 157 Vigilling and other street work | 160 From the schools to the law courts | 164 Ritual and symbolism | 170 The political use of silence | 172 Women's peace camps | 173 Nonviolent direct action: putting the body into play | 176 Prefigurative struggle | 178

7 **Towards coherence: pacifism, nationalism, racism**. 181

Peace, justice and solidarity | 181 National belonging and ethnic otherness | 192 Committed to creative argument | 202

8 **Choosing to be 'women': what war says to feminism** . . . 206

The valorization of everyday life | 208 The trope of motherhood | 209 Male sex/sexual violence | 212 Organizing as 'women-only' | 215 Soldiering: women who want to, men who don't | 222 A feminism evoked by militarism and war | 225

9 **Gender, violence and war: what feminism says to war studies** 231

War and security: feminists' marginal notes on international relations | 232 The sociology of war and militarism: doing gender | 235 Theory grounded in women's experience of war | 239 Masculinity and policy: an erect posture on the home front | 242 Military needs: enough aggression, not too much | 247 Three others: the woman, the labourer and the stranger | 252

Bibliography | 260

Index | 276

Acknowledgements

The research on which this book is based would not have been possible without support from six generous funding organizations. The most substantial grant came from the Joseph Rowntree Charitable Trust, and I would like to thank the trustees, and Nick Perks, the assistant secretary who fostered my project, very warmly for their support. To my surprise and delight I received a generous grant from the French foundation Un Monde pour Tous, through the friendly agency of Patrick Lescure. As in the past, the Network for Social Change trustingly backed my project, as did the Ian Mactaggart Trust, the Lipman-Miliband Trust and the Maypole Fund. My deep appreciation to all of you, and to City University London for furnishing me with an academic home for going on twenty-seven years.

This book is founded on the life experiences of countless women, submerged in war, surviving war, observing and protesting against war. Those experiences were conveyed to me, relived, analysed and theorized, in the words of more than 250 women in fifteen countries. You allowed me to interview you, or joined me in conversations, or sent me emails. Scarcely a word could have been written without you. If there's value in this book it's entirely the product of your love and labour. Its shortcomings are down to me. All of you besides gave me a heartening welcome and eased my way on long journeys. In naming you below, I want to thank you from the bottom of my heart. You are all valued friends, to each other, to myriad other women in our many and complex networks, and especially cherished by me. Thank you!

Before I start in on the long list, however, let me say first that I owe to the following shorter list special gratitude for welcoming me to their homes and continuing my education over breakfast, tea and supper: Marie-Françoise Stewart-Ebel, Indira Kajosević, Diane Cardin-Kamleiter, Joan Acker, Ann Jencks-Guy, Carme Alemany Gomez, Carmen Magallón Portolés, María Vercher, Marta Brancas, Vahida Nainar, Abha Bhaiya, Elisabetta Donini, Charlotte Browne, Mariarosa Guandalini, Anna Zoli, Patricia Tough, Lily Traubmann and Gila Svirsky. A million thanks – it made all the difference.

The following acknowledgements I have ordered in the sequence of visits in my itinerary.

In Belgium My very first interviews were in Belgium, early in 2004, where I gathered information from Edith Rubinstein, Foutoula Ioannidis and Dominique Dauby, active in Femmes en Noir groups in Brussels and Liège; Lieve Snelling and Ria Convents among women of Vrouwen in 'T Zwart in Leuven; and Fanny Filosof and Florence X,[1] among women of the distinctive Collectif Femmes en Noir. Edith Rubinstein also helped me with translation from English to French.

In Turkey I next went to Turkey, on the invitation of Sabancı University, and was guided throughout this visit, and before and since, by activist-thinker-writer-teacher Ayşe Gül Altınay to whom I owe a special debt of gratitude. She introduced me to Nadire Mater and her inspiring work, and to others in their circle of friends in Istanbul. Publishers İletişim have produced two of my books in Turkish translation. I am specially indebted to editors Tansel Demirel and Asena Günal, conversations with whom also helped this present work. I learned about Winpeace from Gönül Dinçer, Nur Bekata Mardin and Zülal Kılıç and had interesting conversations with Banu Açıkdeniz, Zeynep Kutluata and other women of BÜKAK and the Feminist Women's Circle in Istanbul. You will see that I gained a lot from meeting with Pınar Selek, Yeşim Başaran and other women of Amargi in Istanbul. I had a memorable visit to Kurdish South-East Turkey where Ayşe introduced me to Nebahat Akkoç and her colleagues in the women's association Ka-Mer in Diyarbakır, and associated women's centres in Mardin and Kızıltepe. Hilal Demir and Uğur Yorulmaz, antimilitarist activists in Izmir, kept me in touch with their bold activities by e-mail.

In the USA My several weeks in the USA in the early summer of 2004 focused mainly on the international network Women in Black, which features in chapter 2. First, in New York, I met and interviewed members of the Public Library Women in Black vigil, Indira Kajosević, Julie Finch and Pat De Angelis; and from among the Union Square vigil, Anne Wangh, Judy Solomon, Lila Braine, Melissa Jameson, Naomi Braine and Sherry Gorelick. Then, down south in the Gulf Coast WiB group, I had a chance to interview six remarkable women: Barbara Johnson, Diane Cardin-Kamleiter, Edie Daly, Jackie Mirkin, Julia Aires and Kath Madden Moxon. In Oregon I talked with Pat Hollingsworth and Yvonne Simmons about their Women in Black and WILPF groups in Eugene; with Carol van Houten of the Community Alliance of Lane County about her antimilitarist work in schools; and informally with Joan Acker and Sandy Morgen, who welcomed me to the University of Oregon. Ending up on the West Coast, I first had a meeting with Jane Welford and seven friends of Berkeley Women in Black; a helpful hour or two with Jennifer Beach of the WiB San Francisco group; and an inspiring meeting with Jane Ariel, Frances Reid, Penny Rosenwasser and Sandy Butler of Bay Area WiB. Additionally, I had valuable interviews while in San Francisco with Marcia Freedman (a founding spirit of Women in Black in Israel, currently president of Brit Tzedek), Sarah Anne Minkin (graduate student and researcher on military refusal at the University of California, Berkeley) and Terry Greenblatt (Activist in Residence at the Global Fund for Women, in San Francisco, and former director of Bat Shalom) who among other things informed me about the Palestinian/Israeli International Women's Commission (see chapter 5); Medea Benjamin of Code Pink: Women for Peace (chapter 2); and Gwyn Kirk and Margo Okazawa-Rey of the East Asia–US–Puerto Rico Women's Network against Militarism (chapter 2).

In Colombia My induction to Colombia (see chapter 1) began as I listened to presentations at the International Conference on Women against War, 9–11 August 2004, organized by La Ruta Pacífica de las Mujeres, the Alianza Iniciativa de Mujeres Colombianas por la Paz (IMP) and other organizations. Following the conference I had valuable interviews with Marina Gallego Zapatas, co-ordinator of La Ruta, and members Clara Elena Cardona Tamayo, María Eugenia Sánchez and Olga Amparo Sánchez. I also separately interviewed Rocío Pineda of the IMP, an interesting organization that features in chapter 5. I gained also from interviews with Ana Teresa Bernal of Redepaz; Leonor Esguerra of Mujeres que Crean; María Isabel Casas of the Mesa de Trabajo Mujer y Conflicto Armado; and Patricia Prieto of the Grupo Mujer y Sociedad. I also had a lively social supper with Clara Mázo, Elizabeth Sepúlveda and Olga Ramírez of Vamos Mujer of Medellín. Carmen Elisa Alvarez and Clara Elena Cardona Tamayo kindly helped me with spoken interpretation, and Isabel Ramos and Doro Marden with written translation of this case study from English to Spanish. See chapter 1 for the product of this visit.

In Spain In the autumn I went on to Spain, aware of the strong link they maintain with feminist antimilitarists in Colombia. I went first to Barcelona where I sat down with Carolina Costa, Gloria Roig, María Eugenia Blandon and Montse Cervera of Dones per Dones; interviewed feminist activists Clara Bastardes Tort and María Palomares Arenas Cabral; and learned something of Catalan feminist activism from Carme Alemany. In Barcelona and Zaragoza I interviewed four members of the collective that used to produce the journal *En Pie De Paz*, namely Carmen Magallón Portolés (now in the Seminario de Investigación para la Paz), Elena Grau, Isabel Ribera and Montse Reclusa. In Madrid I interviewed, singly or as a group, the following members of Mujeres de Negro (Women in Black) in that city: Almudena Izquierdo, Antonietta Russo, Concha Martín Sánchez, Encarna Garrido Montero, María de Mar Rodriguez Gimena, María Jose Sanz Municio and Yolanda Rouiller, together with Michelle X of Mujer Palabra. I received helpful email communications from Concha Moreno (Valencia), Leonor Taboada (Palma de Mallorca), Sofía Segura (Sevilla), Vita Arrufat Gallén (Castellón) and other women, giving information about Mujeres de Negro groups in their cities. Finally, in the Basque Country, Euskadi, I would like to thank Marta Brancas, Dominique Saillard and Idoia Romano Guridi for interviews and subsequent correspondence that were helpful in shaping my thinking on nationalism, see chapter 7. Thanks, Michelle X and Gloria Roig, for your help with language interpretation and Rosemary Perez for translation into Spanish.

In Serbia and Montenegro Of the activists of Žene u Crnom (Women in Black) in Belgrade I interviewed Staša Zajović, its heart, spirit and co-ordinator, whose writing has also been very important for me. Thanks for interviews also with Boban Stojanović, Cica (Nevzeta) Josifović, Dana Johnson, Ksenija Forca, Tamara Belenzada and Zibija Šarenkapić. I met and chatted with others there too, whom I remember as Cica, Fika, Gaga, Lilja, Melita, Miloš, Nena, Senka and Svetlana. I was able to interview Daša Duhaček, Slavica Stojanović and Jasmina Tešanović, three key women who told the inspiring history not only of Women in Black but those significant feminist partner organizations in Belgrade during the war years – the Women's Studies Centre, the Autonomous Women's Centre and Feministička 94. I benefited also from meeting, at the seminar organized by ŽuC, women of the Women's Association 'Maja' of Kravica, the Women's Association 'Podrina', 'Forum Zena' of Bratunac, the Association of Mothers of Srebrenica and Žepa, and Citizens of Žepa and Srebrenica living in Tuzla. I've gained enormously over the years (as so many of us have) from conversations and correspondence with Lepa Mladjenović, and from her stunning way with the written word. Much of what I learned in Belgrade appears in chapter 3.

In the Pacific region My contact with the East Asia–US–Puerto Rico Women's Netw ɔrk against Militarism, described in chapter 2, occurred in two phases. First, as mentioned above, while in California in May 2004 I had an interview with Margo Okazawa-Rey and Gwyn Kirk, US members and activists, to whom I owe my first introduction to this remarkable Network. Second, later that year, I was fortunate to be welcomed for six days in Manila to attend, as a researcher-observer, the Network's fifth international meeting. The Philippines Working Group of the Network hosted the meeting and several of their member organizations were present. In particular, I had a valuable opportunity to interview Aida Santos of the Women's Education, Development, Productivity and Research Organization (WEDPRO), Quezon City, and received a great deal of practical help and support from Marlea Muñez, then of WEDPRO. Linda Lampera and her colleagues of Nagkakaisang Kababaihan ng Angeles (Nagka, or United Women of Angeles) took me to visit their centre and hear about their work in the prostitution district serving the former US Clark airforce base. I was able to interview Ada Dultra Estepa of Pagkakaisa ng Kababaihan (Kaisa Ka) in the Philippine island of Mindanao; Fatima Pir Tillah Allian, of West Mindanao State University; also Zaida Torres Rodriguez and Carmen Valencia Perez from the Alianza de Mujeres Viequenses, Puerto Rico; and Terri Keko'olani Raymond of DMZ Hawai'i / Aloha Aina. Represented at the Network meeting were women of the South Korean umbrella organization SAFE Korea and some of its member groups, including Durebang (My Sister's Place), Hansori (One Voice), Women Making Peace, Peace and Human Rights Solidarity and the National Campaign to Eradicate Crime by US Troops in Korea. I greatly appreciated the chance to interview, from among the women of SAFE Korea, a group of three activists, Yu Young-Nim, Ko You-Kyoung, and Chang Hee-Won, and also help received from Elli Kim. I learned of the activity of Okinawa Women Act against Military Violence in correspondence with Suzuyo Takazato. My warmest thanks to Don Mee-Choi, Chang Hee-won and Beatriz Herrera for helping me with interpretation in some interviews.

In India My visit to India in December 2004 began in Mumbai, where I was welcomed by Vahida Nainar, chairperson of the board of the Women's Initiative for Gender Justice in Brussels, then at her home in Mumbai. With her I had several long and valuable conversations. Subsequently I was introduced by Sandhya Gokhale to members of the Forum against the Oppression of Women; by Sabah Khan to members of Aawaaz-e-Niswaan; and by Saumya Uma to women of the Women's Research and Action Group. I was able to have good long discussions with members of all three of these remarkable organizations in connection with communal violence and the International Initiative for Justice in Gujarat, described in chapter 1. My next stop was in Bangalore, where Madhu Bhushan and Celine Sugana introduced me to the work of Vimochana, Angala and the Asian Women's Human Rights Council (AWHRC) which initiated Women in Black in India, Asia and other regions of the world, particularly the global South. I enjoyed spending time with Shakun, Lakshmi and other activist women in this cluster of projects, who took me with them to the Women in Black vigil they were mounting in the city centre. Corinne Kumar, of El Taller International, Vimochana and the AWHRC, who has been a key actor in conveying the Women in Black concept worldwide, would have been an inspiring person to talk with. We were reduced to email because she was not in Bangalore at the time of my visit. I then travelled to New Delhi where I learned a great deal about women in the conflicts in Kashmir and the North East States in the course of a meeting with Meenakshi Gopinath, Manjri Sewak and others at WISCOMP (Women in Security, Conflict Management and Peace) about the organization Athwaaz and other activities in Kashmir; and interviews with Binalakshmi Nepram ('small arms' activist in North East India, writer, and editor of *Borderlines*, Journal of Ethnic Wars, Insurgencies and Peace Building), Roshmi Goswami (North-East Network), Sahbah Husain (Aman – Initiative for a Just and Compassionate Society), writer Sonia Jabbar, Syeda Hameed of WIPSA (Women's Initiative for Peace in South Asia), historian Uma Chakravarty (Delhi University). I also had informal conversations with Abha Bhaiya (who enabled me to give a public lecture and introduced me to the work of Jagori) and Urvashi Butalia (of Zubaan Women's Publishing House), and met more briefly Kamla Bhasin, Rita Manchanda and Sheba Cchacchi. Additionally, I gained many insights on the conflict in Kashmir from conversations with researcher Seema Kazi, my housemate in London during this time, and the impassioned Assabah Khan, visiting from Srinagar. My last stop-over in India was in Kolkata at the invitation of Ranabir Samaddar, director of the Manahirban Calcutta Research Group. I had the pleasure of addressing their students on the Forced Migration course and gained greatly from conversations with Paula Banerjee about her engaged research on the North East conflicts. Thanks also to Aditi Bhaduri, Asha Hans, Rajashri Dasgupta and Krishna Bandyopardhyay for helpful conversations in Kolkata.

In Sierra Leone I first heard of the Mano River Women's Peace Network (Marwopnet, described in chapter 1) when I met Rosaline M'Carthy by chance in Bogotá. It was she who welcomed me to Freetown on behalf of the Network and introduced me to some of its members and other activist women. While there I had the privilege of attending a chapter meeting of Marwopnet, and later interviewing Rosaline herself, Nana Pratt (the national focal point for the Sierra Leone chapter of Marwopnet), and members Gladys Hastings Spaine, Mabel M'Bayo, Mabell Iyatunde Cox and Princess Kawa. Agnes Taylor-Lewis talked to me both about Marwopnet and NEWMAP, the Network for Women Ministers and Parliamentarians, of which she is a member. I was lucky to be able to interview Christiana Thorpe (Forum for African Women Educationalists), whose colleague Florie Davies accompanied me on a visit to FAWE's girls' school at Grafton; Florella Hazeley ('small arms' activist in the Council of Churches of Sierra Leone); Maureen Poole (Uniform Solutions to Poverty in Security Sector Families); Memunata Pratt (who heads the Peace and Conflict Studies programme at the University of Sierra Leone); and Zainab Bangura, who is greatly respected for her role in the mobilization of women and civil society that helped to bring an end to the war in Sierra Leone. I also had helpful meetings with lawyer Yasmin Yusu-Sheriff (first vice president of Marwopnet) and Rajiv Bendre, director of the British Council in Freetown, a well-informed observer and supporter of women's activism in Sierra Leone. Altogether I received memorable friendship and co-operation here.

In Italy I visited Women in Black groups in four cities in northern Italy in May 2005. In Torino, nine women of the Donne in Nero della Casa delle Donne welcomed me, made time for me and gave me the benefit of their thoughts. They are Ada Cinato, Anna Valente, Diana Carminati, Elisabetta Donini, Giulia Daniele, Margherita Granero, Patrizia Celotto, Filomena Filippis and Valeria Sangiorgi. In Verona, at a supper meeting with several of the women of the local Donne in Nero group, around the table were: Anna Cipriani, Annamaria Romito Pacini, Mariarosa Guandalini, Rosanna Restivo-Alessi, Vanna Zamuner, Vilma Martini and Yifat (Taffy) Levav. Taffy generously helped me with interpretation. The next morning I had a long combined interview with Mariarosa and Taffy at the latter's home among the vineyards of nearby Soave. In Padova, at a meeting of DiN in the Casa della Donna, I met almost the whole group: Charlotte Browne, Gabriella Rossi, Giuliana Ortolan, Lucia Tomasoni, Manuela Carlon, Marianita De Ambrogio, Mariella Genovese, Mariuccia Giuliani and Maya Giugni. Later I sat down with Charlotte, Giuliana and Marianita for individual interviews. Finally, in Bologna I had interesting conversations, separately and together, with six DiN members: Anna Zoli, Chiara Gattullo, Gabriella Cappelletti, Lorenzina Pagella, Patricia Tough and Piera Stefanini. Luisa Morgantini, active in the Associazione della Pace and a member of the European Parliament, is a significant figure in Women in Black both in Italy and internationally. She has been an inspiration to me and to our WiB group in London since the early 1990s and in particular helped me develop relationships with Italian activists.

In Palestine and Israel Chapter 4 is based on visits to Palestine/Israel in November 2005 and March 2006. The following generously gave time for interviews. In East Jerusalem, I learned about the Jerusalem Center for Women (JCW) and the Jerusalem Link of which it is one of the partner organizations, mainly from interviews with Natasha Khalidi (director of the JCW), Amal Khrieshe Barghouti (board member of the JCW and director of the Palestine Women Workers' Society for Development) and Maha Abu-Dayyeh Shamas (board member of the JCW and director of the Women's Counselling and Legal Advice Centre in East Jerusalem, from whom I also learned about the progress of the International Women's Commission, in which she is a prime mover, see chapter 5). In Ramallah I had very productive interviews with three individual women, Nadia Naser-Najjab (Assistant Professor, Department of Education and Psychology, Bir Zeit University), Raja Rantisi (Associate Professor, Department of Language and Translation, Bir Zeit University) and Rana Nashashibi (director of the Palestine Counselling Centre in East Jerusalem). On the Israeli side of the Green Line, my account in chapter 4 of Bat Shalom's activities nationally and in West Jerusalem is based on valuable interviews with Molly Malekar (director of Bat Shalom of the Jerusalem Link), Lily Traubmann (political co-ordinator of Bat Shalom), Bat Shalom board members Aida Shibli and Khulood Badawi; board member Judy Blanc (from whom I also learned some of the history of Women in Black); also board member Debby Lerman and former Bat Shalom staff member Manal Massalha (both interviewed in London). My account of northern Bat Shalom is based mainly on interviews, while visiting Megiddo, Afula and Nazareth, with Yehudit Zaidenberg, programme co-ordinator, active members Mariam Yusuf Abu Hussein and Samira Khoury, informal talks with Aisheh Sedawi, Vera Jordan and Yael Miron, and many long conversations with Lily Traubmann. Beyond the two organizations of the Jerusalem Link, which were my main focus, I filled out the picture of women's anti-occupation activism in Israel by means of interviews with Gila Svirsky (co-founder and at that time international co-ordinator of the Coalition of Women for Peace); Rela Mazali (writer, researcher and founder of New Profile: Movement for the Civilization of Israeli Society) and Tali Lerner (currently developing New Profile's youth programme); Amira Gelblum (historian, Department of Political Science, Open University who told me about the Community of Learning Women of which she is a joint founder); and with Hedva Isachar (writer and broadcaster, author of *Sisters in Peace: Feminist Voices of the Left*), Samira Khoury (active in TANDI, the Movement of Democratic Women for Israel, as well as Bat Shalom), Sharon Dolev (formerly staff member of the Geneva Accords Campaign, active in the political party Hadash), Yehudit Keshet (co-founder of Machsom Watch), and, at the end of the alphabet, Yvonne Deutsch (a founding director of Kol Ha-Isha, the Women's Centre in W. Jerusalem).

In the UK In relation to chapter 5, I was lucky to catch both Felicity Hill and Carol Cohn on their way through London. Felicity is former director of the office of the Women's International League for Peace and Freedom (WILPF) at the United Nations in New York, subsequently a Peace and Security Adviser to UNIFEM's Governance, Peace and Security Team, and was currently Greenpeace International Political Adviser on Nuclear and Disarmament Issues. Carol Cohn is director of the Boston Consortium on Gender, Security and Human Rights and a senior research scholar at the Fletcher School of Law and Diplomacy in the USA. My account of the NGO Working Group and its efforts to achieve UN Security Council Resolution 1325 owes much to them. I've also gained some reassurance concerning my account of WILPF from advice received from Edith Ballantyne, for many years its Secretary General, and Sheila Triggs, currently UK president of the League and active besides in the London group of Women in Black. The account of 'camping' and other forms of nonviolent direct action is based on interviews with a very experienced trio, Helen John (associated first with the Greenham Common women's peace camp, subsequently with the camp at Menwith Hill, Yorkshire); Rebecca Johnson (centrally involved at Greenham, subsequently founding director of the Acronym Institute for Disarmament Diplomacy); and Sian Jones (involved with Greenham and subsequently an activist at the women's peace camp at the Atomic Weapons Establishment at Aldermaston).

Doing my desk work here in London, too, I've received plentiful help, and I'd like to thank the following. First, Andrée Michel, French activist and writer, for trusting me with her files on French women's anti-war activity. Second, a number of typists, most especially the super-skilled, speedy and perceptive transcriber Lucy Edyvean. Lucas Tobal imaginatively set up my weblog and patiently guided me in the use of the programme. Jill Small turned out time and again after her long working day to apply her astonishing competence to resolving my computer problems. Sarah Masters too saved me from computer disaster several times. This is the third book that Zed have published for me, and as always I value not only the chance to be in their exciting list of titles, but the competent and cheerful help a Zed author gets from the many individuals handling editorial, production, marketing and sales who, most unusually, choose to work as a collective, without hierarchy. Pat de Angelis in New York often contributed moral support on a transatlantic phone line. I owe a lot to my tolerant housemates, Seema Kazi, Maria Petrides and Mariangela Presti (all that undone washing-up), to my daughters Claudia Cockburn and Jess Coburn (for loads of encouragement and affirmation), to my friends in the political street choir Raised Voices (who cheerfully sing themes from my research when I transpose them into badly rhyming couplets). Finally, our local Women in Black group in London has been an unfailing source of fun, solidarity and political wisdom throughout this long project of mine. Thanks, friends!

Note

1 I use 'X' where someone has stated a preference for her surname to be withheld.

To Deniel Lois Coburn
born 27 July 2005

Yes to Peace

Introduction

§ In many countries women show a particular concern about the issues of war and peace. Opinion polls commonly reveal a gender difference, with women less inclined than men to support a war, or at least more hesitant or undecided on the issue. Women who want to actively engage in opposition to militarism and war often choose to organize separately as women. Why are these things so? What do we, as women, or as feminists, think we're doing? What is a feminist 'take' on war? To begin to sketch some answers, I draw in this book on the experience of women located in different countries at different moments in relation to armed conflict, experiencing militarization and war in a range of ways. Some of them are victims and survivors of decades of war, while some of them have seen 'hot' war only from afar. None of us, though, is ever very distant from militarization and 'cold' wars. All the women featured in the book are alike in one respect: they're not just 'peace-minded'; they've chosen to organize collective opposition to militarism and war, in one way or another.

My title, *From Where We Stand*, is chosen as having a tentative feel to it, and being open to many questions. We could unpack it a little. First, note that it's not at all the same as saying *Here We Stand* (banner in hand!). Rather, it invites the question who 'we' may be and how many kinds of 'we' may be packaged in that smallest and largest of words. It leaves unclear (I hope) how much identity may be assumed between the 'me' (the writer) in the 'we', and those others it contains, the women I'm writing about and for. 'From where' evokes a view over a changing landscape in which many things are happening, calling for interpretation. If one or other of us stood somewhere else, even a little to the side, other events would come to view and the perspective on them would be different. 'Stand' is a little too firm for my liking, but at least I hope it may suggest a useful array of possible meanings: an uncertain and temporary footing, perhaps; a geographical location relatively close to the killing, or far from it; or a social positioning that governs our chances as women, whose lives are lived also as members of a certain class or ethnic group.

Finally, I'd like to point out the incompleteness of the title, which is merely a subordinate clause of an unfinished sentence. Standing where we variously do, making sense of what we see, what then? What might we do? I want to suggest that, though the take any one of us has on war and peace is partial, many of us would like to act in concert, for a shared purpose. But what are our various motivations? Are our groups, organizations and networks alike in the way we see militarism and war? Do we (many and varied as we are) have something coherent to say about the violent past and the violent present that might contribute to a less violent future? These are questions to which I shall be able to give only cautious and provisional answers.

Origins of the book

In the mid-1990s, from my academic base in the Department of Sociology at City University, London, I started what would become an incremental research project on and among women working across nationalist divisions in Northern Ireland, Israel, Bosnia-Herzegovina and eventually Cyprus (Cockburn 1998; Cockburn and Zarkov 2002; Cockburn 2004a). Meanwhile, having started to be active in the women's movement against nuclear missiles in the 1980s, some of us in London went on to become a group calling ourselves Women in Black against War. This network had been started in 1988 by women in Israel as a movement opposing the occupation of Palestinian territories, but during the 1990s the idea of Women in Black (WiB) had spread fast and there was soon a worldwide movement of local groups opposing militarism and war more generally (see <www.womeninblack.org>). There was no central organization, but a sense of belonging was fostered by annual international conferences. We valued the exchange of experience, the warmth and the shared anger at the apparently endless and upwardly spiralling cycles of violence devastating our societies. But these conferences also showed us how various we were. If a social movement entails a shared analysis and a common goal, were we a movement at all?

I decided to look for research funding to enable me to learn more. But this study would not be just about Women in Black, I decided. One thing was already clear about WiB: for many women it's something they occasionally 'do' rather than something they permanently 'are'. Women in organizations of many varied names and purposes from time to time go out on the streets 'as' Women in Black. And a lot of women who have never heard of WiB have comparable motivations and similarly feel part of an imagined worldwide movement. So I searched for funding for a two-year study of 'women's movements against militarism and war', if not in global perspective, at least without territorial limits. A large item in my budget was travel costs. The funds enabled me, between the spring of 2003 and autumn of 2005, to travel more than 80,000 miles and make studies of women's activity in Belgium, Turkey, the USA, Colombia, Spain, Serbia, India and the Pacific region, Sierra Leone, Italy and finally Palestine and Israel. I also contribute certain insights based on our experience in England.

These twelve countries or regions are insufficient to give anything like a world picture. There are twenty times as many current or recent conflicts as I touch on here. What about Russia and Chechnya, Sri Lanka, Sudan, Afghanistan, Burma, Congo, Uganda? Each additional country study would have brought to view a substantially different conflict and a fresh kind of response by women. My coverage is sketchy, then, and what's here is in no way representative of the world as a whole. The countries, suggested by my initial reading and existing contacts, were chosen to illustrate different kinds of war and an interesting range of women's initiatives against it. The selection was designed to reveal the kind of phenomena that *can* exist in our war/anti-war universe, rather than to exhaust the range of possibilities or to sum the total.

Research approach

My aim in every country or city I visited was to meet at least one or two members of the principal organizations and networks of women opposing militarism and war, to learn their political circumstances, the nature of the violence they're addressing, their analysis of the conflict and their strategies of action. Altogether I gathered information from more than 250 women and three men. In the case of 163 of these individuals we were in situations formally characterized as an interview. My contact with the remainder was in informal conversation, group meetings and in a handful of cases I sought information by phone or email. Through them I learned about the work of ninety-one groups and organizations – sixty-three of them in some detail. I think of these groups and organizations not as a sample but as a panel, of the kind sometimes assembled for a TV show, but larger. One can pose questions to members of a panel, test ideas against their experience. Some of my panellists are in the front row, in the full brightness of the spotlights, seen clearly, heard in some detail. Others are in the second or third row, now and then contributing something to the overall story of war, the wider picture of women's responses to it. In answer to my questions women described their particular practices and forms of action, among them street protests and nonviolent direct action, mass mobilizations, campaigns of lobbying and media work, education and consciousness-raising, contact and co-operation across war-zones. (I deliberately, but perhaps arbitrarily, excluded organizations whose work was 'only' humanitarian.) I tried to grasp how each group organized and communicated, inside the country and beyond. From each individual I tried to obtain, too, a more general contextual picture of militarization and conflict in her country and of its mainstream[1] anti-war movement.

I was careful about the way I worked with the groups and individuals I visited, about my choice of questions and style of exploring them. Some said, later, that thinking out loud about their situation and practice had been helpful to them as well as me. I tried to transmit useful information from one group to another and one country to another, aware that inevitably I was part of the very international linking processes I was looking to uncover. From concept to publication, producing a book is a long, slow business. I wanted to feed back quickly into the movement the things I was learning. So I set up a website – a weblog actually – and posted there as I went along 'profiles' of the various regions and groups I visited. They comprise a volume of writing equivalent to more than a couple of books. It's my intention to leave these fieldwork reports on the website (<www.cynthiacockburn.org>) so they can be accessed by readers of the book who are looking for more detail. I also tried to spark off discussions on the weblog, to inform my writing as I went along.

As researchers we have a big responsibility, I feel, to the people who give us their time and share information with us. We need to be transparent with them about the nature of the study and the status of the particular conversation we're asking for. We should give people as much control as is reasonably possible over the public use of their words. The way I've proceeded here is to ask, before the interview begins, for agreement to take notes or make a recording.

I promised that the person being interviewed would be offered a chance to read any words and comments deriving from the interview that I might wish to make public. In this spirit, on return from travelling I immediately transcribed interviews and drafted for my informants a country or regional 'profile'. I emailed this to them – my interpretation of what I had learned from them in the light of my particular research interest. I asked them to help me work on the text until they felt comfortable with it, satisfied that it in no way misrepresented them or their circumstances. They discussed the document, individually or collectively, and proposed changes. When agreed – and this could take up to six months – I put the profile on the website. There were a very few, relatively peripheral cases where I failed in this process, where repeated requests to women I had interviewed to give me comment elicited no reply. In these cases I eventually decided (so as not to keep other participants waiting) to post the profile in the form agreed by my other informants.

Sometimes a two-step process was necessary. Where there were divergences of opinion or practice, for instance, between two or more groups in an area, it seemed best (in order to avoid creating misunderstandings or animosity between them) to return to each, first, that part of the profile concerning *them*, only later putting together the various parts, separately negotiated and agreed, for all to see simultaneously as a single profile. There was one case where I was unable to find words that could satisfy both parties to a conflictual situation, despite the care we all put into this work, and I reluctantly abandoned the material. When a first draft of the book was complete I made it available on the website and contacted all the women and groups mentioned by name in the text, asking them to do a computer search of the document for mentions of their name or the group name, and send me their views within a month. The final version responds as much as possible to their comments.

Some concepts and theories

I've deliberately avoided long and deep discussions of theory, either theories of gender or theories of war, because I'd like the book to be readable not by academics alone but by anybody who has an interest in feminism, war and peace. On the other hand, feminisms are themselves theory-based movements, and it's useful to know where a writer is coming from, how and why she's using a certain terminology.

To help me understand women's organized responses to war you'll see I've drawn on that materialist feminism, inspired by Marxist thought, for which a formative moment was the 1980s (for instance Hartsock 1985; Harding 1986). One special value in this work for me is that it never neglects the dimension of economic exploitation and relations of class, a necessary component of the multi-dimensional, holistic approach to power and violence I believe to be appropriate for any understanding of militarism and war. Another is the creative ways the work has adapted certain Marxist concepts, in particular that of alienation, and used them as tools for a feminist understanding of gender (for instance O'Brien 1981; Jónasdóttir 1994).

Also indispensable has been the concept of a sex/gender system (or gender order) as a necessary feature of all societies, and male supremacy (patriarchy) as the form in which we experience it (e.g. Connell 1987). I understand gender as a relation of power, and as something produced and reproduced in social processes. I see women, as well as men, as participating actively in, and sustaining, patriarchal power relations and thus gender hierarchy. I see men, as well as women, as damaged by the gender order we live in, and note that some men are making a bold and perceptive critique of it and opting out of its oppressive and violent practices. I take particular note of the body (as the military do), starting from a belief that, as Connell suggests, while biology is not determining, bodies do have their agency. With all its structures, chromosomes and hormones, the body is an arena, a site 'where something social happens' (Connell 2002a: 47–8). I see gender processes as both shaped by and shaping social structures, by which I mean the family for instance, but also those that seem to be (but are not) institutions purely of class and ethno-national power. In this field of militarism and war, the process of forming masculinities is specially important and this leads me to a concern with sex/sexual violence (drawing for instance on Price 2005). A few years ago such a preoccupation might have been termed 'radical feminist'. I see no contradiction in bringing these various dimensions of feminist analysis into play together, and perhaps this is a time when for many women (especially women active around issues of war) such a move will be welcome.

One development out of the materialist feminist work of the 1980s mentioned above was the notion of 'standpoint'. My choice of title, *From Where We Stand*, among all its other meanings, alludes to standpoint theory (e.g. Hartsock 1985 and 1998; Harding 1986;

Stoetzler and Yuval-Davis 2002). But we need to be careful here. We can't assume that women, even carefully specified women (white middle-class English women, Moro women of Mindanao) share a standpoint. There's a useful understanding, often associated with 'standpoint', that different meanings are made by differently positioned people, so that knowledge is not universalizable. Knowledges are 'situated' (Haraway 1991). In my usage, 'standpoints' are not individual, but generated collectively by movements. In this book I've tried to evolve from the many activist accounts I gathered, by the end of chapter 8, a sketch of a putative antimilitarist feminism which I then, in chapter 9, adopt as standpoint to obtain a gendered perspective on militarism and war.

I use the ugly terms 'positionality' and 'intersectionality' because they are unavoidable in this context (see for instance Anthias 2002; Anthias and Yuval-Davis 1992; Johnson 2005). We need 'positionality' because it lets us see and speak of the way individuals and groups are placed in relation to each other in terms of significant dimensions of social difference. (But note that I use the word 'location' to refer to another difference that emerges in these stories: women's physical or temporal proximity to or distance from violence and war.) For the purposes of this study I emphasize positioning on three dimensions of power, not only that of gender but also those of class and race. Though there are others, I suggest these three are particularly relevant when considering militarism and war. By class I mean to refer to ownership and lack of ownership of the means of production and differences in relationship to property and wealth, over which people often take up arms. Race I use as shorthand to refer to the outcome of a social process of differentiation, hierarchization and disempowerment on the basis not only of skin colour and phenotype, but also of territorial association, culture, religion, community, ethnicity and national identification. It is clearly a second key factor in war. Race is about 'foreigners'. Dealing with this dimension I often use the related terms ethnicity and ethno-nationalism.[2]

The concept of positionality is specially useful in pointing to identity (as ascribed) and the self (as experienced) as being something complex and unpredictable, since we are each positioned in more than one dimension of difference. It suggests power relations: one's positioning in terms of class, race and gender entails power or impotence relative to another. I often use the terms 'othering' and 'other' in the book.[3] In principle, the self can be brought into being in a way that suggests an on-going creative relation with the non-self. Alternatively, and all too often, the non-self is differentiated as an alien and inimical other. In being 'named', the other is simultaneously excluded or marginalized as inferior or dangerous (e.g. Connolly 1991).

'Intersectionality' is a term that highlights the way dimensions of positionality cross-cut each other, so that any individual or collectivity experiences several simultaneously. A 'woman' or 'man' is also, always (among other things), ethnically identified and a member of a given social class (and so on). But I will suggest, and this is most important to my concluding argument, that intersectionality applies not only to the experience of individuals and groups but also to *systems*. Structures and practices of economic power, 'racial'/ethno-national power and gender power intersect and are mutually constitutive. War is the most violent expression of the antagonisms they embody. The main argument of this book, therefore, is that war cannot be explained, as it normally is, without reference to gender.

The shape of the book

The early chapters of the book contain 'portraits' of particular countries, wars and organizations. The later chapters are more conceptual. I open in chapter 1 by presenting contrasted conflicts on three continents – in Colombia, India and Sierra Leone. Three women's initiatives are examined, one in each country. In Colombia the three-sided war, between leftwing guerrillas, rightwing paramilitaries and the state's army, is primarily a class war. It continues unabated. In India I look at what is by contrast an ethnic conflict, a pogrom in which Hindu nationalist extremists attacked the Muslim minority. Though the main events took place in 2002, the violence simmers on, creating tension and anxiety about a future renewal of massacre and rape. In Sierra Leone, a decade of anarchic and brutal civil war has ended, but fear of renewed violence remains. Here, in the absence of distinct class or ethnic lines of division, the part played by gender in the violence shows up with particular clarity. I show the way these conflicts have affected and continue to affect women's lives, and some very different strategies women have evolved in these contexts, looking for a way out of violence and war.

From these localized conflicts I turn in chapter 2 to the other extreme, the global 'war on terror' since 11 September 2001 that's changed (and cost) lives, heightened racism and curbed human rights. Here I introduce three transnational women's activist networks with a wide geographical reach.[4] They are Women in Black, Code Pink: Women for Peace, and the East Asia–US–Puerto Rico Women's Network against Militarism, contrasted movements responding in different ways to distressing factors in the contemporary political environment, including the thrust of corporate capital to control world markets, US militarization with a global reach in a unipolar world, and the use of self-immolation as a weapon of the desperate that targets the innocent to threaten the powerful. One feature of their environment is a mainstream anti-war movement, usually comprising an alliance between peace movements and the left.[5] The persistent masculinism of these movements has often been a factor propelling women into women-only organizing.

The women's anti-war groups I encountered tended to represent themselves as having three self-ascribed tasks. The first is to inform and educate as wide a public as possible about the gendered nature of militarism and war and the suffering, courage and achievements of women in armed conflict. Second, they must challenge the militarization of their own societies, monitor and contest their policies on war, fighting, defence policy, immigration and civil liberties. But, third, and simultaneously, they wish to foster communication, connection and solidarity between women divided by war. The spaces these lateral moves have to span are of two main kinds. The first is the physical and experiental distance between women in war-delivering and war-afflicted countries. The second is the rift opened up by war between women immediately involved, that is between those the authorities identify as 'us' and those called the 'other', the 'enemy', whether they live beyond the national borders or inside them.

In chapter 3 we see feminist anti-war activists in Serbia attempting to sustain meaningful connection with women in other parts of the former Yugoslavia in defiance of the ethnic othering perpetuated by nationalist war-makers. We see some of the moves made by women in Spain and Italy to support that work, and the way theory and practice, especially the concept of transversal politics, has evolved through such links. In the following chapter I look at the three-way relationships between Palestinian women in the occupied territories, Palestinian women citizens of Israel and Israeli Jewish women, the way they address racism, oppression and armed conflict, and the difficulties they meet in sustaining meaningful alliances as women defined (in both societies) as enemies.

In chapter 5, I describe the best-known, longest-lived and most thoroughly structured transnational women's anti-war network, the Women's International League for Peace and Freedom (WILPF). Its ninety-year lifetime enables me to review some of the early history of women's peace activism. In the last decade, WILPF has played a role at the heart of a wider and more amorphous network also described in this chapter, the mixed bunch of organizations and individuals that devised, lobbied for and obtained the landmark resolution passed by the UN Security Council on 30 October 2000: UNSC 1325 on *Women, Peace and Security*. It is a heartening example of feminist internationalism, but the story also reveals compromises involved in working at institutional level. We also see clearly in this chapter the importance to the movement of individual women, often academics, who become involved as writers and consultants.

One reason women often give for stepping out of the mainstream anti-war movement is that it frees them to make their own choices as to forms of organization and action. Chapter 6 reviews the range of kinds of structure women peace activists choose to inhabit and the organizational processes they favour. Some new and different women's organizations are introduced here. I identify some characteristic activist methods developed by women in the struggle for peace and justice – the silent vigil, for instance, camping and the use of symbolism. Particularly important for women, we see, is the principle that the means of activism should 'prefigure' the desired ends.

The question remains: do these women activists so widely scattered around the world, doing their various things, share an analysis? If we speculate that these many movements might be or might become 'a' movement, a definable current in the great river of global, social movements, how coherent is it? In chapters 7 and 8 I pick up issues I found women debating among themselves, some of which represent divergences either at a conceptual level or in practice. In chapter 7 I cluster some of these issues around the notions of 'pacifism' and 'nationalism'. Are we pacifist, and if so what does that mean? Does 'justice' take priority over 'nonviolence'? What do we think about external 'intervention'? The word 'nationalism' too was continually slipping in and out of our discussions, evoking disagreement. Is nationalism by definition a bad thing, are nation states necessary evils? Or is national identity and belonging a legitimate need, and a national 'homeland' something to which everyone has a basic entitlement? Racism entered our conversations as well. Is it unavoidably the concern of any antimilitarist, anti-war movement? And do we have a political responsibility for certain victims of racism – those whom war casts up on 'our' shores as refugees, migrants and asylum-seekers? I suggest that women of differing positionality and in diverse locations in relation to war are unlikely to agree on such issues, but having different knowledges in play need not mean incoherence. I discuss the relational skills our movements may need in order to achieve coherent dialogue without imposition of a 'line'.

Pacifism, nationalism and racism are issues addressed by the mainstream movement as well as by women. Gender seldom is. In chapter 8 I select certain gender issues I found women debating, such as motherhood, male violence and women's and men's relation to soldiering, and use these themes to explore further 'what war says to feminism'. I conclude this chapter with a formulation of the particular kind of feminism my reading of the philosophy of the many individuals and groups described in this book suggests to be characteristic of women's movements opposing militarism and war.

In chapter 9 I turn the question around and, adopting the anti-militarist feminist standpoint thus achieved, ask, 'What do militarism and war look like from here?' What's fresh about the perspective we gain from our activism? What might we want to say to war studies and the mainstream anti-war movement? I briefly enter the field of international relations and sociology, to compare mainstream and feminist understandings of militarism and war. I sketch a feminist theory of patriarchy on which many women anti-war activists implicitly or explicitly draw, and suggest that this male-dominant gender order, and in particular the proper constitution of masculinity by cultural means, are key to the reproduction of both systemic male supremacy and military capability. I give examples of this process at work in the assuring of appropriately masculine national cultures disposed to war, and the grooming of actual men for war fighting.

I conclude by noting the historical simultaneity about five thousand years ago of the emergence of economic class stratification; city and state formation involving 'racial' differentiation; and a sex/gender system characterized by male supremacy. All three developments involved coercive othering – constituting the labourer, the stranger and the woman. Their most violent expression was war, which became institutionalized in this same epoch. I suggest that still today these three systems of power relations intersect and are implicated in war-making. We're accustomed to considering war an effect of the first two, but the import of this book is that it cannot be fully explained without reference to the third. A gender analysis is an indispensable addition to the miserably inadequate tool-kit with which we currently strive to dismantle militarism and interrupt the cycle of war.

Notes

1 I use the adjective 'mainstream' here and elsewhere in the book in specific counterpoint to 'women's' or 'feminist'. For example, by 'the mainstream anti-war movement' I mean the movement, larger and broader than the women's anti-war movement, whose members are both men and women. By 'the mainstream discipline of international relations' I mean that academic discipline minus the critical feminist element within it.

2 When I use the term race it is in the understanding that it is a racist concept. Please refer to further discussion in chapter 7 [page 199] I have consciously chosen not to use quotation marks around it.

3 Henceforth I take these terms into regular usage and drop the quotation marks around them.

4 I use the adjective 'transnational' in reference to networks that have members or member organizations in three or more states (Moghadam 2005). In the main I limit the use of the adjective 'international' to describing those institutions, or their scope and practices, such as the United Nations, that involve an alliance of governments. But sometimes a more casual use of the word, along with 'worldwide' and 'global', has been unavoidable.

5 These terms will crop up often in this book. For 'mainstream' see note 1. By 'peace movement' I mean organizations, networks and alliances for which issues of militarism, war and peace are the principal focus. Some are religious. By 'left' I mean an array of tendencies, movements and parties, many of them extra-parliamentary, whose principal focus is anti-capitalist and anti-imperialist. By 'anti-war movement' I mean movements that today are commonly coalitions of the peace movement and the left. To illustrate from the UK: the big demonstration of 15 February 2003 was organized by the Campaign for Nuclear Disarmament and the Muslim Federation of Britain in alliance with the Stop the War Coalition which comprises the Socialist Workers Party, members of the Labour left and several smaller left parties. The Coalition has many other affiliated associations, including political parties and trade unions, and individual subscribers.

ONE
Different wars, women's responses

§ Armed conflict takes many forms. It may be all-out war between alliances of nation states, as in the First and Second World Wars. It may, as in the Cold War, be a stand-off between over-armed superpowers, unable to unleash their weaponry for fear of destroying themselves in destroying the other. It may be asymmetrical conflict between guerrilla forces (or 'terrorists') and a repressive power they seek to overthrow; or a war of retribution in which states with overwhelming might terrorize a weaker enemy, as in the 2001 invasion of Afghanistan to destroy the Taliban and Al-Qaeda. It may be a nationalistic project of ethnic cleansing, or spasmodic civil strife between the armed forces of class interests.

The diversity of conflicts generates a diversity of responses. And women in countries or regions caught up in armed conflict have differing scope when it comes to organizing action for peace. In this chapter we'll see three wars internal to states, but of rather different kinds. The first, in South America, is a three-way conflict, half a century in duration, in which the Colombian state army, guerrilla forces and rightwing paramilitaries fight a war with a class dimension. The second is a religious pogrom resulting in mass murder in the Indian state of Gujarat in 2002. Here the enemy 'other' is clearly seen in ethnic terms. Third, in Africa, we'll see the collapse of Sierra Leone into a decade of anarchic violence that ended in 2002. The motives in this war were obscure, but the absence of evident class and ethnic othering permits an unusually clear view of violent masculine subcultures at work. In the three countries we'll also see contrasted responses by women: mass mobilization in the first case, a panel of enquiry in the second and alternative diplomacy in the third.[1]

'Violence came here yesterday': the women's movement against war in Colombia

Some of us join a movement against war when we're jolted into an act of compassion and responsibility by something we see on TV news. But there are others among us who create such a movement because it's the only thing left to do, because violence walked into our village, our street or our home once too often. That's how it is in Colombia. The women's movement against war there is women 'coming out' in rage, rebellion and determination against fifty years of political violence that has wrecked generations of lives. You have no need of the media to tell you about this kind of violence. It is local, intimate. You can see it inscribing one new scar after another on the bodies and minds of those you love.

Since the nineteenth century there have been only two political parties of any significance in Colombia, the Conservatives and the Liberals. They have been alternating monopolies of power, whose rivalry has divided the country as effectively and as violently as if they had been warring ethnic groups. Peasants, workers, resources and territories were divided and recruited by the Liberal and Conservative elites for their conflict. Progressive movements trying to cut through this clientilism were wiped out (González 2004).

The outbreak of two decades of struggle, termed 'La Violencia', began in 1948 with the assassination of a popular leftwing Liberal leader Jorge Eliécer Gaitán (Sánchez and Meertens 2001). By the 1960s a large-scale leftwing guerrilla movement was active, spurred by poverty, gross inequality, the exclusive nature of the political elite and continuous stalling by successive governments on the crucial issue of land reform. The strongest and most widely known guerrilla force was, and remains, the FARC (the Fuerzas Armadas Revolucionarias Colombianas or Revolutionary Armed Forces of Colombia, associated with the Communist Party, formed in 1964). The guerrillas built support for their social and economic programmes in areas of the country where capitalist exploitation of workers and peasants was giving rise to the greatest resentment. Unfortunately, they funded their organizations by extortion, kidnapping and (increasingly today) 'taxes' on the production, processing and sale of cocaine, and in doing so lost their political credibility.

The government's armed forces, intent on finding and eradicating the guerrilla movements and suppressing popular discontent, have killed, imprisoned and tortured tens of thousands. The state's inability to uproot the armed fighters led wealthy landowners, the business class and the drug traffickers to raise and fund their own armies, shadowy militias, now grouped under a single association of paramilitaries, the AUC (Autodefensas Unidas de Colombia,

United Self-Defence Forces of Colombia). They have been active in both rural and urban areas, battling the guerrillas for control of their territories. Their strategy is to attack guerrilla bases, real or imagined, cordoning, massacring and expelling civilian communities. They contain many criminal elements, are deeply involved in narcotics, and are known to receive the tacit support of elements in the state military.

For Colombian men it's difficult to avoid bearing arms. Poverty, lack of prospects, fear for their families and the need for 'protection' drive them into the dangerous embrace of one side or another. Necessarily, many Colombian men have been brutalized by their involvement in fighting. It starts early. More than 11,000 children are enrolled into guerrilla and paramilitary units (Human Rights Watch 2004a). But women fight too. According to the AUC, women constitute 12 per cent of their ranks. The estimate for FARC is as high as 40 per cent.

The government of the USA compounds the violence in Colombia. Its triple agenda is securing the region against leftwing insurgency, protecting US oil and other business interests and stemming the flow of narcotics to US markets. In 2004, the year I visited Colombia, it donated $680 million in aid, putting the country among the top five in the world in terms of receipt of US military assistance (Human Rights Watch 2004b). US Southern Command has 1,500 military personnel in the country. Its approach to the narcotics problem involves programmes of fumigation from the air that destroy, along with coca plantations, subsistence crops and people's health. US policy favours rightwing Colombian administrations such as that of the current president, Álvaro Uribe, a hardliner heavily criticized by local and international human rights organizations. Uribe took Colombia into Bush's Coalition for the invasion of Iraq. Since 11 September 2001, US official statements have rhetorically linked FARC with Al-Qaeda and encouraged the view that terrorism in Colombia is yet another legitimate target in the international 'war on terror' (Tate 2004).

The effect of war on everyday life and on women In the last ten or fifteen years, despite a series of peace negotiations between the government and several of the armed actors, the lives of ordinary Colombians have become even less secure. During the 1990s the annual number of violent deaths varied between 25,000 and 30,000, representing a national rate of 80 per 100,000 inhabitants, one of the highest in the world. An estimated 13 per cent of these were political killings of, overwhelmingly, civilians (Meertens 2001). Torture and mutilation remain commonplace and hundreds are held hostage. Sexual violence against women is endemic, used by all three armed actors to punish women for associating with 'the wrong side', or to punish enemy men. Most cases go unreported. But in the city of Medellín alone in the period 1995 to 2001, 3,486 instances of sexual violence were reported. In 1,785 of these the aggressor was not known to the victim and it is believed that many of them were politically motivated rapes, a retaliation by one armed group against another (Gallego Zapata 2003). Many women have been tortured and killed in an obscene and clearly misogynistic manner. Women are often kidnapped into sexual servitude and forced to do domestic labour for guerrillas or paramilitaries. Contraception is difficult to obtain, and abortion is illegal. The danger of travelling to hospital and lack of facilities in rural areas mean women must often give birth at home, with resultant deaths. Donny Meertens, a feminist academic at the National University, explains:

> Whereas earlier traditional power-holders – including guerrillas in their old strongholds – could offer some protection to their local population, the present frequent power-shifting renders this nearly impossible. Protection is replaced by terror as the most easily available mechanism for obtaining popular quiescence. All armed combatants understand territoriality as a zero-sum game in which no neutral space exists, and no room for negotiated solutions is available. The civil population is caught in the paranoiac logic of '*si no estas conmigo, estas contra mi*' (if you are not with me, you are against me) …
>
> In a situation where it is not safe to assume any responsibility nor to make any accusation, the only way to refer to acts and perpetrators of violence is in a neutral form: *violence came here yesterday*, as if it were an autonomous force and not a human act. (Meertens 2001: 38)

Increasingly, in many areas, the only response left to ordinary people is to abandon their homes. Colombia has the world's largest internal displacement crisis after Sudan. In the three years to 2005 alone, more than 3 million people, over 5 per cent of the population, were forcibly displaced because of the armed conflict (Human Rights

Watch 2006). These IDPs gather in vast precarious settlements on the edge of towns and cities. They are disproportionately women. Many are heads of households. Of those, many are widows of men killed in the conflict. Maintaining the primary bonds of family and community was the women's role, so women experience their sundering even harder than men. But they're quicker and better than men in adapting to the new circumstances, learning how to deal with the institutions and inventing ways of keeping themselves and their families fed (Meertens 2001). The war pursues displaced Colombian women even into the cities. The armed actors control many urban areas, policing women by rape, carrying out exemplary assassinations of women leaders, dictating moral norms – even threatening girls with death for sporting pierced navels or drop-waist jeans.

Partly as a result of the conflict, the new Colombia is a nation of city-dwellers. Migration from rural areas to towns and cities began in the 1970s and today 70 per cent of the population is urban. The country has a wealth of natural resources, yet 60 per cent of Colombians live in poverty, while some are super-rich. In matters of health and hunger the country is more comparable to Africa than to the rest of Latin America. Added to the material immiseration, many women, men and children live continually with the memory of dead and 'disappeared' loved ones, and a terrible nostalgia for an irrecoverable place and time.

The women's movement against war in Colombia There's a long history of peace negotiations in Colombia. Successive presidents have swung between a maximalist concept of peace, with social and economic changes under discussion, and a minimalist agenda of agreement to disarm particular groups in exchange for electoral representation. Neither approach has succeeded. Until recently, civil society has been excluded from these official peace processes. Indeed, Colombian civil society has scarcely existed apart from those civil organizations that are fronts for armed interest groups. But in the early 1990s social mobilization for peace took off, first in war-ravaged areas like Urabá and Magdalena Medio. Gradually, more social sectors and more regions became involved. A Committee for the Search for Peace was formed and the Catholic Church set up a National Conciliation Commission (Rodriguez 2004). One important initiative, in 1993, was the forming of Redepaz, a National Network of Initiatives for Peace and against War, which, in October

1997, organized a national 'Mandato', a referendum which generated over 10 million votes for peace – more than the combined votes for all candidates in the previous presidential election. A permanent Civil Society Assembly for Peace was formed in 1998, and in 1999 mass demonstrations around the country brought out an estimated 8 million people under the slogan 'No Más' (No More) (ibid.).

These civil society initiatives have involved both women and men. But, recently, women's organizations with a gender analysis of war have gained in significance. So much so that this emergence of women in organized opposition to war was described to me by Olga Amparo Sánchez, an academic feminist and anti-war activist, as the third of three big leaps forward for women in Colombia, on a par with winning the right to vote fifty years ago and achieving a reform of the Constitution in 1991. The logic of the movement lies in the reality of Colombian life. Women are raped and abused by the men of all sides of this conflict. The sustenance of everyday life, especially for indigenous women and peasant women, is made perilous or impossible by the operations of the armed actors. It's not surprising if women are sometimes pushed by their circumstances across a threshold, the line that separates passivity and fear from courage and resistance. In many parts of the country, male leaders of human rights and peace organizations have been assassinated or disappeared. Class-based workers' and peasants' movements have been repressed or irredeemably corrupted. Women and women's organizations are therefore among the few surviving bearers of any type of democratic demands. Increasingly, they are bringing together issues that used to be the domain of separate NGOs; on the one hand those of human rights and on the other those of peace. As Patricia Prieto, of the Grupo Mujer y Sociedad (Women and Society Group) said to me, in interview: 'It's on women's shoulders. They are holding things together. They are the weavers and maintainers of the social fabric.'

La Ruta Pacifica de las Mujeres The largest and internationally best-known women's organization for peace in Colombia, formed in the mid-1990s, is La Ruta Pacifica de las Mujeres por la Negociación Política de los Conflictos (Women's Peaceful Road for the Political Negotiation of Conflicts).[2] It's an alliance of more than 300 organizations and groups of women in eight regions, among them several substantial projects such as the Casa de la Mujer (the Women's

House) in Bogotá, Vamos Mujer (Women Let's Go) in Medellín and Mujeres que Crean (Creative Women), also in Medellín. These and other member NGOs represent and include women of many specific 'identities': women of the tribes of indigenous peoples of Colombia; Afro-Colombians whose presence derives from the slave trade; young women; peasant women; women of the urban poor; displaced women. Membership is also open to individuals.

The central office of La Ruta Pacifica is in the capital, Bogotá, but they also have 'regional coordinations' with street addresses in several other towns. The network is managed through monthly meetings of the regional coordinators. Communication is mainly by phone. Although email is used, and they have a website (<www.rutapacifica.org.co>), they can't lean heavily on the Internet as an organizing tool because many of their constituent women and groups lack computers and Internet access.

Their principal leaflet introduces La Ruta Pacifica as:

> a feminist political project, national in character, working for a negotiated end to armed conflict in Colombia and to render visible the effects of war in the lives of women. We declare ourselves to be pacifists, antimilitarists and builders of an ethic of nonviolence in which the fundamental principles are justice, peace, equality, autonomy, freedom and the recognition of otherness.

They describe their politics as follows. First and foremost, peaceful and antimilitarist resistance 'that redeems the sacred value of life and thence of the "everyday", of sensibility, the respect for difference, solidarity and sisterhood'. They stress dialogue at various levels, seeking local (both urban and rural) and regional dialogue within the populations close to the armed conflict, and also women's active participation in the national processes of negotiation leading to a peaceful route out of conflict. They call for a culture of nonviolence and co-existence. They use 'international human rights', especially women's human rights, as a rallying point. They demand processes of memory, truth, justice and reparation because only such processes 'will permit the recovery of hope and the process of reconciliation in our country'.

La Ruta Pacifica are more unequivocally pacifist than most other women's NGOs in Colombia. They call for the demilitarization of civil life and are uncompromising in their rejection of a resort to arms on whatever pretext. In Colombia almost everyone in civil society condemns the mercenary and brutal paramilitaries. Some might excuse the state's use of force, due to its electoral legitimacy. Yet others would excuse the violent actions of the guerrillas, on grounds of their proclaimed programmes for social and economic reform. La Ruta Pacifica are women who no longer believe the armed conflict can end capitalist exploitation of the poor, and make no exceptions in the name of 'just wars'. Their political writing, however, shows that La Ruta Pacifica's analysis of Colombia's wars is holistic, continuing to encompass more than the gender dimension. They link peace with the internationally defined rights of the human being, as well as those of women. They denounce the multinationals for 'economic genocide' and for exploiting Colombia's rich bio-diversity and natural resources. They call on Colombian factory- and landowners to take responsibility for those causes of conflict in which they are implicated, to support economic redistribution and involve themselves in the movement for peace. They write and speak about environmental destruction and sustainable development, using the terminology of eco-feminism. They speak of the challenge of 'constructing citizenship and democracy' while conflict continues.

La Ruta Pacifica are also more explicitly feminist than some other women's organizations in Colombia. They call feminism and pacifism their two 'bulwarks' (baluartes). They are explicit in condemning violence against women whether domestic or military, and in affirming women's sexual and reproductive rights. 'We say "no" to domestic slavery, to the intervention of the armed actors in private and emotional life; "no" to using women's bodies as booty of war (botín de guerra).' Constituting its membership as 'women', María Eugenia Sánchez told me, was a conscious decision in La Ruta Pacifica. 'It's a political choice to be a women's organization, it's not *exclusion*.' The choice is theoretically grounded. Patriarchy and patriarchalism are concepts the group use without hesitation. This distinguishes them from the mixed-sex peace organizations, some of which are in fact affiliated to La Ruta. The latter contain many women members, some of whom participate as individuals in La Ruta's activities, though the organizations as a whole do not share its gender analysis.

A slogan used by La Ruta Pacifica from their very first action in 1996 was a conscious echo of the women's strategy against war in Aristophanes' play *Lysistrata*, written 2,400 years ago. They said,

'No parimos hijos ni hijas para la guerra' ('We will not give birth to sons and daughters for war'). It was the idea of Rocío Pineda, one of the founding members of La Ruta. (We shall meet her again in chapter 6 in connection with the Iniciativa de Mujeres por la Paz.) Rocío wrote a startling article on these lines in 1997 (Pineda 2003). She quotes Lysistrata's words to one of the military commanders in Aristophanes' play: 'Look: when we are spinning, if the skein gets tangled we take it off the spindle, we tease the threads first this way, then that way. If you let us, we'd deal with this war in the same kind of way, sending ambassadors to one side and the other' (ibid.: 68).

In this article, Rocío challenges women's loyalty to their men. She cites the 30,000 violent deaths in Colombia during the preceding twelve months. She invites women to question themselves: who are these men we love? Whose are these bodies that we desire, eroticize? What were they doing just before they made love to us? How can we take into our arms, she asked, someone who's killed, who's left some child fatherless? She told me, looking back on those days: 'It was possible to think this way, then. To think: if we want to, women can stop war. Even if weapons are strong. We can simply refuse to make love with men who carry guns, we can refuse to conceive children for them. This is a source of power that women have. Why not use it? Then we would have no more young men for militarism to recruit.'

'No parimos' ('we won't give birth') early became, and still remains, an important slogan for La Ruta Pacifica. In that initiating moment, Rocío had meant it not merely as a slogan but as a strategy. But, she says now, philosophically, it's hardly surprising it didn't catch on. 'To tell women not to make love with men, that's a highly irreverent and non-respectable idea in any society.' All the same, I was struck by Olga Amparo Sánchez, in her talk at our conference, describing patriarchalism as 'a relation in which women's love, freely given, is exploited by men'. She was quoting Anna Jónasdóttir (Jónasdóttir 1994). This seemed to me a sign that Lysistrata-thinking is still alive in La Ruta Pacifica.

What most characterizes La Ruta, though, is their extraordinary strategy of mass mobilizations, in which women travel in large numbers from all over the country to bring solidarity to women in a given region. Their first action was a national mobilization in 1996 that transported more than 2,000 women in forty coaches from all over Colombia to the desperately war-torn area of Urabá. It was the first time Colombia, in all its history, had seen women in such numbers taking a political initiative in the absence of men. The mobilization to Urabá was an act of solidarity with women who had survived massacres in which many of them had lost husbands, partners and children. Official information suggested that a lot of these women had been raped in the course of those events. These atrocities galvanized a handful of women activists, who felt they had to 'do something'. They chose 25 November, the international day of action against violence against women, for a 'convergence' on Urabá.

Women were at first afraid at the prospect of this risk-laden project, involving travel through disputed territories. Urabá was an ultra-violent area. For many of the participants it would be more than a forty-eight-hour journey. For many it meant going against their family's wishes. And for some it would be the first journey of their lives out of their own locality. Each woman took a decision for herself whether or not to join the action, talking through their fear in preparatory workshops all over the country. Later, many felt these workshops had been as life-changing as the journey itself. Over a period of ten years La Ruta have organized a sequence of symbolic acts of solidarity of this kind, building a sense of connectedness between women all over Colombia.

The women have given a lot of thought to the deployment of symbols in all of their actions – planting seeds, weaving cloth, using light and colour with meaning. They are consciously deconstructing the pervasive symbolism of violence and war and substituting a new visual and textual language, with creative rituals and other practices that 'recover what women have brought to the world'. (I discuss symbolism as a political methodology further in chapter 6.) At the same time, La Ruta are immensely practical. Each activity is painstakingly prepared in a process that is essentially feminist and formative. Each results in a statement for issue to the media, setting out its intentions and the women's principles, hopes and demands. The persistent theme of La Ruta Pacifica and other women's initiatives for peace has been the recovery of 'everyday life' – expelling violence from the home and the community. One mobilization, for example, took 3,500 women in ninety-eight coaches to Putumayo on a 'Journey of Solidarity with Women of the South'. Putumayo is a coca-growing area, terribly afflicted by the fumigation policy sponsored by the USA's anti-narcotics programme under Plan Colombia. 'For the demilitarization and recovery of civil life', they wrote on their banners. 'La fumigacion = la miseria.'

La Ruta's videos of these massive woman-to-woman pilgrimages leave no doubt of the extraordinary innovation they represent, and the great warmth and optimism they generate. Indeed, the odd thing about Colombia is that, while you know it's scarred by violence and suffering, you're immediately attracted by both its stunning physical beauty and the warmth and humour of its people. In my interview with María Isabel Casas, of La Mesa Mujer y Conflicto Armado (Working Group on Women and Armed Conflict), she told me: 'I love Colombia as though it were a person … Colombia's crazy. It's a combination that's difficult to explain. From outside, people see us as a lot of crooks and killers. And it *is* a murderous place. It's sadistic. But it's also a creative place. Colombia is tender. Colombia is passionate. I can love in Colombia. We can dance and enjoy friends … [But] everything that's beautiful here is being killed. What we're defending is a very special life energy. They're going to do away with it. So many people are leaving. We're losing our vital energy. And what's being killed isn't just bodies, it's all the wealth of a diverse culture. This country gives me so much and I want to give something back, to help towards a solution.'

War against women: a feminist response to genocide in Gujarat

In February 2000, in the Indian state of Gujarat, a segment of the majority population, proclaiming Hindu religious and national identity, committed genocidal acts against the minority identified as Muslims, with active support from the authorities. More than 2,000 people were murdered, overwhelmingly from among the Muslim community. Hundreds of thousands were driven from their homes, 113,000 finding refuge in relief camps. An estimated 38,000 million rupees-worth (£500 million) of Muslim property was destroyed, including 1,150 hotels burned in Ahmedabad city alone, 1,000 trucks burnt and 250 mosques destroyed (*Communalism Combat* 2002).

This spasm of nationalist violence, though shocking, did not really come as a surprise. The ethnic partition of India, consequent to the end of British rule, was accompanied by extreme and protracted violence between Hindus, Sikhs and Muslims. The transfer of population between the successor states was massive, yet not total: many Muslims remained in India, where today they constitute a minority of 13 per cent, relatively poor, marginalized and politically under-represented. In the on-going cold war between India and Pakistan, Indian Muslims have always tended to be both hostage and scapegoat, represented as inspired by, or even agents of, the 'enemy' state. Uma Chakravarty told me how, especially in the light of the nuclear arms race between the neighbouring countries, 'communalism, militarism and patriarchy fall into a common frame of reference for some of us – the discourses can't really be kept separate'.

From the late 1980s, Indian Muslims were increasingly threatened by a growing Hindu rightwing movement seeking political power. Hinduism is in principle a loose combination of diverse beliefs and practices, and is not derived from authoritative texts. However, a Brahminical (upper caste) and patriarchal Hindutva culture, embodying an aspiration to an ethnically pure Hindu nation, was spreading in the majority population. It was led by the Sangh Parivar, a movement that includes the Rashtriya Swayamsevak Sangh (RSS), an ideological institution of the Hindu right; the Vishwa Hindu Parishad (VHP), a Hindu religious order, with an outspoken youth wing, the Bajrang Dal; and the Bharatiya Janata Party (BJP) the political arm of the Hindutva movement (Bose 1999).

Between September and November 1989, a wave of anti-Muslim violence inspired by the Sangh Parivar afflicted Northern India. On 6 December 1992, a mob of Hindu extremists, apparently with official sanction, demolished a 464-year-old Muslim holy place, the Babri Masjid mosque, to recover what they claimed to be the site of an earlier Hindu temple at Ayodhya. This evoked widespread triumphalism in Hindu communities throughout India, while Muslim communities and organizations, as well as numerous human rights organizations, women's groups and progressive political parties, massively protested. Many died in the ensuing violence (Bose 1999). In the elections of 1995 the Hindu nationalist BJP gained political control in Gujarat state and three years later won partial power at national level, entering a coalition government. Many Indian democrats already believed that Congress had betrayed the officially secular nature of the Indian state. Now remaining constraints on the Hindutva movement were removed.

After the demolition of the Babri Masjid, squads of Hindu activists had set about constructing a Ram temple at the Ayodhya site. In late February 2002, a train carrying many such 'kar sevak' volunteers to Ayodhya had acted aggressively towards Muslims at stations along the way. On 27 February, as the Sabarmati express made its return journey, an incident occurred at Godhra, in Gujarat, in which one carriage of the train burned and fifty-nine people died of asphyxiation. Despite the lack of clear evidence, and in the absence of proper investigation, the rumour quickly spread that this was ethnically motivated murder by Muslims. Influential politicians at both national and state level implied this to be so, and some suggested the hidden hand of 'terrorists' from Pakistan. Their statements appeared to predict and, worse, to legitimate violent reprisals against Indian Muslims (Varadarajan 2002).

The pogrom in the state of Gujarat occurred in the three days following the incid nt on the Sabarmati express train. Political leaders holding various positions in the Gujarat ministries and bureaucracies, deeply penetrated by the Sangh Parivar, were actively involved in promoting the violence. In an article 'When Guardians Betray', Teesta Setalvad documented many instances of the police leadership doing the bidding of the RSS and VHP, and described how they had packed the force with Hindutva supporters and penalized officers who defended Muslims (Setalvad 2002). The Indian state itself appeared to be complicit in the carnage, at times through active involvement, and at times by turning a deaf ear to pleas from the victimized community. The national administration was slow and ineffective in its interventions. Three days elapsed before a detachment of the Indian army was sent in, by which time the worst was over.

Although the massacre was widely represented as a backlash against the incident on the train, there was evidence that it had been planned long before. The mobs carried lists of Muslim properties obtained from a survey conducted by the local authorities. Swords were widely used by the killers, and these, together with trishuls (iconic three-pointed spears) and other Hindutva paraphernalia, had been assembled and distributed in advance. Cans of petrol and gas cylinders for torching properties and people were widely available. In short, it was a well-planned pogrom, consciously pursued by organizations of the Hindu right with the connivance of state and central government (Varadarajan 2002).

The mainly Brahmin Hindutva ideologues had successfully co-opted Hindus of all castes, and many Sikhs, Jains and Buddhists, into their notional Hindu nation. While Christian communities were threatened, it was principally Muslims they identified as 'other'. On the other hand, many secular and moderate Hindus, and also some women and men from tribal, Dalit (Untouchable) and other non-Muslim communities, were appalled by the upsurge of fascism. Among the many civil society organizations that responded to the massacre were women's organizations. Most contributed humanitarian help, but some also campaigned for justice, raising issues of women's human rights in and after armed conflict. One investigative study, published as early as 16 April, was undertaken by a panel of six women sponsored by the Citizens' Initiative, Ahmedabad. They concluded that the sexual violence in the pogrom was being 'grossly underreported' (Women's Panel 2002: 2). In May 2002, three months after the massacre, women's groups working in Gujarat took the matter further, establishing a project, the International Initiative for Justice in Gujarat (IIJG), to address from a human rights perspective the massive sexualized attack on women. Key actors in this were two Mumbai-based women's groups, the Forum against the Oppression of Women and Aawaaz-e-Niswaan (Women's Voices), who mobilized a number of other women's organizations.[3]

Founded in 1980, the Forum is the oldest feminist group in Mumbai and has its origins in the movement against rape, to which they brought a totally fresh analysis, representing sexual violence as a relation of power, of patriarchy operating through state, communal, class, caste and gender structures. They challenged the inadequacies of the law, the regime of impunity that protected the police and the powerful, and the communal cultures of honour and shame that placed blame on the victim. They've always tried to create spaces within the women's movements for women from marginalized sections, be they tribal women, women from Muslim communities or women who identify as lesbians. Forum are an activist group of between twenty and twenty-five women, mainly of Hindu background, strongly secular in their politics. They are mostly educated women, with full-time jobs of various kinds, such as lecturer, engineer, architect and doctor. Some work in NGOs. They are an open group, with no office, no full-time workers, no regular funding. They say of themselves:

> Our desire to be accountable to our own commitment and thought process was the reason we maintained our autonomy from any

> political party or funding-related logistics. This has helped us take up without hesitation issues that deeply concern us – be it the question of sexual minorities' rights or demanding gender-just laws which would not be confined by religion, caste or sexual orientation. (personal communication by email)

Aawaaz-e-Niswaan was formed in 1987. Their membership was, and is still, women mainly of Muslim background and their activism concerns the rights of Muslim women – though, like the Forum, they prefer not to stress cultural identity. They told me: 'We often have to spend fifteen minutes explaining we're a feminist organization, not a Muslim one.' At the start, Aawaaz were unfunded and unregistered, 'an informal space'. Today they have more than a thousand members, with between fifteen and twenty women attending the regular Saturday meetings and a wider circle participating in campaigns.

The women of Aawaaz-e-Niswaan both provide a service and work on campaigns and advocacy. They see their organization as an 'intellectual space in which we can clarify our politics'. They conduct campaigns (for instance, against dowry deaths and police violence) in a predominantly Muslim community that's deeply conservative, where many women wear the burkah and are in purdah, and unhesitatingly raise issues that no one else in the community cares or dares to address, such as child marriage, marital rape, divorce and the rights of sex workers. One activist, Akeela, told me: 'Talking about sexuality is important for us. There are very strong patriarchal controls on sexuality. It's so personal. But in Aawaaz-e-Niswaan we see control of sexuality as bondage of the person, her mind and body. Our thoughts are under attack. We have to confront it as part of our feminism. '

Forum and Aawaaz-e-Niswaan have worked together on various issues at different times. In 1992–93, during the riots that followed the Babri Masjid incident, there was violence by Hindutva extremists in Mumbai, as elsewhere. The Muslim areas were under curfew. The women of the Forum were at this moment driven seriously to confront the fact of their (mainly) Hindu background and used the mobility that being Hindu gave them in order to reach out to different parts of the city. The two organizations combine different strengths and skills in working together. Forum women have the advantage of higher education in the English language and skills of

THE CULTURE OF
INTOLERENCE
KARNATAKA
LAND OF

The pogrom against Muslims in the Indian state of Gujarat in 2002 was deeply gendered. The women's association Vimochana in Bangalore, like the Forum and Aawaaz-e-Niswaan in Mumbai, point up the links between male violence against women in the home, at community level and in the state and international relations. Here they mount a Women in Black vigil on the steps of the civic centre.

communicating, while Aawaaz have stronger links to the grassroots, and particular insight into problems of the Muslim community. Sabah Khan said: 'Aawaaz has learned a lot from Forum, but at the same time there have been instances when we have had to sit and explain things. The radical politics of Forum enriches our understanding and fieldwork. We have a lot of love and respect for them. Whenever we've needed help they've been there for us. Even though they have no funding, they sometimes contribute money from their own pockets. They've always ensured we didn't die. It's a real commitment they have.'

The trust between the Forum and Aawaaz was the sturdy bridge that carried the IIJG project. The coalition they assembled for this purpose decided on a three-fold strategy. They would bring to bear *feminist knowledge* about sexual violence in relation to reactionary nationalisms. They would take a *juridical approach*, relating the facts on the ground to legal statute, which would mean including lawyers in the panel. And they would *internationalize* the inquiry. By May 2002 it was clear that the Indian legal system was not going to deliver justice to the Gujarat victims. The women's hope was that by invoking international law and bringing international pressure they might shame the Indian authorities into action.

Working from a preliminary list of thirty, they assembled a panel of nine women with highly appropriate experience, including lawyers, writers, academics and campaigners from several different countries.[4] Although the panel was carefully selected to draw women from three continents, six countries and a variety of cultures, they steered a careful course in conceptualizing this composition. In their report they acknowledged their individual positionality but they took care not to label themselves according to 'identity'. Neither did they collapse the group into political unanimity. Instead, they emphasized a precisely defined common value, demonstrating a clear feminist standpoint. They wrote:

> The feminists who form the IIJG come from different locations, in terms of their race, class, ethnic origin, religion and other status; they are all women, located within the specific nexus of power in relation to their subject positions. Without an assumption of commonality of all positions on social and political issues, they stand together as a community of feminists from across the world who refuse violence and discrimination on the basis of race, religion

and other identity-based differences and who believe in justice and human dignity for all. (IIJG 2003: 142)

The coalition set about obtaining funding and preparing a dossier of existing information about the pogrom. The nine panellists assembled in Mumbai in December 2002 and, after a briefing, separated into three groups of three, each going out to gather testimonies from survivors in separate areas of Gujarat. They visited many sites of violence and relief centres, and had contact with forty-one organizations, meeting 181 women and 136 men, who gave evidence about incidents of violence occurring in eighty-four different urban areas and sixty-six villages in seven districts of Gujarat (ibid.: 7). The Forum, Aawaaz and other local organizations provided organizational support, fielding bilingual note-takers, transcribers and interpreters.

The investigation by the IIJG bore out the facts already publicized about the pogrom, the deaths, the destruction of property and the complicity of the state. But it produced more and detailed evidence of the extent to which communal violence had been gendered and its violence sexual. Men had goaded each other to action with taunts of effeminacy. Women's testimonies revealed 'the specific targeting of women, as part of a conscious strategy to terrorize the Muslim population of Gujarat'. Sexual violence had been used 'as an engine of the mobilization of hatred and destruction … the sheer magnitude of the trauma recounted by women even nine months after the violence was overwhelming' (ibid.: 11).

The panel heard first-hand evidence of multiple instances, not only of rape and gang rape of women, but also of the insertion of iron bars and swords into the vagina, the cutting open of the belly of pregnant women to extract the foetus, cutting off of breasts and mutilation of genitals, and rapists declaring the intention of inseminating women with 'Hindu' offspring. Men in the mob were everywhere taunting and molesting women, seizing them and stripping them of their clothes. Even police officials were exposing their penises to terrorize Muslim women and humiliate Muslim men. In many cases these acts were done publicly and repeatedly in front of family members and children. 'There were many women bleeding, injured, naked. Many women had bite marks on their breasts … women were raped with wooden rods,' a witness said (ibid.: 127).

The panel concluded 'the woman's body was a site of almost

inexhaustible violence, with infinitely plural and innovative forms of torture'. But, worse, these acts were in many cases only 'the torturous prelude to killing, often by torching the raped woman alive or throwing her to a fire'. Women's bodies were in many cases deliberately rendered unrecognizable to make legal redress or retribution less likely. The fact that many raped women died, and the reluctance of surviving women to speak of their ordeal, made it impossible to establish numbers. But it's certain that many hundreds of Muslim women were subject to these crimes (ibid.: 34, 112). What's more, the panel found distressing evidence that Hindu women participated actively in the violence in Gujarat, inciting rape and murder. As in many other patriarchal and misogynist cultures, women play a significant and proactive part in the Hindutva movement (Bachetta 1996).

The IIJG study produced evidence that nine months after the massacre the ethnic aggression was continuing in different but still frightening forms, and with less media attention. Muslims and dissenting Hindus still had reason to fear mob attacks, and victimization by the police. There was widespread trauma and mental illness, and there were adverse effects on women's reproductive health. There had been a retrenchment of Muslim culture in these threatening circumstances, with greater control imposed on women and girls in the name of 'protectiveness', while male community leaders were 'increasingly insisting that women should fit into their narrow definition of what a "good Muslim woman" should be'. Those Muslims who were leading the recovery process, trying to help people shift from being 'victims' to being 'survivors', were being harassed or imprisoned. That the climate of Hindutva hatred in Gujarat had not diminished was clear enough when the BJP was returned with a substantial majority in the state election in December (IIJG 2003: 87, 91).

The drafting of the report was a collective process, each panellist taking responsibility for a section. Five panellists met six months later to do the editing. The book, *Threatened Existence: A Feminist Analysis of the Genocide in Gujarat*, was eventually published on Human Rights Day, 10 December 2003. Vahida Nainar told me, two years later, how a feminist ethics had informed the process from start to finish: 'It was such a comfortable process to be in! It was the first time I had experienced that. Whoever came was of the same mind: "we want this to happen". Everyone was equally committed and after the visit each one invested as much time as they could. There was respect for each other's views, sensitivity to each other's thinking. There was good listening.'

To me, what's most striking about the report is that, unlike any other 'commission of inquiry' you ever read, a feminist principle is there in the very conceptualization. The panellists are not anonymous, disembodied, official representatives of civil society. Rather, each takes space to say what the experience meant to her, as a woman, and the impact the stories of torture and murder had on her within the context of her own life.

Sierra Leone: women, civil society and the rebuilding of peace

Contemporary wars in Africa can be understood only in the light of the continent's subjection to the slave trade and European colonization. People and wealth were stolen on a vast scale. Coastal cities were developed for the limited purpose of sustaining these operations, while the interior was ravaged or neglected. Local cultures were diminished and damaged. Inequalities and enmities were created between and among local populations (Reader 1998). Liberia and Sierra Leone, adjacent countries on the West African coast, were both founded on European/American initiative as homelands for returned slaves. Slaves from America were relocated in Monrovia, Liberia; groups from Britain were sent to Freetown, which would become the capital of Sierra Leone. The forebears of the returning slaves had not necessarily originated in this region. The returners were unprepared for conditions in Africa. Many died. Relations between the surviving immigrant population and the tribal societies of the hinterland were often difficult and sometimes exploitative. Today, forty-five years after independence, Sierra Leone is still extremely poor. The population is debilitated by infectious disease and life expectancy is only forty-two years. More than two-thirds of adults are illiterate. In 2002 the country had the lowest rating of all countries in the world on the UNDP Human Development Index (UNDP 2004).

A formative factor in Sierra Leone's post-colonial history was the long rule of the All People's Congress party (APC), a regime that became increasingly centralized, corrupt, brutal and authoritarian (Bangura 2004). In 1991, after a brief restoration of multi-party politics, an army calling itself the Revolutionary United Front (RUF) entered Sierra Leone from neighbouring Liberia. It was a mixed force of Liberian and Sierra Leonean combatants led by Foday Sankoh. Sankoh had struck a deal with Liberian rebel Charles Taylor and his National Patriotic Front of Liberia whereby the latter would provide base facilities and training for Sankoh's subversive project in Sierra Leone in exchange for support for their own bid for power in Liberia.

The RUF's initial targets were the traditional chiefs and office holders, local traders, the more prosperous farmers and religious leaders, who were subjected to forced labour, various forms of humiliation and public beheadings (Abraham 2004). The state army was sent to counter-attack but, subsequently, disaffected young soldiers returned from the front and stormed into the city. Calling themselves the National Provisional Ruling Council (NPRC) they went on to control the country for four years until, in 1996, elections brought to power the current President of Sierra Leone, Ahmad Tejan Kabbah (Kandeh 2004a). However, peace processes notwithstanding, war continued between the elected government (virtually without an army), the genocidal RUF, renegade soldiers and foreign peacekeepers. Some of the most brutal events occurred in the storming and sacking of Freetown by rebel forces in 1997 and 1999 (Abraham 2004). Peace was eventually achieved in January 2002, but not before between 50,000 and 70,000 people had died, between one-third and two-thirds of the approximately 5.5 million inhabitants of Sierra Leone been forced to flee their homes, and 70 per cent of the country's educational facilities and 84 per cent of its health centres had been destroyed (Gberie 2004). The atmosphere at the time of my visit early in 2005 was cautiously optimistic.

The African continent is beset by war. With 10 per cent of the world's population it currently experiences 60 per cent of its civil war deaths (Bergner 2005). In terms of its atrocious sadism, however, the eleven-year war in Sierra Leone may have been in a class of its own. The killing was random and wanton. A particular feature of the violence was the hacking off of hands and feet by machete, leaving victims alive but maimed and helpless. It's estimated that there were 10,000 living amputees by the end of war (Abraham 2004; Kpundeh 2004). An estimated 4,500 children were recruited into the fighting forces. The RUF abducted under-age boys, many as young as nine or ten, mainly from the rural areas. They plied them with mind-bending drugs and often forced the child first to kill a member of his own family, leaving him no option but to run away with the rebels. They were quickly made to witness and participate in every kind of atrocity, including eating body parts of victims. It was not only the RUF that committed such atrocities. Many destitute children enrolled themselves voluntarily into the state army (let's call it Army with a cap A) and the Civil Defence Forces, but once enlisted were used in similar ways, terrorized into inflicting terror. One twelve-year-old forcibly recruited into the Army, when interviewed by Sierra Leonean authors, for example, recounted how he was required to make RUF captives dig their own graves and 'depending on orders given we will plug eyes, cut off the nose, ears, fingers and then bury them half dead' (Abdullah and Rashid 2004: 248).

The war was, of course, profoundly gendered. The fighters were overwhelmingly young men, both urban and rural, bonded in a masculinist subculture of drugs and drink. Several commentators on the war mention 'raray' boys or 'bayaye', a particular stratum of politically unsophisticated 'lumpen' youth, as having been a resource for all fighting groups. Their disruptive potential became more seriously criminal after gaol breaks during the disorder in the capital city in 1997 and 1999 (Gberie 2004; Rashid 2004). An unknown and incalculable, but certainly very large, proportion of women and girls were repeatedly, brutally, raped in these years, by individual men and by gangs. Their genitalia were injured with sticks, bottles and weapons, so that many died of their wounds. Many pregnant women were cut open and their foetus removed. Sometimes their killers gambled on the sex of the unborn child. Thousands of girl children were captured by the rebels and pressed into service as cooks and carriers, forced into sexual servitude as 'wives' of rebel males. Many became pregnant and bore unwanted children while still no more than children themselves.

To many, the war in Sierra Leone defied explanation. There was no apparent motive for hatred – no ethnic, national or religious project. Foday Sankoh was influenced by the credo of President Gadhafi of Libya but he was never at pains to win people to a revolutionary ideology. On the contrary, RUF brutality seemed designed to alienate ordinary Sierra Leoneans. Political scientists and sociologists have puzzled over the question 'why?' They have invoked banditry, hedonism, barbarism (Bangura 2004), and the 'instrumentalization of disorder' (Chabal and Daloz 1999). Certainly it was a conflict more about 'greed' than 'grievance' (Berdal and Malone 2000). A major resource in the war, perhaps its principal purpose, was control of diamond extraction. The RUF made an estimated $125 million a year from the sale of illicitly mined diamonds, exported to Western diamond merchants with the assistance of unscrupulous international middlemen. Sankoh paid Taylor with diamonds for his sponsorship of the RUF. The Army likewise adopted illicit diamond mining, and the ruling group also took their share (Smillie et al. 2000; Koroma 2004). But as the country was reduced to dereliction it may have become a simple calculation: in a hungry country 'whoever has weapons eats first' (Kapuściński 2002: 225).

It's easy to see that the belligerent parties, led by men and galvanized by a particular masculinity, had material interests in prolonging the war in Sierra Leone. It was civil society that was desperate for peace and democracy (Kandeh 2004b: 179). From the start, women's organizations played an important part in the civil society movement to end the war. In 1994, in preparation for the United Nations Fourth World Conference on Women in Beijing, more than forty Sierra Leonean women's organizations had come together to create a Women's Forum. The following year a national consultative conference was announced. Zainab Bangura, among other women, noticed that the invitation list included scarcely any women. They called for representation, and then went on to prepare a women's case for 'elections now'. When I interviewed Zainab a decade later, she said: 'We hadn't known democracy in all my lifetime.' They were not going to let this opportunity slip. 'We met in advance, we organized an agreed position. We printed copies of our nine main points and distributed them to all the participants at the conference.' It was a neat move: many participants, having no time to read the long official document, voted for the women's well-thought-out and simple manifesto.

Elections were held and a government formed. But the civil society movement, and the women's movement in it, often had occasion to be on the streets in the turbulent years that followed. When the government was overthrown by yet another military coup, civil society quickly responded with a broad-based Movement for the Restoration of Democracy (MRD). 'Again we marched!' Agnes Taylor-Lewis told me. 'In Sierra Leone, women have always been marching – and praying!' The march that is most burned on their memory is that of 6 May 2000, when women went en masse to

Foday Sankoh's house to demand the release by the RUF of UN personnel they were holding hostage. The even bigger mixed march two days later would result in twenty-two dead, among them one woman participant.

When I visited Sierra Leone in 2005, three years after the end of the fighting, the women I met had a clearly gendered perception of what had happened in Sierra Leone during the terrible 1990s and a conviction that women, as a sex, had the potential to intervene nonviolently for peace, and had particular reasons for doing so. As soon as conditions made it possible, a number of women established projects to empower girls, women and civil society. It's characteristic of Sierra Leone that many women work from a base in one of the numerous Christian denominations or the Muslim mosques. Zainab said: 'It's the women that hold the mosques and the churches together here.'

Mabell Cox, a Christian Scientist, told me of her project helping commercial sex workers to address HIV/AIDS. Christiana Thorpe was the inspiration behind the Forum for African Women Educationalists whose educational project for young women war survivors I visited. Florella Hazeley, the Advocacy Officer of the Council of Churches of Sierra Leone, is a key person in the campaign to gather in small arms and light weapons. She told me, 'When you say small arms, it's a man's face that comes to mind. Women are usually seen as the victims. You don't think of women holding, trading and smuggling small arms. But they do.' I found a retired British police inspector, Maureen Poole, organizing with women in the Army, police and prison service – and with the wives of male personnel. Memunata Pratt told me about her research and teaching in the Gender Research and Documentation Centre and the programme of Peace and Conflict Studies at Fourah Bay college. And Agnes Taylor-Lewis told me about Fifty-Fifty, the energetic campaign for equal representation of women in political parties and elections. But I went to Sierra Leone specifically to visit the women of the Mano River Women's Peace Network (Marwopnet). This unusual alliance was founded with the help of the Africa Women's Committee for Peace and Development (AWCPD) of the Organization of African Unity, the West African Women's Association (WAWA) and of Femmes Africa Solidarité (FAS).[5] At the Sixth African regional conference of women in November 1999 in Addis Ababa, FAS facilitated a fringe meeting of women from Guinea, Liberia and Sierra Leone

– neighbouring countries related through war. These women had for some time been talking to each other about the need for a strategic alliance between women's organizations in the three countries to strengthen their involvement in peace-building.

The following year FAS and AWPCD sponsored a foundational meeting in Abuja to which each of the three countries fielded a government minister, two parliamentarians, a journalist, a representative of the private sector and five representatives of women's NGOs and civil society organizations. Delegates from various UN and OAU agencies also attended. The new network was named for the Mano River that forms a border between parts of Guinea, Liberia and Sierra Leone.[6] By then Liberia had experienced seven years of war, Sierra Leone ten years, and the fighting was not yet over. Guinea had taken in 300,000 refugees from its two neighbours, 80 per cent of them women and children. The cross-border trade in drugs, diamonds and arms affected all three countries. Rosaline M'Carthy told me: 'The really distinctive thing about Marwopnet is its regional flavour. It's not that there were not peace groups locally, there were. But we felt we would have more influence with the politicians if we acted together.'

In some ways the network anticipated United Nations Security Council Resolution 1325 on women, peace and security, which would be passed the following October (see chapter 5). From then on the world would pay a little more attention to the gender-specific impact of armed conflict, the under-valued capabilities of women for conflict prevention, peacekeeping, conflict resolution and peace-building, and their potential for being active agents in peace and security. But the thinking that led to Resolution 1325 was already in the air, and the Marwopnet initiative was a sign of it.

Immediately on return from Abuja, the fledgling organization was swept into the civil society demonstrations against Sankoh in Freetown. Then they went by helicopter to make contact with RUF women in the bush. Before long they had drawn up a constitution for a 'non-political, non-sectarian, non-discriminatory and non-profit-making organization', with three country chapters and a rotating presidency. Nana Pratt, the 'focal point' for Marwopnet's Sierra Leone chapter, is based in the Freetown office, maintaining connection with her counterparts in the two other countries by email and phone. Getting financial support is a struggle, for their travel costs are necessarily high. Language is another problem – English is spoken in Liberia and Sierra Leone, but Guinea is francophone. 'But,' Agnes Taylor-Lewis told me, 'we are very alike in the clothes we wear and the food we eat.' And Mabel M'Bayo added: 'We are *women*, after all. We can argue about things, but then we can work out agreement point by point.'

Marwopnet characteristically acts on two fronts. The first is advocacy and intervention at the very highest level of the government and its opponents. This strategy is an instance of what Louise Diamond, a conciliation trainer in the USA, has termed 'multitrack diplomacy'. More precisely, although the Marwopnet women themselves do not use this terminology, their dealings with presidents, ministers, military commanders and rebel leaders, from their footing in civil society, may be seen as 'track-2 diplomacy', i.e. supplementing the standard diplomatic moves of political leaders, foreign secretaries and ambassadors by involving the interventions of neutral non-state actors, including NGOs (Diamond and McDonald 1996). Explaining their high-level approach, Rosaline M'Carthy observed: 'In the last analysis it's the men at the top who run the show.'

A classic case of 'track-2 diplomacy' occurred in 2001. In early summer that year relations between Liberia and Guinea deteriorated badly. Serious tensions arose in Guinea due to the influx of people fleeing from the terror in Liberia and Sierra Leone. Local Guineans resented the incoming refugees, particularly because the latter received international aid, while the host population, also desperately poor, did not. There was much animosity between President Lansana Conté of Guinea and President Charles Taylor of Liberia, whom he blamed for sponsoring the rebel insurrection in Sierra Leone as well as unleashing terror in his own country. Conté refused at this point to have any further dealings with Taylor, while Taylor expelled the Guinean and Sierra Leonean ambassadors from Monrovia. On 7 June 2001, the Liberian members of Marwopnet, supported by women who had flown to Monrovia from the other two chapters, obtained an audience with Taylor. Nana Pratt said: 'It was being collective that was our strength.' They urged him to meet the other two heads of state to discuss the deteriorating security position in the sub-region. Under pressure from the delegation of women, Taylor agreed to such a meeting and also to re-establishing diplomatic relations by recalling the ambassadors.

On return to Freetown, women of the Sierra Leone chapter then visited President Tejan Kabbah to inform him of the agreement they had won from Charles Taylor and tell him of their intention to visit the Guinean head of state. Though sceptical about its prospects, he endorsed the women's mission. In late July a three-country delegation from Marwopnet obtained an audience with President Conté in Conakry. A democratically elected president, he was known to feel concern about 'women and war'. One of the Liberian participants, Mary Brownell, began by stressing the human suffering caused by war and the overriding need for a new peace initiative. At first Conté was intransigent. No way would he attend a summit with Charles Taylor! Then Mary Brownell told him, 'You and President Taylor have to meet as men and iron out your differences, and we women want to be present. We will lock you in this room until you come to your senses, and I will sit on the key.' A report of this event in *Africa Recovery* continues:

> When her comments were translated into French for Mr. Conté, there was a long silence. 'Then he started laughing,' she recalled. 'He couldn't believe it! Finally he stopped laughing and said, "What man do you think would say that to me? Only a woman could do such a thing and get by with it."' In the end Mr. Conté agreed to attend the summit and he credited the women for changing his mind. (*Africa Recovery* 2003: 18)

Some months later a joint secretariat committee of foreign ministry officials of the Mano River countries started meeting. Then, in March the following year at an African heads of state meeting in Rabat, the King of Morocco brought the three men together in the anticipated summit. Relations improved. Marwopnet's initiative had worked.

Marwopnet's second strategy is to reach out to the remotest regions of the country, especially to the Mano River basin shared by Liberia, Guinea and Sierra Leone. 'Above all,' Mabel M'Bayo said, 'the borders are the crucial thing for us.' Despite the terrible roads, the lack of adequate vehicles and the petrol shortage, they decided to prioritize outreach. The Sierra Leone members told me how, in 2000 and 2001, they started visiting refugee camps, IDP camps, amputees' camps, transit and demobilization centres, and continue to do so. Some of the camps are for locally displaced people, others shelter refugees who have crossed from Liberia. The women take with them sacks of manioc, fresh water supplies and other kinds of relief. They listen carefully to what local women have experienced, what they're feeling, and what they need. Through these journeys Marwopnet are trying to establish what they call an 'early warning system'. 'We want to train women to be watchful,' Nana Pratt said, 'to know what the indicators of war are. For example, to be alert to the smuggling of drugs, the movement of small arms and light weapons, strangers appearing in their district.' Women traders do a lot of the commerce across the border between Sierra Leone, Liberia and Guinea. They see what goes on. If women don't feel confident in the neutrality and honesty of local politicians they can report instead to Marwopnet, who will pass information to the security services.

One particular incident can illustrate Marwopnet's 'border work'. At the village of Yenga, near the border between Sierra Leone and Guinea, a number of Guinean soldiers and their families had entered Sierra Leone and occupied the village. At first they claimed it was part of Guinea, citing the boundaries marked on some old colonial map. Marwopnet saw the potential for violence at Yenga. They went to the Ministry of Foreign Affairs and eventually accompanied President Tejan Kabbah on a trip to the area where he met Prime Minister Diallo of Guinea and Chairman Gyude Bryant of Liberia. Diallo conceded that Yenga was indeed Sierra Leonean territory. In response to the soldiers' protests, it was agreed they might stay for some more months until they'd harvested the crops they'd planted. Some months later, while I was in Sierra Leone, Yasmin Jusu-Sheriff went down to Yenga to check that the Guineans had kept their word and crossed back over the border. She found them still there, harassing local people. Marwopnet bring together their two strategies by enabling women directly affected in local areas to speak for themselves to the highest authorities. They now took a delegation of women from the region to President Kabbah at State House, so they could raise their concerns with him directly.

For their work at both levels, among political leaders and at the grassroots, Marwopnet have gained wide recognition. Though the key activists are women of the urban elite, the acclaim the organization has received simultaneously acknowledges the potential for peace-building of women throughout West Africa. Memunata Pratt, lecturer in gender and conflict, told me: 'People will say "men in Sierra Leone have let us down". In other words, they have been the ones in the position of power, and look what a mess the country has got into. Patriarchy has negated processes of development.

Masculinity in men has led us into trouble, so there's a crisis of confidence in masculinity.'

That's why it made sense to turn to women. Mabell Cox said: 'Listen, we have the skills! We're mothers, we're carers, we're nurturers, we have love and compassion. Women have insight. We can persuade, we can influence people.' In Sierra Leone, war begins and ends in the family. Mabel M'Bayo said: 'In the provinces women told me "peace begins at home". We are the ones who can reconcile society. It was our young people who went to war.'

However, the most terrible thought with which I came back from Sierra Leone was this: that in a country beset by fear, where one aspect of that fear is the fear parents feel *for* their children, another is the fear they feel *of* their children, especially their sons, many of whom have been turned into drug addicts, murderers and rapists and whose first victims have often been their own families. Then again, flying back to London, I was reading a book by a Sierra Leonean woman who imagines herself called to return to her country after the war to help reconcile her uncle with his only surviving relative, a grandchild who had been abducted into the war after being forced to kill his grandmother. You can hear the compassion in her understanding of this child. She wrote: 'He feels a gun being pressed into his hands, another gun pressed to his head. He cannot respond: his hands are small. He cannot speak: this is not what he wants. He wants to play the instrument, to sing again and feel the sun on his face and limbs' (Jarrett-Macauley 2005: 208).

I also read an article which quoted from a Human Rights Watch report on Sierra Leone, where I found the following account by Zainab, a twenty-four-year-old market vendor. She said:

> Late one evening, a 10-year-old with a pistol came, alone, into our house. He told my husband his commander was hungry and wanted one of our chickens. While my husband was catching the hen, that boy sat down to wait. He was thin and exhausted. I brought him a biscuit and water. He said he was tired and weak and as he left with the chicken he turned to me and said, 'thank you, mam'. Later my neighbours criticized me for giving him the biscuit. I said I didn't care if he was a rebel or not. He's still somebody's child. (Abdullah and Rashid 2004: 238)

We've seen that much of the lethal energy in the Sierra Leonean and Liberian wars came directly from violent masculine subcultures. So Marwopnet's insistance that women are a major resource for peace here is unsurprising. Some women, for complex reasons, became perpetrators of violence. But others, they are certain, can bring to bear on a society riven by hate and fear a compassion and kindliness they have learned and practised in everyday domestic and emotional life.

§

We've seen how localized armed conflicts in Colombia, Gujarat and Sierra Leone gave rise to three distinctive local women's initiatives. But each of them was partly shaped by connections beyond their national borders. The international links were of four kinds. They involved funding, recognition, solidarity actions and intellectual expertise.

The inspiration and energy that drive La Ruta Pacifica in Colombia are those of Colombian women. But their self-organization has been backed by substantial funding over a period of years from a Swiss programme for the promotion of peace in Colombia, SUIPPCOL, a coalition of charities and human rights organizations which itself receives funds from the Human Security Division of the Swiss Foreign Ministry. SUIPPCOL's work is intended to complement Switzerland's official diplomatic endeavours for peace in Colombia. We saw that the Mano River Women's Peace Network, though born of the political imagination of women of Guinea, Liberia and Sierra Leone who had lived through a decade of war, was helped into being by another Swiss agency, Femmes Africa Solidarité, based in Geneva. FAS also helped Marwopnet with small grants for particular projects, as did the UK High Commission in Sierra Leone, UNAMSIL (the United Nations Mission in Sierra Leone) and the Urgent Action Fund (UAF). Thirdly, Indian women looking to fund their initiative for justice for the women raped in the Gujarat emergency obtained help from the Global Fund for Women (based in San Francisco) and, again, the UAF.

International recognition for local women's groups sometimes comes in the shape of a prize that in turn brings publicity and can attract more funding. When La Ruta Pacifica won the Millennium Peace Prize awarded by UNIFEM and International Alert, María Eugenia Sánchez told me: 'Two things flowed from the award. It gave us international recognition. But also it woke us up. We saw, yes, we are in the world, now we have to live up to our reputation, people out there are watching us!' Marwopnet were awarded the United Nations Prize for Human Rights in 2003, presented ceremonially in New York by Kofi Annan, the UN Secretary General. They've also gained recognition regionally. In December 2000 they were given delegate status at the twenty-fourth summit meeting of the Economic Community of West African States. They have observer status on the Joint Security Committee of the Mano River Union and have been present at meetings of MRU foreign ministers. The network was asked by the United Nations Department of Peacekeeping Operations for advice on 'best practices'.

As to solidarity action, its effect is particularly visible in the case of La Ruta, and it has come about mainly through their linking up with the international network Women in Black, of whom we shall see more in chapter 2. In 2000 they joined with the Organización Feminina Popular to create a Women in Black (Mujeres de Negro) movement in Colombia. Vigils in the characteristic style of Women in Black, that's to say, silent and dignified, opposing violence, militarism and war, began to be held on the last Tuesday of each month in a number of Colombian cities and towns, constituting a sustained, visible and widespread public statement of women's opposition to war. This development has usefully linked La Ruta Pacifica to the Women in Black worldwide network. In particular they've benefited from sustained solidarity on the part of WiB groups in Spain, with whom they have a common language. The Spanish left and the Movimiento de Objeción de Conciencia (MOC, the Conscientious Objection Movement) has long had links of solidarity with Latin American liberation, anti-imperialist and left movements. Women in Black in Spain, especially the group in Madrid, and Dones per Dones who 'do' Women in Black in Barcelona, are in frequent contact with La Ruta office in Medellín. They've organized rallies and demonstrations in Spanish cities to alert people to the continual drain on life, health and well-being caused by the vicious war in Colombia and the implication in it of the US government. While they do not raise money directly for La Ruta Pacifica and the Organización Feminina Popular because they are not themselves a registered NGO, they do lobby the Spanish government for a responsible foreign policy towards Colombia and for grant-aid for women's projects. They've helped put Colombian women in touch with the Spanish Ministry of Foreign Affairs. Several Spanish and Catalan women have visited

Colombia and there have been return visits by Colombian women to Spain. It's Mujeres de Negro in Spain who organize the Spanish-language international email list for Women in Black internationally, putting considerable time and energy into translating items of news between English and Spanish, and this has been helpful in gaining worldwide visibility for La Ruta and the OFP.

The transfer of intellectual expertise between women internationally is most evident in the case of the International Initiative for Justice in Gujarat. As we saw, the Indian women had no confidence that women's demand for justice would receive a response from the Indian government, since earlier inquiries into episodes of violence had failed women. The judiciary are too often Hindutva extremists. Public prosecutors fail to charge rapists and, when they do, courts fail to deliver judgments against them. This is why the women went for an international and law-based approach. Five panellists brought an international element to the IIJG and four of these had experience of legal processes at international level. Rhonda Copelon was a professor of law in the USA and director of the International Women's Human Rights Clinic. Vahida Nainar was chair of the board of the Women's Initiative for Gender Justice, a network that intervened in the International Criminal Court (ICC) process from a gender perspective. Anissa Helie was coordinator of the UK-based office of Women Living Under Muslim Laws, an international solidarity network focusing on the rights of women from Muslim countries and communities. And Gabriela Mischkowski, a co-founder of Medica Mondiale, an international NGO based in Germany working to support war-traumatized women, had been monitoring the treatment of rape by the International Criminal Tribunal on the Former Yugoslavia. The expertise thus assembled on the panel led them to frame their work in terms of rape as an aspect of genocide, a 'crime against humanity'. Their calculation was that, although the Indian government had not acceded to the Rome Statute founding the ICC, none the less, under international law, in cases of genocide where the state in question fails to take legal action there's a universal obligation on the international community to do so.

A fifth panel member was Nira Yuval-Davis, a professor in gender and ethnic studies in the UK, well known for her theoretical work on gender in relation to nationalism (Yuval-Davis 1997). She and Anissa Helie had been significant members of the feminist, UK-based association Women against Fundamentalisms. Together they brought to the work of the IIJG a highly relevant understanding, clearly visible in their report, of the way religious political projects such as the Hindutva movement are essentially patriarchal, with an ideology defining masculine and feminine in ways profoundly detrimental to women's autonomy. The project became an example of 'transnational feminist ideology in action' (IIJG 2003: 8). Theorization of their work enabled them not only to account for Hindu women's complicity in the pogrom but also to avoid, in defending the rights of Muslims, falling into the trap of validating the subordination of Muslim women within their own community. This became important as Muslim community leaders were observed, in the wake of the massacre, to impose yet more restriction on 'their' women. As the Colombian women say, 'Ni guerra que nos mate, ni paz que nos oprima' ('No to a war that kills us. No to a peace that oppresses us').

Notes

1 The Colombian and Indian studies refer to the situation when I visited in the second half of 2004, that of Sierra Leone to early 2005. For my contacts and sources please refer to Acknowledgements.

2 I mention a second significant Colombian women's network, the Alianza Iniciativa de Mujeres Colombianas por la Paz (IMP), in chapter 6.

3 Other groups involved were Stree Sangam (of Mumbai); four Delhi-based women's organizations: Saheli, Jagori, Sama and Nirantar; the Citizens' Initiative (of Ahmedabad); the People's Union for Civil Liberties (PUCL); Shanti Abhiyan (of Baroda); the journal *Communalism Combat*; and the Organized Lesbian Alliance for Visibility and Action (OLAVA, Pune). Several women's organizations working in Muslim communities in the state of Gujarat were also involved but for reasons of safety preferred not to be publicly named. Farah Naqvi was a member of both the Women's Panel and the IIJG.

4 The panellists were Sunila Abeysekara, director of Inform, Colombo, Sri Lanka; Rhonda Copelon, Professor of Law, City University of New York and director of the International Women's Human Rights Law Clinic; Anissa Helie, director of the international activist organization Women Living Under Muslim Laws; Gabriela Mischkowski, historian and co-founder of Medica Mondiale, Germany; Nira Yuval-Davis, then Professor of Gender and Ethnic Studies at the University of Greenwich, UK; Uma Chakaravarti, feminist historian from Delhi University; Vahida Nainar, researcher in Gender and International Law, Chairperson of Women's Initiatives for Gender Justice, the Netherlands, board member of the Urgent Action Fund, USA, co-founder, Women's

Research and Action Group, Mumbai; Farah Naqvi, co-founder of Nirantar and an independent writer and consultant on issues of women, democracy and development, Delhi; and Meera Velayudan, formerly of the Institute for Environmental and Social Concerns, Coimbatore. There was no panellist from Pakistan because to include one was felt to be too inflammatory to Indian public opinion; and though a participant was anticipated from Bangladesh she did not attend because of fears for her safety in her own country.

5 Femmes Africa Solidarité was founded in June 1996 by Synergie Africa, UNIFEM and other US agencies, with funding from the Economic Community of West African States. The activists were African women leaders representing different nationalities and professions, motivated by the explosion of violent conflicts tearing apart the fabric of society in Africa. It is based in Geneva and has a branch in Dakar.

6 There already existed from 1973 a Mano River Union in which the three states were supposed (in principle) to co-operate for political and economic purposes. Marwopnet is, however, only rhetorically, not structurally, related to the MRU.

TWO

Against imperialist wars: three transnational networks

§ In chapter 1 we saw three women's initiatives, each grounded in a particular territory, each trying to douse a local conflagration. But there are some instances where women have initiated a project that was intended from the start to be transnational, or that pretty soon spontaneously leapt over national borders. This tends to happen when large machineries like the North Atlantic Treaty Organization (NATO) are involved in war, when the US bid for global dominance is clearly visible, 'Western' strategic interests are invoked, and where worldwide conflict seems to threaten, as in today's so-called 'war on terror'. In this chapter I'll introduce three transnational women's networks: Women in Black, Code Pink: Women for Peace, and an interesting alliance with the irreducible name East Asia–US–Puerto Rico Women's Network against Militarism. I shall introduce a fourth, the longest-lived and most structured of women's international peace networks, the Women's International League for Peace and Freedom (WILPF), in chapter 5.

Women in Black and Code Pink, although differing in many ways, share a primary concern which differs from that of the East Asia–US–Puerto Rico Network. The period in which the Women in Black idea, originating in Israel, caught on and spread worldwide was the 1990s. The impulse was the shock of the 'new wars'. Many women who had been active against nuclear weapons in the 1980s breathed more easily when the Cold War ended. But where was the 'peace dividend'? Hope turned to dismay as the Gulf War erupted and was rapidly followed by murderous nationalist conflicts in Croatia and Bosnia, genocide in Rwanda and finally war in Kosovo/a and the NATO bombing of Serbia. 'Stop war' was Women in Black's message in these years. Code Pink joined Women in Black on the anti-war scene after the events of 11 September 2001. Like Women in Black, they chose the streets as their main arena and 'war' as their focus. In fact the title of their book, published in 2005, was *Stop the Next War Now* (Benjamin and Evans 2005).

In recent years both networks have necessarily been preoccupied mainly with the policies of the USA and its allies, including Israel, as the source of many injustices and much violence. The USA has a very long history of intrusion into the affairs of other countries with the purpose of maintaining an 'open door' for its business interests. In the period from the end of the Second World War to the late 1980s, the CIA and the military intervened persistently in countries as near as Haiti and Nicaragua, as far as Congo and Vietnam, to forestall egalitarian movements and instal compliant regimes, the rationale being the supposed threat from the Soviet Union in the context of the Cold War (Blum 2003). The left, in the USA and elsewhere, continually protested against these illegal acts.

US international relations, however, entered a new phase when the Republicans won the election in 2000, bringing George W. Bush to the presidency. Gathered around him in the new administration were neo-conservative ideologues and businessmen, many of whom had been members of the influential group the Project for the New American Century (PNAC) that had been quite explicit in its aim of rallying support for America to pick up the reins of world dominion. The USA had supported the break-up of European colonial empires during the twentieth century in the interests of 'free trade'. Now the notion of empire, a US empire this time, was being rehabilitated. The PNAC's Statement of Principles issued in 1997 had railed at the Clinton administration's neglect of US national interests abroad saying: 'We aim to change this. We aim to make the case and rally support for American global leadership.' They urged modernization of the military, 'to challenge regimes hostile to our interests and values' and to preserve and extend an international order 'friendly to our security, our prosperity, and our principles' (PNAC 1997). Important figures in the PNAC were Dick Cheney and Donald Rumsfeld, later to become Bush Junior's Vice President and Secretary of Defense respectively.

Already in 1998 the PNAC had urged the removal of Saddam Hussein from power in Iraq (PNAC 1998). Then came the attack of 11 September 2001 on the World Trade Center in New York and the Pentagon in Washington DC by means of hijacked civilian aircraft. The blame was swiftly pinned on Islamic fundamentalist jihadists Al-Qaeda. Bush proclaimed a righteous 'war on terror', in which any group actively opposing US interests, or those of US allies, anywhere in the world, became fair game – especially if they were Muslims. The Bush clique seized the opportunity to take a military initiative in the Middle East that would be a cautionary demonstration of US muscle, secure crucial oil supplies and reassure the rightwing Israeli leadership. It began in late 2001 with the bombardment and intervention in Afghanistan, at the cost of some 3,000 civilian lives, in a failed bid to apprehend or kill Osama Bin Laden and the Al-Qaeda leadership.

In January 2002 George W. Bush made a speech denouncing Iraq, Iran and North Korea as countries constituting 'an axis of evil'. In June, addressing West Point cadets, he warned that deterrence was not enough protection against shadowy terrorist networks and first spoke of the need for pre-emptive action (Burbach and Tarbell 2004). By September 2002 pre-emption and unilateralism had been enshrined in the National Security Doctrine of the US (US Federal Government 2002). Bush set the intelligence agencies to search for evidence that Saddam Hussein possessed weapons of mass destruction and had connections with Al-Qaeda. Still lacking that evidence, and overriding the opposition of many member countries of the United Nations General Assembly and Security Council members France, Russia and China, the USA, together with the United Kingdom and a coalition of other countries on which they had successfully leaned, invaded and occupied Iraq (Gareau 2003). They did so in defiance of 'the largest global demonstration in the history of humanity' when on 15 February 2003 an estimated 11 million people went on the streets in seventy-five countries in a last-minute bid to halt the aggression (Burbach and Tarbell 2004: 9).

It's these events that have been the main impetus for the activism of Women in Black and Code Pink: Women for Peace, in the USA and elsewhere in the world, particularly in countries whose governments supported the USA. They've been dismayed by US refusal to use its hegemony over Israel to achieve justice for Palestinians, and by its conduct in Iraq, with daily news of many dead and injured. They are incensed by the award of enriching contracts for the repair of Iraq and its oil facilities to US companies, in some of which individual members of the Bush administration have a financial interest. They've also been spurred by related domestic developments, particularly the passing of 'anti-terrorist' laws, such as the US PATRIOT Act (October 2001), that target immigrants with arbitrary arrest and unregulated detention, and curtail civil liberties in other ways.

Women in Black – for justice – against war[1]

When I travel, then come back to London, I don't feel the journey is really over until I touch base at the stone statue of Nurse Edith Cavell in central London around which we hold our Women in Black vigil every Wednesday evening. There's something calming about vigilling, holding yourself in silence and stillness as city workers and tourists mill around you and the taxis and buses stream past. The view down to Trafalgar Square changes with the seasons – sometimes wet pavements that reflect the streetlights, trees crisp with frost in winter, a certain gaiety among the theatre-goers on summer evenings. What restores me as I stand there once again is the presence of other women at my shoulder, some known to me, some not; the confidence I can have in the carefully thought-out message we are trying to put across; and, more than anything, the feeling that women are doing this in hundreds of similar vigils around the world.

So what is Women in Black? Not an organization. It has so far avoided any formal structure. Each vigil is autonomous. Although there are charismatic personalities, no one 'holds office'. In a way WiB is just a formula for practice – the silent vigil in a public place, wearing black, holding signs, offering leaflets. But then again, no – since many Women in Black groups do other things instead or as well as vigilling. Some parade in costumes, lobby parliaments, blockade military establishments, enter forbidden zones or give support to refugees fleeing war.

The movement began in Israel. Judy Blanc, who lives in Jerusalem, told me how she and others on the left, men and women both, had come together the first night of the 1987 Palestinian intifada to think about how to dramatize their own opposition to the occupation. Let's do a 'black' vigil, they thought. They had in mind something like the Argentinian Madres of the Plaza de Mayo or the South African women's Black Sash movement. At the first vigil outside the Cinematec in Jerusalem they were seven – two of whom were men. 'The next week,' said Judy, 'it was in Zion Square – just women and better organized.' The number of WiB vigils snowballed and at a certain moment there were more than thirty around Israel. They would stand every week on a Friday, usually for an hour from 1 till 2 p.m., at some prominent place such as a major crossroads. The Israeli vigils were never totally silent in the way many of those in other countries would eventually be, but the message was quietly put across on placards. The most common was the raised black hand bearing the words 'End the Occupation'.

Gradually, as you can read on the WiB international website (<www.womeninblack.org>), Women in Black spread from Israel to become a worldwide phenomenon. Italian women came to Israel to support Palestinian and Israeli women working to end the occupation and took home the WiB formula, creating Donne in Nero groups in many Italian cities. These in turn, as Yugoslavia collapsed into war in the early 1990s, carried the idea to Belgrade where a group, which would eventually match the Israeli group in influence, adopted the name Žene u Crnom protiv Rata (Women in Black against War). From Jerusalem, Rome and Belgrade, WiB spread worldwide. Already in 1992 Vimochana and the Asian Women's Human Rights Council were holding Women in Black vigils in Bangalore, India. Corinne Kumar, in the context of the AWHRC and El Taller International, based in Tunisia, would go on to organize WiB vigils involving thousands of women, first at the NGO Forum of the UN Fourth World Conference on Women in Beijing in 1994, and subsequently at World Social Fora in Mumbai, Bamako, Lahore and elsewhere, often giving birth to local WiB groups along the way, many in the global South.[2] Some WiBs call themselves Women in Black against War, while others address violence more generally, focusing for instance on trafficking and prostitution. At the time of writing in 2006, WiB groups are thought to exist in at least thirty countries and 300 locations, from Katmandu to Manchester. It's impossible to make an accurate census of 'membership' because groups come and go, not all of them record their existence on the website, and we do not know how many women are involved in each.

'Justice for Palestinians and peace for Israelis' has remained an important theme in Women in Black internationally, the more so since the Israeli provocations and renewed intifada of October 2000, the subsequent building of the Separation Wall and the advance of Jewish settlement in the West Bank (see chapter 4). Some groups, notably Jewish WiB groups in the USA, still focus exclusively on that issue, and we shall see an example below. Other localized conflicts as they flare up and die down – in Bosnia, Rwanda or Sudan, for instance – enter and leave the agenda of WiB groups around the world. But most significantly, Women in Black, like the broader anti-war movement of both men and women, have felt driven to mobilize against US/Western war policies. After the events of 11

September 2001, Women in Black groups took to the streets calling for law, not war. A few months later they would protest against the shattering attack on Afghanistan, one of the poorest populations on earth. And at the time of writing, and for the last three years, the invasion and occupation of Iraq by the USA and its allies has been a key issue in WiB vigils.

While Women in Black groups in several countries and regions will feature as we go along in other chapters of this book, here I shall single out two groups in New York, partly because of the significance of their location and partly for the contrast they represent. These are not the only Women in Black groups in or near New York, but they are the two longest lived and most internationally known. One holds vigils in Union Square on a Thursday, the other stands on the steps of the Public Library on a Wednesday. The Union Square group are mainly Jews, mainly addressing the New York Jewish community in order to influence opinion (and US policy-making) on the Israel and Palestine issue. The Public Library group are of more mixed composition and reach out more generally on issues of violence and war to 'the person in the street'.

New York: Women in Black at the Public Library I stood with the Women in Black vigil on the steps of the Public Library on 42nd Street in central Manhattan one dismal afternoon in May 2004, five women under dripping umbrellas. One stood out in the rain holding her damp leaflets towards the passers-by. It reminded me a lot of London. This WiB began in 1993, in response to the descent of Yugoslavia into nationalist violence. That January there had been a women's march of protest from Central Park to the United Nations. Soon afterwards a group of women began to hold regular vigils in front of the UN building, focusing their protest on the appalling sexual violence against women in the Bosnian war, just then filling the newspaper headlines. The vigils continued monthly, now modelling themselves on Women in Black (Žene u Crnom) in Belgrade.

A year later Indira Kajosević, a young postgraduate political science student at the University of Belgrade, came to New York with a study grant. In Belgrade she had been an active member of ŽuC. It had been the one political environment in the midst of Belgrade's rampant Serb nationalism where, as daughter of a Montenegrin Muslim father and an Albanian mother, she could feel secure and

Women in Black groups characteristically hold silent vigils in visible spaces. This group stands every Wednesday, rain or shine, on the steps of the Public Library in New York.

But many groups break with the formula and invent distinctive local forms of action. Bay Area Women in Black (below) have made giant puppets with which they celebrate Jewish festivals while opposing the occupation of Palestine.

Photo: Joan Bobkoff.

welcome. 'They were maintaining a safe place for all of us,' she said. Some of the New York women had already flown to Yugoslavia for a ŽuC international 'encounter'. Now the presence in New York of Indira and other women from the former Yugoslav region strengthened the vigil's engagement with the situation there.

They moved the vigil from the draughty, and largely empty, UN plaza to the steps of the Public Library, where they would be seen by more passers-by. They visited schools, organized talks, developed a website and issued public statements. With varying frequency they would maintain their street presence all through the 1990s, and were strengthened by the publicity when in 2000, Women in Black Belgrade came to New York to receive the UNIFEM and International Alert Millennium Peace Prize.

Public Library WiB has always been relatively small, with a core group of six or seven very active women, building to fifteen or twenty at certain moments. In age they're mainly in their forties and fifties today, mainly white, middle-class American women. Jewish membership did not increase in 2000, as it might have done when Israel and Palestine hit the world's headlines once more, because the Union Square (Thursday) vigil group would then establish itself, with a strong appeal to Jews opposing Israeli policies. In the early years some very well-known women, including actors, academics and lawyers, and peace-workers from WILPF, the Quakers and the War Resisters' League, stood with the Public Library vigil. Since then it has been sustained by a small but steady group made up (as one put it) of 'more modest' women.

This WiB don't stress academic or intellectual analysis and don't engage each other regularly in political discussion. At times they get together in a nearby café after the vigil to talk things over, but all of them are busy with other commitments, often tired and ready for home. 'We're lacking an overtly intellectual approach to the thing, maybe,' Pat de Angelis said. 'But in our city, we're so bombarded with information and argumentation that we feel the need to step back into something simple.' So they don't so much choose their actions on the basis of an analysis collectively hammered out, as respond to their own reading of the political news and to deep feelings of conscience that each has good reason to believe the others share. Consequently, they've chosen a vigil practice that's consistent and simple in form. They hold one large banner, reading 'Women in Black against War'. They maintain stillness and cherish silence.

The only person to engage with the public is Pat, who hands out leaflets and will answer questions. The others just want to be 'silently thoughtful'. Julie Finch said: 'We shall be silent, but we won't be silenced. That's a play on words I feel is powerful.'

The Public Library group greatly value the national and international connectedness that being a Women in Black group gives them. It has felt good to take the banner and link up with other WiBs on the big national demos in Washington DC. They joined a worldwide WiB mobilization on 1 November 2003, called by the Mexican women's organization Justicia para Nuestras Hijas (Justice for Our Daughters), to protest against the failure to prosecute perpetrators of the rape and murder of hundreds of Mexican women in Chihuahua and Ciudad Juarez. At the moment of 9/11 this group acquired a special s gnificance among WiB internationally. Within days of the fall of the Twin Towers and Bush's bellicose response, they came out on the Public Library steps with a clear call for 'justice not vengeance'. It was not an easy message for many New Yorkers to hear. Indira, who was the main coordinator of the vigil just then, said: 'It was hard to be on the street at that time. We were spat on. But there were lots of women coming to us, needing something. It was as if they thought of us as some kind of "headquarters".' The group received a lot of phone calls and email messages at this time, from women across the USA, asking how they could start their own vigils.

Since then the concerns of the Wednesday vigil have been wide. There's an implicit feminism. They single out women's experience and women's issues for particular emphasis. They respond as women to the reality that (as Pat put it) 'women are being hurt, both themselves and their loved ones'. Their theme ranges from violence itself, including local incidents of racist violence or sexual violence against women, to any outbreak of aggression on the world stage. But it's the immediate phenomenon of war they address, rather than the longer-term issue of US neo-imperialism, militarization and global projection of force. They are aware of that constant, if less visible, reality, but don't work on it as a group, leaving individuals to pursue it in other contexts.

So what's the strategy for getting an effect across the rather wide spectrum of issues the Public Library group address? It's creating awareness in people they encounter, one by one, on the street. It's not that they don't consider the lobbying of politicians and development of media contacts to be important. They do try to get their message out there, but are frustrated by the difficulty of obtaining page space and air time. They say: 'WiB can't be everything. What we do in the vigil, that's a common, simple message to the world.' And the people who see the vigil, in the rush hour on 42nd Street, are many and varied. There are a lot of tourists, a lot of office workers. And Pat finds it interesting that 'the hands that reach out for the flyers, the people whose eyes meet mine, are most often people of colour. Sometimes they say "thank you". They know the effects of war are going to fall on their children, who often enrol in the military to get an education.'

For her, the main strategy of the vigil is 'planting seeds in people's minds'. This springs from her own experience. She remembers moments when her own mind was turned around, seeing people being arrested for anti-nuclear activity in 1955, being touched by the death of Martin Luther King. She's alert to the potential for violence in herself. She feels: 'We have to start with individuals. Each of us lives in our own present, our own backyard. We have to work for peace and justice in our own lives, primarily.' Then we have to model the possibility of standing up, for something and against something. 'Yes, we're *for* peace. But *no to war* – not in my name.'

New York again: Women in Black in Union Square The Public Library or 'Wednesday' vigil group and the Union Square or 'Thursday' group don't communicate very much. They'll stand side by side at major rallies, and there's an overall sense of mutual supportiveness. They are all New Yorkers and all 'women in black'. But they attract a different kind of vigiller, due to contrasts in inspiration, focus, audience and style. Union Square WiB has had two distinct lives. It sprang up very soon after the start of Women in Black in Jerusalem and, like most groups in Israel, became inactive three years later with the onset of the Gulf War and during the Palestinian–Israeli peace talks that led to the Oslo Accords. Then, in September 2000, Ariel Sharon took his provocative walk at the Al-Aqsa mosque in Jerusalem, Palestinians protested, Israel reacted with unwarranted violence and the second intifada erupted (see chapter 4). That was when Union Square WiB was revived.

When I visited them in early 2004, the weekly Thursday-afternoon vigil had a regular attendance three times as large as that of the Wednesday group, and on occasion they would draw up to sixty or seventy people from an email list of a couple of hundred. Most of the core group are Jews, ranging in age from thirty to eighty-five, many of them past or present members of Jews for Racial and Economic Justice (JFREJ) and Jews against the Occupation (JATO). The vigil is organized as a long line of women, and a few men, wearing black. It's silent, in the limited sense of no loudspeakers, chanting or shouting. But (as in Israel) the vigillers do move about and chat with each other. 'We just can't keep quiet,' they say. Besides, this is a moment to exchange information, since they don't spend a great deal of time together apart from the vigils. In fact they told me, 'You have to understand this isn't a *group* at all. It's who shows up.' Organization is minimal. They usually have a meeting once a month, immediately after the vigil, in a nearby café. A rotating steering group keeps the show running. But Naomi Braine plays an important role in gathering information from the Internet. She subscribes to the circulation lists of Israeli feminist organizations such as New Profile and the Coalition of Women for Peace (see chapter 4) as well as the Women in Black US and international mailing lists. She trims the incoming news to manageable proportions and forwards it around the group.

The focus of this vigil is quite clearly Israel/Palestine. The message is simple but they make sure certain words – 'Jews', 'Women' – are prominent. A large black banner reads: 'End the Occupation' in English, Hebrew and Arabic. Smaller placards state: 'End the Occupation of the West Bank and Gaza'; 'Israeli and Palestinian women say the Occupation is killing us all'; and 'Stop the Wall: don't say you didn't know'. The vigil is well sited. Union Square is on the edge of Greenwich Village and has often been a venue for public assembly and protest. Judy Solomon told me: 'I love it that in our area ordinary people, cabbies, cyclists, kids, people of colour of all ages, they see us and lots will give a thumbs up sign. It's good for people to see that not all Jews agree with Sharon.' Like the Public Library group, they see their role as educational. Lila Braine said: 'It's important for people to see us there and read our leaflets. It's additional information. It helps to counteract all the misinformation there is about. It's important to stand out there and say that not every Jew supports the Israeli government. It gives courage to other Jews.'

This vigil often attracts an aggressive response from passers-by – mainly from dogmatic Zionist Jews offended by its message of compromise and reconciliation. At times the women are all but assaulted – people scream in their faces, hit the placards. It's not only their views about Israel and Palestine but their gender and sexuality too that incense their critics. Naomi Braine, who like several members of the core group is a lesbian, wrote to me: 'The harassment is very gendered and homophobic. The harassers are largely men, and they explicitly attack us as women (Arafat's whores etc.). They also use a lot of homophobic language, calling the men who stand with us faggots, calling us lesbians, focusing in particular on those of us who are perceived as "butch".'

The Union Square vigil group believe the harassment is worth enduring, because their small but persistent presence on the street says something more than the placards they carry. Melissa Jameson told me that, for her: 'Exercising free speech in the USA, especially now, is crucial. If you don't use it, you lose it. We stand in a commercial area and at the end of the working day people come out and see us making a political statement. WiB is free speech in practice ... Speaking your mind politically is important. It's good to bring these taboo subjects of politics and religion out of the closet. And thirdly, it's about "speaking truth to power".'

Given their focus on Palestine and Israel, the Union Square WiB group have to position themselves within a wider Jewish political environment. They find themselves to the left of some left Jewish organizations, wishing to be more challenging of mainstream Jewish opinion. They want to acknowledge that Israel is the main perpetrator, uses more force, has greater power and carries greater responsibility than the Palestinians. But some are to the left of them, with a position ('Free Palestine', the 'Right of Return' of Palestinians to Israel) that some of the Union Square WiBs read as unacceptable, threatening the very existence of Israel.

Women in Black in the US context Despite its usual focus on Palestine and Israel, in the aftermath of 11 September the Union Square group of course responded to the immediate situation. Naomi says: 'You had to talk about the "war on terror" at that moment. And, being us, we couldn't *not* talk about Israel. So it was both. We spoke about what our country was doing, how Sharon was using it as a cover to intensify his own actions.'

In opposing the 'war on terror', both of the New York WiB groups, and the scores of others across the USA, have to find a place in relation to the wider, mixed-sex, anti-war and anti-Bush movement. They attend the demonstrations of the national coalition, United for Peace and Justice, which includes the American Friends Service Committee and the War Resisters League, relatively comfortable environments for women. But in the coalition they encounter also hardline leftist organizations such as ANSWER, that are much more masculinist, even violent, in words and style. Neither tendency voices a gender perspective. Neither articulates the sex-specific experiences of war or recognizes masculinities as being implicated in militarism and violence.

On the other hand, the contemporary women's movement in the USA, for its part, seldom takes up the issue of war. A significant component of it could be termed 'liberal', in the sense of women seeking equality with men of a relatively prosperous class. A more radical component is focused on reproductive rights. This has been very visible in the Million Women marches, organized by the National Abortion Rights Action League (NARAL, or Pro-Choice America). Terry Greenblatt, in San Francisco, recalled the April 2004 march, a few weeks before my visit. The organizers had made no connections with the international issues, she said. 'They lack a materialist analysis. They don't see the link between patriarchy, nationalism and militarism, in the way the right wing and fundamentalists absolutely do see it.' Consequently, the women marchers who chose to put on their placards the dual statement 'Out of our bodies – Out of Iraq' were a small minority and had seemed out of place.

There remains the other choice WiB groups have to make – how much emphasis to give to Israeli policies in Palestine, how much to the Bush administration's 'war on terror' and its domestic spin-offs. In this respect many of the US WiB groups are situated at points along the same spectrum as these two in New York. In San Francisco I met and spoke with members of three other vigils, that call themselves Berkeley, San Francisco and Bay Area Women in Black. Each expressed in its political activism a rather different, and acutely conscious, take on the Palestine/Israel issue in relation to global issues.

The context for these differences is the prevailing antisemitism, not only in US society as a whole but also among a minority in the left and anti-war movements who too readily engage in a hate discourse that elides Israeli rightwing 'hawks' with 'Israelis', and 'Israelis' with 'Jews'. Whether this is motivated or merely careless, the effect is the same. Fear of exacerbating antisemitism makes some anti-occupation Jews cautious about the kinds of public statements they themselves make. It makes them highly sensitive to the detail and language of non-Jews' campaigns against the occupation. It silences some thoughtful Jews and non-Jews altogether. There's a great deal of pain involved in these debates. Risks are taken with each other's feelings. Certain WiBs risk being seen as insensitive to Jewish trauma, flying dangerously close to the wind of antisemitism; others, more Israel-focused, risk having their 'nuances' interpreted as compromising with Jewish existential neuroses.

Another question is afloat among Women in Black, not only in the USA but also in Israel. Would it have been preferable for WiB, worldwide, which started in Israel in protest against the occupation, to continue to be focused only on this? In a decade and a half there has been an exponential growth of the movement, not only to encompass a geographical range unimaginable to the women who stood in Jerusalem in 1988, but also to take on a very wide spectrum of wrongs, from violence against women and in the community, to wars of many different kinds, the arms trade, militarism as a system, and Western neo-imperialist bellicosity. Some WiB women are bemused and a bit dismayed by this proliferation. This is no longer the movement they intended. Focus has been lost, energies dissipated, they feel. But others welcome the promise of a truly international movement, a presence in the global South as well as the North, confronting not just one armed state and the injustice and violence it perpetrates, but militarism and war in general.

Code Pink: Women for Peace

Code Pink is another women's initiative against war that's become something of a phenomenon in the USA and is starting to break out like a colourful rash in other countries. I met one of its founders, Medea Benjamin, in May 2004 in her home base, the San Francisco offices of the Global Exchange, an international human rights organization dedicated to promoting environmental, political and social justice. In 2002, terribly distressed by the bombing of Afghanistan in the first phase of the US 'war on terror', Medea and other women visited that country and made contact with women. On return they held press conferences highlighting civilian casualties and the situation of Afghan women. They could gain little attention from the media. But Medea had come back from that trip feeling, she said, 'a great need for a women's focus. There was so much aggressive male energy about. Bin Laden saying it's OK to kill thousands. Cowboy Bush killing thousands more in Afghanistan. Hussein's mafiosi in Iraq. I felt: a pox on all your houses.'

The movement she, Diane Wilson, Julie Evans and others then started was inspired by a joke. The state security services were terrorizing people in the name of anti-terrorism with their 'Code Red' alerts, their 'Code Orange' alerts. We could send up this system, the women thought. Why not 'Code Pink' – Code *Shocking* Pink? They decided to go to Washington DC in October 2002 and start some pink actions. At first there were just six of them, in the rain, at Vietnam Veterans Memorial Day. The Iraq war was looming, and they wrote on their placards 'Support the Vets, Stop the War'. In spite of this disarming message, they only escaped being physically attacked by the Vets because the latter were (they admitted) inhibited by the flimsy pink gowns the women demonstrators were wearing.

A month later the women sent out a call for a women's camp. The inspirational thought, Medea said, was 'massive numbers like at Greenham Common. An ongoing encampment. We had a vision of pink tents all across Lafayette Park, opposite the White House, until George Bush agreed not to go to war. We imagined thousands of women dropping their lives to come and join us! It didn't happen.'

Not even a hundred turned up. It was freezing cold and by nightfall there were only eight women left. They weren't allowed to put up more than one tent, and at 5 a.m. they were evicted from that, too. The next night they took tarps. The police dismantled them. Meanwhile, the women were attempting a fast. 'That was hard! We thought what the hell are we doing here? Thank God the police came on the third night and said "out". After that we decided to do our action just from sun-up to sun-down. We kept it up for four months with a rotation of women. Even that took a lot of organizing. It was a terrible winter.'

Other women's groups supported the camp. WILPF did a weekend, so did Washington DC Women in Black, some trade union women, even businesswomen. They achieved a good deal of publicity. Reporters from several countries called by, sure of recording a sound-bite against the war. The women ended their action on International Women's Day, 8 March 2003, with a 1,000-strong march and rally, 'very positive and joyful'. Writers Alice Walker and Maxine Hong Kingston were there, and Amy Goodman, host of the progressive daily radio news programme 'Democracy Now!'. 'We worked hard to get arrested,' said Medea. But arrested they were, and those few hours in gaol were 'a great feeling'. Alice Walker wrote about this:

> The arrest went smoothly. I thought the police were considerate, humane. Some of us tried to help them do their job by sticking our arms out in front of us, but the handcuffs go behind, not in front. We sang in the paddy-wagons, we sang later in the holding cells. We recited poetry to each other and told stories from our lives. And all the while, there was this sweetness. Even though the floor of the cell was cold, where some of us had to sit, and even though the toilet wouldn't flush ... I felt happier than I'd felt in years ... None of us could live with ourselves if we sat by and did nothing while a country filled with children, a lot of them disabled, homeless, hungry, was blown to bits using money we need in the United States to build hospitals, housing, and schools. (Benjamin and Evans 2005: xiii)

When Code Pink started campaigning, their trade mark was a play on words. In the USA, when you are fired from a job your employer hands you a 'pink slip', a notice of dismissal. So Code Pink gave highly publicized 'pink slips' to delinquent Congress-persons. Except that in this case it was not a bureaucratic form but a sexy bit of pink underwear. Favoured personalities, by contrast, were decorated with an outsize pink medal of commendation. At times, however, external events precipitate more anger and distress among Code Pink women than can really be expressed by wearing bright pink. They disrupted a House Armed Services Committee hearing, where Donald Rumsfeld, then Secretary of Defense, was stating his case for war with Iraq. When the invasion started they went in a screaming horde to Rumsfeld's house, some dressed as soldiers, covered with blood as if hit by a bomb. They took 'body parts' and a coffin. 'We even scared ourselves,' Medea said. 'But it was cathartic.'

As anticipated in the 2002 visit to Afghanistan, Code Pink combine their practice of chromatic and extrovert action with a practice of solidarity travel. This was a relatively thinkable step for them because the Global Exchange had already been pioneering 'people to people ties' for fifteen years. They went back to Afghanistan, accompanied by some of the families who lost members in the attack on the World Trade Center. They visited Iraq, before the invasion, to show support for Iraqi women. There they used music and dance, humour and street theatre ('blood for oil', 'smoking guns'). Diane Wilson, co-founder of Code Pink, who had served in the US military, was one of the visiting group. Her preoccupation was not only the impact on Iraqi civilians of the impending war but what it would do to young military recruits on both sides. She later wrote: 'During my time as an army medic in the Vietnam war, I saw firsthand ... what happens to eighteen-year-old boys conscripted into wartime service: their descent from innocent enthusiasm into a hell of drugs and violence and numbing withdrawal' (ibid.: 70).

Visiting Iraq before the invasion, Code Pink had to struggle continually to avoid being co-opted by Saddam Hussein's regime. Yet, when they've returned since, they've had Coalition forces calling them 'Ba'athists'.

In addition to their anti-racism and gender analysis, Code Pink have a class analysis. They delivered protests against the Iraq war not only to the administration but also to the capitalist corporations, whom they see as war's ultimate winners. In September 2003 Paul Bremer, the US senior representative in occupied Iraq, issued his Order 39, opening Iraqi business to unrestricted foreign investment and permitting the repatriation of all profits (Iraq Coalition 2003). Code Pink did some classic 'shareholder' interventions, gaining access to the meetings of corporations to expose the scandal. And Naomi Klein, a Canadian writer and Code Pink supporter, wrote

> If every last soldier pulled out of the Gulf tomorrow and a sovereign government came to power, Iraq would still be occupied: by laws written in the interest of another country, by foreign corporations controlling Iraq's essential services, by 70 percent unemployment sparked by public sector lay-offs ... Any movement serious about Iraqi self-determination must call for an end not only to Iraq's military occupation but to its economic colonization as well. (Benjamin and Evans 2005: 191)

During 2005, Code Pink: Women for Peace allied with Cindy Sheehan, mother of a soldier killed in Iraq, who had made media headlines for her very personal and impassioned protests to George W. Bush. In January 2006 they launched a campaign bigger than anything they had attempted till now. The aim was to bring together women across borders worldwide in a call for the withdrawal of all foreign troops and foreign fighters from Iraq, for the representation of women in the peace-making process, and for a commitment to women's full equality in post-war Iraq. Among the 200 prominent endorsers were writers, film stars, congresswomen and academics. In Iraq itself the Organization of Women's Freedom in Iraq and Iraqi Women's Will signed up to it (Code Pink 2006). The campaign involved, as a first step, gathering 100,000 signatures by 8 March, International Women's Day. Medea said: 'We're unleashing a global chorus of women's voices shouting "Enough!"' By now, three years after the invasion, the war had cost the lives of (possibly) 100,000 Iraqis, 2,182 US troops and 98 from the UK. Hundreds of journalists and humanitarian workers had been killed. The promised elections had produced more, not less, insecurity. Suicide bombers were still immolating themselves and murdering others on a daily basis. Crucial services like electricity and water were still lacking and women's rights were under attack. Yanar Mohammed wrote: 'Iraqi women are devastated now, and it will take us decades of struggle to regain a peaceful and civilized life. The US occupation has planted seeds of ethno-sectarian division, preparing Iraq for a civil war, and has blessed religious supremacy over and against human and women's rights' (ibid.).

Like Women in Black, Code Pink have avoided organizational structure. 'We're afraid of it, the burden of it,' Medea says. Organizing is limited to 'who'll do what and when'. Funding is chancy. For solidarity travel, the women involved each raise enough to cover their own travel costs. The eight women of the core group communicate mainly by conference phone calls between Los Angeles, Washington, New York and San Francisco. They do a weekly alert to their ever-growing e-list of 60,000 addresses, and depend on their website (<www.codepinkalert.org>) as a first line of information. With more and more Code Pink groups springing up in the USA (250 at the last count) and others in the UK and Ireland, Canada, Brazil, Germany, Iran, Fiji and Australia, all asking for guidance, they are aware that more analysis and clarity are going to be needed. But they are determined it shall not be at the cost of their spontaneity and inventiveness, their ability to startle and surprise.

East Asia–US–Puerto Rico Women's Network against Militarism

The East Asia–US–Puerto Rico Women's Network against Militarism (the Network) is quite different both in focus and organization from Women in Black and Code Pink. Its efforts are not directed towards putting out flames, preventing an impending war or stopping a current war. They deal with the slow-burning problem represented by the military system itself, the structures of preparedness and control that, whether armed conflict is current or not, deform everyday life in many countries.

The United States military expenditure is massively larger than that of any other country. The military budget requested for 2006 is $441.6 billion, to which must be added $49.1 billion for pursuit of the Afghan and Iraq wars and a further $41.1 billion for homeland security. It has increased by 93 per cent in the last five years, is six times higher than that of the second biggest spender (Russia) and will soon be equal to the military expenditure of all other countries of the world combined (Shah 2005). Congressional Budget Office calculations suggest that to fully fund the Pentagon's current plans, average annual costs from 2010 to 2020 might exceed $530 billion per annum (O'Hanlon 2005). This high degree of militarization affects many aspects of US life. It both produces and is sustained by a military–industrial complex in which business corporations, politicians and military are closely knit. Whole sectors of the economy depend on military purchasing. Large numbers of young men and women experience military service, the culture is shaped to the celebration of military exploits, and expenditure on necessary social provision is curbed.

Much of the US military budget is spent overseas. A far-flung system of US military bases is not new. It began in 1898 when the USA defeated Spain and took control of the Philippines, Guam, Hawai'i, Puerto Rico and Cuba. It was massively extended during the Cold War years. In a comprehensive study made as the USSR disintegrated, Joseph Gerson found the USA to have at that moment, possibly the height of its overseas deployment, more than half a million military personnel in 375 bases and a further 1,500 facilities in other countries, excluding ports and airfields to which the US military also had regular access. He wrote of the effect of the US presence on local societies: 'Bases bring insecurity; the loss of self-determination, human rights, and sovereignty; as well as the degradation of the culture, values, health, and environment of host nations.' Their purpose has been from the start, and remains today, ensuring 'that US economic interests have privileged access to the resources, labor, and markets of these regions' (Gerson 1991: 9, 12).

The East Asia–US–Puerto Rico Women's Network against Militarism is a collaboration between twenty or so organizations, and some individual women, active against militarism in South Korea, Japan, the Philippines, Hawai'i and Puerto Rico, in addition to the USA.[3] Their mission, they say, is 'to promote, model, and protect genuine security by creating an international women's network of solidarity against militarism. To strengthen our common consciousness and voice by sharing our experiences and making critical connections among militarism, imperialism, and systems of oppression and exploitation based on gender, race, class and nation' (Network 2004).

'Military security' in the Network's view is an oxymoron, and they organized a sequence of Women's Summits to Redefine Security, in Washington DC and Okinawa between 1997 and 2000. '[T]rue security,' they write, 'requires respect for land, air, water, and the oceans, and a very different economy with an emphasis on ecological and economic sustainability, not the pursuit of profit' (Kirk and Okazawa-Rey 1998: 319). The Network call for the 'de-militarization of cultures and national identities'. They are specifically woman-focused, aiming to 'promote solidarity and a healing process among the diversity of women who are impacted by militarism and violence' (Network 2002). They are equally specific in their critique of gender: 'Masculinity in many countries, including the United States, is defined in military terms. We need a redefinition of masculinity, strength, power, and adventure; an end to war toys and the glorification of war and warriors' (ibid.).

In a video I heard Aida Santos, the Network country contact for the Philippines, say: 'The basis of militarism is the strengthening of the patriarchal system.' And in everything Network participants do they mark an intersection of gender with race and class, showing how poor women of colour are worst affected by the many aspects of militarism, including military service, 'paying double every time'.

The participant groups keep in touch through email, coming together for a working meeting every two years. I had the chance to be an observer at their fifth international meeting in Manila in

November 2004. In South Korea and the Philippines, the countries in which the participating groups are most numerous, the women have set up umbrella organizations (SAFE Korea and the Philippines Working Group, PWG) to manage regional coordination for the Network. The relationships are complex and challenging, not only because of differences of positionality, country by country, but because they must work in five languages: Japanese, Korean, Tagalog, English and Spanish. They take great care with the quality of facilitation and interaction, making space for festivity and celebration and, as I've found feminists doing in so many countries, using ritual and symbolism as a means of bonding.

The damaging effects on local populations of the projection of US military force in the Americas and around the Pacific are many. The various Visiting Forces Agreements between the USA and regional governments are the 'armed wing' of a foreign policy directed towards installing and sustaining rightwing regimes that can be trusted to serve the interests of the United States of America. US-sponsored governments tend to be strong on militarism and weak on human rights and democracy. They prioritize the interests of capital over those of people and, being susceptible to pressures from the US-dominated international monetary institutions, they incline to skimpy public sector service provision and extremes of wealth and poverty. US military expenditure in its client states exacerbates class and gender inequities. In South Korea, for example, billions of dollars pumped into the country over three decades contributed to the rise of the masculinist military elites that for a long while dominated politics and society (Moon 1998).

East and South East Asia are gaining strategic importance for US policy-makers due to the huge population and rapid economic growth of China and the potential of oil reserves in the South China Sea. As the USA seeks undisputed hegemony in the region, neighbouring countries become pawns in the game. Internal conflicts, such as that between the Philippine government and insurgents in the Muslim island of Mindanao, are being reinterpreted as aspects of the global 'war on terror', so as to legitimate US interference.

There are, however, three other effects of US militarization that concern the women of the Network and they were on the agenda of the meeting in Manila in November 2004: military prostitution; the population of Amerasian children that results from liaisons between US servicemen and local women; and environmental pollution.

Women of the East Asia–US–Puerto Rico Women's Network against Militarism monitor US military strategy overseas, campaigning against its harmful effects on local lives. Member groups came together for a working meeting in Manila in November 2004.

Trying on characteristic Moro headscarves brought by women of the Philippine island of Mindanao as gifts for Network women from other countries.

The Network challenges the US and client state governments on infringement of land rights and pollution by toxic residues from military exercises. Women of South Korea (above) and the Philippines (opposite) work also for the rights of prostitutes exploited by US servicemen in the extensive red-light districts that surround military bases.

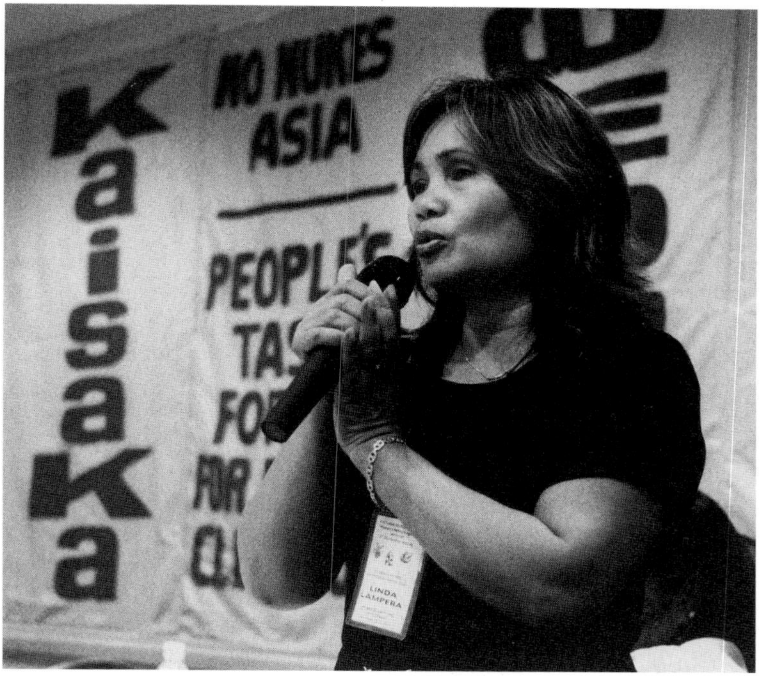
Kaisaka
NO NUKES
ASIA
LINDA
LAMPERA

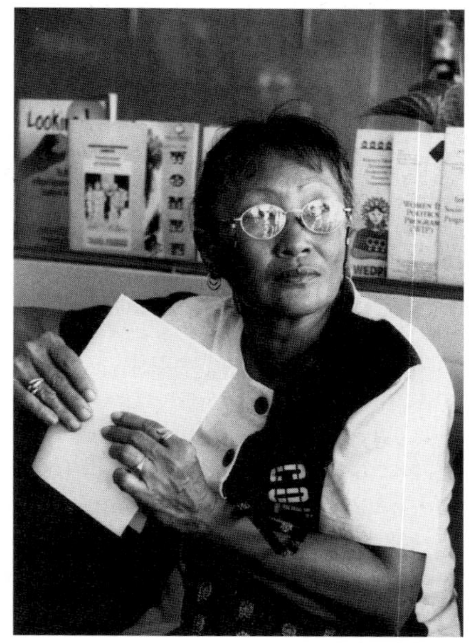

The women of SAFE Korea made clear to me the difference between the nature and aims of the mainstream peace movement and their own women's movement against militarization. They told me: 'In Korea, the peace movement has been simply regarded as a reunification movement and its main focus is in relation to the "big" issues – economic, military and political – to the neglect of the actual lives of people and the experience of women. We want to work differently from this mainstream, and go beyond its narrow nationalism. We want to focus more on the impact of militarization on *daily life*. The victims are often marginalized people, often poor. We want to emphasize the human rights of the individual, the value of each life.'

As women elsewhere, women in Korea are disadvantaged and marginalized, so the impact of militarization on women is neglected by the mainstream. The SAFE women want to bring to it a women's voice and a feminist analysis.

Everywhere the US military goes, prostitution follows. In South Korea, women in military prostitution work mainly from clubs in the ever-growing 'camp towns' (kijichon) near US military establishments. They're not only Korean women but also come from the Philippines, Russia and other countries, admitted through immigration as 'entertainers'. They face problems of surveillance, of violence, confinement and illegality in their work status. Often migrant women's passports are confiscated and their entry into prostitution is not voluntary but forced. A leading organization supporting the rights of women entertainers and women in prostitution in the camp towns is Durebang (My Sister's Place), a member organization of SAFE Korea and long-term participant in the Network. They offer support and professional counselling to women, who come to them with accounts of exploitation and abuse in their work, but also with problems related to childcare, marriage and divorce from US soldiers. Durebang co-operate with migrant workers' groups and women's shelters and also necessarily work closely, if critically, with police and immigration departments. Together with other women's groups they achieved the passing of a law in September 2004, remarkable for protecting the rights of prostituted women and punishing patrons and pimps. But business interests are fighting back. Owners and sex-trade businesses have organized prostitutes to hold hunger strikes and rallies, and have successfully manipulated media to suggest that these women themselves oppose the new law.

Women of the Philippines Working Group who hosted the Network meeting in Manila showed us how the problem of military prostitution continues even when the bases have gone. The USA withdrew from the huge Clark and Subic bases in the Philippines in 1991. Instead, the Visiting Forces Agreement now gives the USA a right of access on demand to more than twenty different locations. Yet Angeles and Olongapo, where the red-light districts originally sprang up to service the US servicemen of Clark and Subic, are still centres of prostitution, with more trafficked women and more very young women and girls than before. Today the clients are mainly sex tourists, though US servicemen on 'R & R' also continue to call by when their ships put into port. The women's groups that are involved in eradication of prostitution in both South Korea and the Philippines face continual threats and vandalism from those with vested interests in the sex industry. Linda Lamperer, coordinator of Nagka, a self-help organization of present and former prostitutes in Angeles, took us to visit their small café and office. Weeks later she sent photos of bulldozers demolishing it by order of the local authority.

Another enduring legacy of the bases is children of mixed parentage, born to local women, fathered by US servicemen. In the Philippines, South Korea and other countries there are scores of thousands of such children, many of them now adult. Durebang were making a film about the rights and needs of Amerasian people, who are made to feel unwanted, meet with discrimination and suffer mental ill-health. Under South Korean government policy, some 10,000 Amerasian children have been shipped off to the USA for adoption.

Finally, there is grief and grievance over land. The US bases have a voracious appetite for territory, owning or leasing large areas, displacing the traditional inhabitants and polluting soil and water irretrievably. We heard that Women Act against Military Violence in Okinawa were currently supporting citizens taking to the water in boats and wetsuits to resist the building of an off-shore heliport that would destroy coral reefs. Women from Puerto Rico told us how people of the island of Vieques, formerly occupied by the USA, had been obliged to live between a massive arsenal on one end of their island and a bombing range on the other. Now the people of Vieques, suffering illnesses caused by arsenic, mercury and lead poisoning, the result of the dropping of 7 million pounds of explosives a year for sixty-two years, were struggling to get reparation for the contamination of the land. Carmen Valencia Perez of the Vieques Women's Alliance told me they do it in the spirit of householders: 'Vieques is our house. Women are head of the household. Women care for people and society.'

> Hawai'i is the linch-pin of US military strategy in the Asia-Pacific region. The Commander-in-chief of the Pacific Command (CINCPAC), based in Honolulu, governs what native Hawai'ian activists have described as a 'transnational garrison state'. It is spread over 105 million square miles and stretches from the east coast of Africa to Mexico, includes 43 countries and over 60 percent of the world's population. The Pacific Command, they assert, has 300,000 military personnel in the theater, including 100,000 forward deployed troops in the Western Pacific. (Kajahiro 2003: 2)

Fifty-four per cent of military land holdings in Hawai'i are the indigenous people's national lands, wrongfully appropriated by the US state. The Kanaka Maoli, or Hawai'ian native peoples, for whom an important cultural value is *aloha 'aina*, or love for the land, have been engaged in unremitting struggle to get these culturally significant areas back from military use. Many of the leaders are women. Like the Puerto Rican women, they use a feminine language of care. 'Caring for the nation is, in Hawai'ian belief, an extension of caring for the family that includes both our lands and our people. Our mother is our land, Papahanaumoku, she who births the islands' (Trask 1993: 94).

The various stories told at this meeting, from Mindanao, Okinawa, Puerto Rico and Hawai'i, all made starkly clear how the struggle for respect for inhabitants, land rights and justice in development are inseparable from the struggle for demilitarization and decolonization. They also showed how connected are the interests of the populations of the affected countries. For example, we learned that the USA was seeking to acquire more land in Makua Valley, on the Hawai'ian island of O'ahu. For what purpose? It would be used by the Stryker Brigade to train soldiers in the use of its 300 new 20-ton armoured assault vehicles. Why is Makua Valley so favoured? It seems the terrain is similar to that of the Philippine island of Mindanao, viewed by the USA as a nest of Islamic 'terrorists'. The soldiers trained in Hawai'i will be ready to be sent to the Philippines

– and to Indonesia, South Korea, Okinawa and the Pacific island nations – for use against anyone who opposes US interests.

So the Network pitch their efforts towards ending the projection of US force overseas, but its work has relevance within US society, too. When I interviewed her in May 2004, Margo Okazawa-Rey said militarism had scarcely entered popular discussion in the USA till now. 'War is understood, yes, but that our society is organized conceptually around military values, that isn't generally understood. Nor is the concept of nation. Because we are Number One we don't see it. Our work has been aimed at surfacing these things. In fact, 9/11 has helped us do that.'

The women of the US group have a rather different role in the Network from those of the other country groups. Living in the USA, they are in a good position to monitor US militarism as a mind-set and US militarization as an unfolding practice, and to provide briefings for the Network. They show the connection between the processes and impacts of US foreign policy and those of US domestic policy, and examine the complex effects on poor communities, particularly communities of colour. World military expenditure for 2005 was estimated to be $1,001 billion, of which 48 per cent was US spending (SIPRI 2006). Yet the USA has the highest infant mortality rate in the industrialized world, Gwyn Kirk told the meeting in Manila. And there are 2 million in prison. The US armed forces are experiencing a labour shortage. More reservists are being called up and recruitment intensified. Individuals convicted in the courts are sometimes offered military service as an alternative to incarceration. With a reduction in education, training and other social budgets, for some young people of colour enlisting in the military is the only viable option.

The US women reminded Network participants that 'full-spectrum dominance' is now official US policy. It means worldwide control of land, air and sea – and space. This reconceptualization of US foreign and defence policy explained many of the changes reported at the meeting by women from the various regions. An on-going restructuring of the US military presence, with the possibility, for instance, of some base closures in South Korea and Japan and plans to relocate some troops from Okinawa to Guam, means women of the region are dealing with a constantly shifting situation and highlights the importance of co-operation. In her address Gwyn Kirk said:

We come from very different places in terms of power and privilege, but we share an analysis ... Women's concept of security is different. What we mean by it is an environment that is sustainable for life, redistribution of wealth and human rights ... [We see] an exploitative system that generates despair, violence and self-hatred. Millions are displaced from poor regions to serve the rich. Looking in this direction things look very bad ... [But] in our network we share a love of land and life, the sturdy connections of women and men, opening space for change – of hearing, imagination, creativity, connection and courage. Looking in this direction there is hope.

Notes

1 This section draws on research visits to twenty Women in Black groups – seven in the USA, four in Italy, three in Belgium, two in Spain, and one each in Colombia, India, Israel and Serbia. In addition, I write this section not only as a researcher but also as an insider, being involved in the London vigil group of Women in Black and also in the international Women in Black Communications Development subgroup. More information about the network can be found on our international website, <www.womeninblack.org> and on those of many local WiB groups.

2 Large one-off vigils have also been mounted by AWHRC and El Taller in conjunction with the series of 'Courts of Women' they have organized in twenty-five different locations worldwide, described in chapter 6.

3 Please see Acknowledgements for a list of the Network women and organizations who contributed the information and ideas appearing in this section.

THREE

Disloyal to nation and state: antimilitarist women in Serbia

§ In this chapter and the next I introduce two women's organizations that have come into being in situations of armed conflict and whose activism is what might be called a refusal of othering. One is located in the contemporary state of Serbia,[1] the other in Israel and its Occupied Territories. The two organizations face a similar political challenge: both states are governed and socially dominated by nationalist political forces that distinguish people on grounds of ethnic or religious identity, attempt to drive the resultant 'peoples' into particular territories and eliminate or marginalize those who don't comply. However, the history and circumstances of the two regions are different. The project of the women living in Palestinian space has been to *come together* in defiance of politically inspired differentiation as Jewish settlers, in the first half of the twentieth century, entered and eventually established a state on land inhabited by a population mainly of Palestinian Arabs. The project of the women living in Yugoslav space has been to *hold together* in the face of a violent late-twentieth-century movement differentiating 'Serbs', 'Croats' and 'Muslims'.

It's important to emphasize that in neither case is this lateral line-crossing on the women's part done just for the feel-good factor. These are not facile exercises of reconciliation that overlook injustices. Both groups are simultaneously involved, at a cost, in actively challenging the political authorities. The women in Israel acknowledge the wrong done by the Zionist movement and Israeli state in the massive displacement of Palestinians and, later, the occupation of Palestinian territories and oppression of Palestinian people. The women in Serbia recognize the asymmetry of power in their region, and the particular culpability of the Serb nationalist regime for the destruction of Yugoslavia and the crimes the wars involved. In both regions, in other words, these are *political* projects – feminist, antinationalist and antimilitarist. They aim to have an impact on contemporary political realities.

Another dimension of connection will show up in this chapter. As war broke out, women of Italy and Spain, among others, established links with women in the Yugoslav region. So the feminist 'identity work' described here was being carried on not only across the contentious new internal borders laid down by the nationalist extremists, but also across the age-old frontier separating 'Europe' from its disruptive other down there in the south-east, 'the Balkans'.

The Federal Republic of Yugoslavia: the manipulation of national identity

The name 'Yugoslavia' means land of the 'southern Slavs'. In the sixth and seventh centuries of the Christian era, Slavs migrated southwards into the area now known as the Balkans, with the effect that today, with few exceptions and despite differences of religion or culture, the population is uniformly Slav. These southern Slavs were later differentiated by religion, however. In the Middle Ages the boundary between the rival Christian empires based on Rome and Byzantium fell across the region, giving rise to distinctive populations of Roman Catholic and Orthodox Christians. From the late fourteenth century, for 400 years the Ottomans held sway over most of the region, and during this period many Slavs converted to Islam. (Above and in the following brief history I draw mainly on Malcolm 1994; Silber and Little 1995; and Woodward 1995).

The late nineteenth century was a period of nation-state building in Europe and elsewhere. Serb and Croat national movements developed among Orthodox and Catholic Christians respectively, challenging the Ottoman Empire as it began its long decline. The ferment of Balkan nationalisms would spark the First World War. But a competing project of unity was also current among the southern Slavs. After the war, this convergence resulted in the creation of a 'Kingdom of Slovenes, Serbs and Croatians'. Renamed 'Yugoslavia', this political entity held the population together until the cataclysm of the Second World War. In 1941 Nazi Germany occupied much of Yugoslavia and put local fascist collaborators in power. Elements of the population fought on both sides in a massively destructive war that cost 2 million dead and a legacy of extreme bitterness, particularly between the fascist Croat Ustaša, and the Serb monarchist Četniks.

On the defeat of nazism and fascism in 1945, it was neither of these groups but anti-fascist Partisan forces led by Josip Broz that emerged to take political control of Yugoslavia. The Partisans were mainly, though not uniquely, Serb by culture. Broz, known as 'Tito', was in fact of Slovene and Croat parentage. Under his charismatic leadership a one-party communist Federal Republic of Yugoslavia was established within the sphere of influence of the Soviet Union, from which it would later split to build a more open and non-aligned communist state with a mixed economy.

In Federal Yugoslavia, the nationalist aspirations of the two dominant ethnic groups were contained within internal 'republics' of Serbia and Croatia, alongside those of Montenegro, Slovenia, Macedonia and Bosnia-Herzegovina.[2] Each of the federated republics had large ethnic minorities (as many as one-quarter of all Serbs and Croats lived outside 'their' borders) but individual rights were guaranteed. There were large populations of Muslims, not only in Bosnia-Herzegovina, but also in Serbia and Macedonia. Religious identification was discouraged by the League of Communists and there were many mixed marriages, so that by the 1980s a strong socialist and secular Yugoslav identity had developed in a post-war generation for which nationalism was an error of the past.

However, rivalry for power among the leaders of the republics led in 1963 and 1974 to changes in the constitution that gave them more control over their local economies. In 1980 Tito died, leaving a power vacuum. The Yugoslav economy was failing. The USA and other capitalist countries, intent on eradicating communism everywhere, were pressing neo-liberal economic reforms on Yugoslavia. Loans kept the country afloat, but conditions imposed by the international institutions led to high unemployment, aggravating class inequalities and causing social unrest. The hegemony of the League of Communists was eroded as the political elites in the republics whipped up nationalist feelings in a bid to extend their power. In 1990, in the first multi-party elections, nationalist parties dominated the voting and the disintegration of Yugoslavia gathered pace.

The Serb and Croat nationalist projects were competitive. Each sought a larger, geographically coherent and secure territory for 'its' people. The principal territorial target in both cases was Bosnia-Herzegovina, with its large, though by now mainly non-religious, Muslim population. Serb and Croat extremists fomented hatred of each other; but both these camps vilified Bosnian and other Yugoslav Muslims. To achieve a system of ethnically 'pure' nation states in Yugoslavia was bound to be insanely costly of lives and livelihoods.

Not only would territorial segregation be physically difficult to achieve, since many people were by now dwelling in 'mixed' areas, there were an estimated 2 million people in the region who were either in mixed marriages or children of mixed marriages and who had no 'homeland' in which to be residing except 'Yugoslavia'. At the time of the 1981 census the 'mixed' Yugoslavs already outnumbered the substantial ethnic minorities – Albanians, Montenegrins, Macedonians, Muslims and Slovenes. Only Croats and Serbs outnumbered them (Korac 1998: 14 citing Petrović 1985).

The worst fighting was necessarily therefore in the most 'ethnically mixed' and ideologically 'Yugoslav' areas. Slovenia, relatively unmixed and economically prosperous, slipped out of the Federation first, declaring itself an independent state in June 1991. Croatia followed suit. Serbia intervened militarily in support of an insurrection by the Serb minority in Croatia. The Serb–Croat war alone cost 20,000 deaths and a third of a million displacements. The conflict in Bosnia-Herzegovina would be even worse. The mainly secular Muslims of this very mixed republic were now beleaguered in a rump Yugoslavia dominated by Serbia, a plight that played into the hands of a defensive Bosnian Islamic nationalism. In 1992, Slobodan Milosević, Serb leader in Belgrade, now in control of the Yugoslav national army, supported Bosnian Serbs in a murderous programme of 'ethnic cleansing' to clear a swathe of northern and eastern Bosnia for a purely Serb population. Within weeks Serb forces had control of 70 per cent of Bosnia-Herzegovina. Eventually Bosnian Croat nationalists supported by Croatia launched 'a war within a war', making their own bid for Herzegovina and additional portions of Bosnian territory.

By the ceasefire in 1995, the Bosnian conflicts had cost an estimated 200,000 dead. Across the former Yugoslav region, between 4.5 and 5 million people had been uprooted from their homes. An untold number of women and girls had been raped, for rape became a tool in the ethnic cleansing and was employed with particular ferocity by the Serb paramilitaries in Bosnia (Amnesty International 1993; Stiglmayer 1995). The Dayton Peace Agreement brokered by the USA reflected the disastrous policy of the Western governments' several interventions for peace, that is, territorial segregation of Bosnia on ethno-national lines. Serb aggression was rewarded with a virtually separate 'republic', the Republika Srpska, comprising 49 per cent of the land area of Bosnia-Herzegovina.

War was not yet over in the Balkans, however. In Kosovo/a,[3] a region of contested autonomy in southern Serbia, armed insurgency was on the point of turning to open warfare. National-minded Serbs and the Albanian, mainly Muslim, majority both regard Kosovo/a as their own by historical right. The Milosević regime had recently emphasized the Serb claim to Kosovo/a by cracking down on Albanian political and cultural institutions. Now, in 1996, as hostilities in Bosnia came to a close, the struggle intensified in Kosovo/a. The non-violent Albanian Kosovan national movement lost influence to the armed Kosovan Liberation Army, while Serbian security forces took brutal measures to maintain control and protect the Serb minority. During 1997–98 an estimated 300,000 Kosovan Albanians fled or were driven from their homes. Monitoring by the Organization for Security and Co-operation in Europe and mediation by a 'contact group' of six nations achieved little. In a dramatic shift of strategy, in March 1999 NATO bombed Serbia and Montenegro, destroying bridges, roads and buildings in Belgrade and other cities, and attacking Serb units in Kosovo/a. In June 1999 Milosević accepted defeat. He lost the September 2000 elections and mass civil disobedience ensured his permanent removal from the presidency. Kosovo/a, its political status still unresolved, is at the time of writing still run as a United Nations protectorate.

A feminist response to nationalism and war

In the peaceful 1970s, when the Second World War was thirty years in the past and the disintegration of the Federation as yet unthinkable, a lively feminist movement sprang to life in Yugoslavia. The activists were young women of the post-war generation, who tended to identify themselves simply as 'Yugoslavs'. They had gained from the sex-equality policies of the League of Communists that gave women rights and opportunities earlier than in many capitalist countries. But they were impatient of the way these formal policies, which as in other communist countries relied mostly on women's 'emancipation' through their entry into the paid labour force, had left men still in power in the Party, the state bureaucracy and public enterprises, while male authority in the family also remained intact (Morokvasić 1986).

In 1978 an international feminist conference was held at the Student Cultural Centre in Belgrade. The event prompted confrontation with the official communist women's organization which claimed these women were 'negating the leading role of the working class', and kick-started autonomous feminism in Yugoslavia (Drakulić 1993). Small but lively groups flowered in the cities of Zagreb, Belgrade and Ljubljana, where the first lesbian feminist group, Lilit, was formed. The issue of gay and lesbian rights became part of a struggle for democracy inside and outside the League of Communists in these years (ŽuC 1998: 59).

However, ten years on, with Yugoslav state socialism in retreat, nationalist ideologues were proclaiming a 'demographic threat' from Muslims and urging pro-natalist policies. The task of the patriotic woman was no longer building socialism by her labour power but regenerating the (various) nations through mothering their sons (Bracewell 1996). Women's reproductive rights came under attack, and likewise their public status. In the 1990 elections, unprotected by the 30 per cent 'quota' of parliamentary seats previously guaranteed by the communist regime, women's political representation collapsed almost entirely (Drakulić 1993). Within twelve months the feminists in Belgrade, Zagreb, Ljubljana and Sarajevo, marginal under nationalism as they had been under communism, were now cut off from each other by impending civil war. When next they travelled to each other's cities they would be the unwilling citizens of new countries and need passports to cross a network of international borders. Lepa Mladjenović, when we were together in London in 2000, recalled what the new reality had felt like. Soon after fighting broke out in Croatia, she'd gone to meet a train from Zagreb at the Belgrade railway station. 'We heard that the train was strangely delayed. The report was first that it was an hour late, then several hours. Then two days. I still didn't understand then that there was a war going on. An important moment for me. Such a sad thing – the lost train. I didn't know, nobody could know, that that train would be five years late! In 1997, I went again to the railway station. The train was back! But now it was from the *international* ticket window I had to buy a ticket to Zagreb, not the local one. I was crying.'

The feminists in Belgrade, isolated in the heartland of Serb nationalism, responded to the threat of war by redoubling their activism. Staša Zajović was already involved in the Centre for Anti-war Action, an organization of both men and women, working against forced mobilization. She noticed that 'the peace movement was … repeating certain patriarchal models, using patriarchal language and ignoring the inequalities between women and men' (Zajović

1994: 49). She began to feel the need for a specifically feminist initiative against the terrifying upsurge of patriarchal militarism now dominating politics, pervading the media and swaggering in the streets.

Around this time a group of Italian feminists came to offer support to the Belgrade women As already touched on in chapter 2, they had for some years been supporting Women in Black in Israel, and now called themselves Donne in Nero. Staša and other Belgrade women adopted the name too, and on Wednesday 9 October 1991 held their first street demonstration as Women in Black against War (Žene u crnom protiv rata). They chose high ground for their vigil: Republic Square in the monumental heart of the city. Their public demonstrations would continue weekly for years, throughout the Bosnian war and the ensuing conflict in Kosovo/a. Even at the time of writing ŽuC mount a 'Women in Black' event in the Square on significant dates. The early Women in Black vigils were classic in form: silent and still, involving women dressed in black carrying simple messages on banners and placards, their case explained to passers-by in leaflets. Undeterred by verbal and sometimes physical violence from nationalists, they kept up a regular presence on the streets, the only anti-war group to do so. At first, as several of them attested, it felt strange to be standing there in public. Women's political action on the street was something for which, as Lepa wrote, there was simply no tradition in Yugoslavia. She said, we 'created our own tradition, sense and language' (ŽuC 2001: 12). 'Don't speak for us – we'll speak for ourselves,' they were saying (ŽuC 1998: 5).

In addition to keeping a defiant presence out of doors, Žene u Crnom also set up house in a rented apartment, which became a refuge for draft resisters and deserters. When the wars started, an estimated 300,000 Serb men of military age went into exile rather than fight in a civil war between Yugoslavs (ŽuC 1994: 32). But many more were trapped, faced with compulsory enlistment to fight and kill people they couldn't consider an enemy. Some went into hiding on threat of conscription, others fled their units later. Giving emotional, moral and political support to these men who refused to fight was one of the practical ways in which women acted on their feminist and antimilitarist ideas. Some of the men in turn became valued members of ŽuC. Together they went on to build a Conscientious Objection Network that, far from fading out once hostilities ended, has grown into a widespread movement, an intrinsic part of the contemporary struggle to demilitarize the country.

Feminist analysis and counter-information

A conscious gender analysis of the unfolding realities in Yugo-space has always been one of Žene u Crnom's strengths. Their articulate critique of patriarchal nationalism and militarism, widely published, not only in leaflets for local use but in English for an international audience, influenced anti-war activist women in many other countries. But the analysis didn't come from Žene u Crnom alone. They were the mechanism that kept up the street action, but they weren't the only feminist initiative in Belgrade. The analysis, the slogans and campaigns were generated by several feminist projects, linked by an overlapping membership and a shared feminist, anti-nationalist and antimilitarist politics.

One of these sister organizations was the Autonomous Women's Centre against Sexual Violence (Autonomi ženski centar protiv seksualnog nasilja, AWC), to which I return below. Another was the Women's Studies Centre (Centar za ženske studije, WSC) which offered courses and activities focused on women's issues and feminist theory. I learned about this from Daša Duhaček, one of the founding group. It was a project planned before the war but only established in 1992. Hundreds of women of all ages found in the WSC the women's culture and feminist ideas they were hungry for. It still thrives today, under a different name. As the Centre of Women's Studies and Gender Research it now also offers accredited courses inside the University, where Daša has an academic position in the Faculty of Political Science. As well as helping make feminist knowledge freely available to women in Belgrade, Daša now says, the WSC was making an input of theory to anti-war activism. Back in the war years she had written that they meant 'theory, not as an approach opposed to praxis, but as a way of praxis, a powerful tool. It works steadily, patiently, persistently,' she said, 'and reveals its effects only in the long run' (Duhaček 1994: 75).

At the same time, surprising as it seems, there was also feminist publishing in Belgrade during the war years. In 1994 Jasmina Tešanović and Slavica Stojanović set up Feminist Publisher 94 (Feministička 94). In the following ten years they would publish thirty-five books. Some of them would be Jasmina's own, because she was not only 'scribe' to the women's initiatives but also a rare thing, a feminist essayist and diarist in Serbia, writing against the war in the midst of the war. Back in the 1990s, Feministička 94 and other such small independent presses represented a new kind of publishing in which 'the book is nearer to the author, the authors are nearer to the readers: the infra-structure is built from one enterprise to another' (Tešanović 1994: 88).

So the Women's Studies Centre set out to develop the conceptual foundations of a women's response to these terrible times. It enabled a lot of women to grasp the gendered nature of this war and to think of themselves as feminists. Feminist Publishing 94 contributed to this too. With Žene u Crnom (and 'as' ŽuC too, since they were all Women in Black whatever else they were and did) they developed a clear analysis of the system that had dragged them into war, of its sexism, nationalism and militarism (ŽuC 1998: 20). They never allowed themselves to forget that those mainly responsible were ideologues and politicians of their own city. 'We have the same Zip code.' And, they believed, you must first challenge the murderers of the state in which you live. In the early days they were not unanimous in their take on 'nationalism' and 'national identity', but soon a strong and clear antinationalism emerged as a key principle of the group. The analytical work they did helped them clarify their stand of principled disloyalty and non-compliance with the nationalist state and it informed their unremitting output of counter-information.

The close partnership of Žene u Crnom, the Women's Studies Centre and Feminist Publisher 94 was also, at a more personal level, a vitally important resource in harrowing times for the individual women who founded them. When I interviewed her in 2004, Daša said: 'I never believed Yugoslavia would fall apart. When it did, *I* fell apart. This became my space of resistance and sanity and solidarity.' Jasmina said of this feminist political environment they had created in the midst of war: 'It was a process to become political, to catch up with the events. We didn't know what we were doing at first. Life was shit … We had to do it to survive. We had to meet, talk, prepare food together. What I liked very, very much was that we all said what was on our mind, not trying to be politically correct or emotionally correct. If someone was crying we'd respond. If a woman was talking like a nationalist we'd talk about it with her. I had so many prejudices at the start. We faced them all.'

Addressing the deadly issues of identity and place

While the world's media tended to represent ethnicity as the *cause* of the Balkan wars, Yugoslavs such as the Belgrade feminists on the contrary saw renewed ethnic identities as a *goal* of the war-makers, a desired outcome of the wars. The nationalist ideologues were using reworked histories, innovatory policies (such as changes to the language and to the names of streets and villages) and extreme physical violence to reinvent, deepen and drive irrevocable wedges between ethnicities that had become too *in*active, for their liking, in the years of Federation.

Feminist theory, as well as their own bitter experience, told the Belgrade activists these nationalist and militarist moves were patriarchal politics. As feminists they had refused gender stereotypes. Perhaps this increased the likelihood they would rebel against authority once more now, rejecting the politics of ethnic naming and othering. They would not be told how to live their identities, nor how to react to those of others. They would work to sustain pre-war bonds of friendship and mutuality and to build a conscious solidarity among women across the new, violently enforced, emotional and territorial lines drawn to separate them.

So the philosophical basis of this activism was feminism. But they didn't invoke sisterhood between women similarly positioned as victims of war, rather between women with similar values, seeing nationalism and militarism in a similarly intersectional way: as gendered, manipulating masculinity and femininity for purposes of ethnic political power. But this was never going to be simple, even between former friends let alone a wider public. Other women had been swept into the ethno-national discourse and now related to the activists, however *they* might wish to reconstruct their identities, as bearers of the name 'Serb' (or 'Croat', 'Albanian', 'Bosnian Muslim'). Many women, of similar ascribed ethnic identity but divergent political belief, bitterly blamed them for treason. Many old friendships foundered in the new mistrust.

The work of understanding these othering processes, learning from the new circumstances how to deal with their own and other women's desperate feelings of belonging, displacement, alienation and loss, began right there in Belgrade within the women's organizations. Some of the activist women had themselves been displaced to Belgrade by the war. One was Jadranka Miličević, a Bosnian 'Serb' who had come there from the Bosnian city of Sarajevo. Lepa

Mladjenović, a nominal 'Serb' living in Belgrade, wrote a moving account of the costs of 'living at the wrong address for your name', especially if it was an address they were shooting at.

> Jadranka removed her children from the wrong address, from the center of Sarajevo, and came with them to the center of Belgrade ... One part of Jadranka's family stayed in Sarajevo, her past, friends, her people ... The whole time, I have been at the right address, in the centre of Belgrade, with the right name for this city. The two of us met at a women's meeting immediately after her arrival. Since then, we have experienced different news and events in a similar way. We were concerned by the women, children and men who suffered, who didn't have anything to eat, or who lived under shellfire. It was immediately clear to both of us that pain should be transformed into political action. (ŽuC 1997: 107)

The women quickly set about 'transforming their pain', but at first the most needed 'political' action was humanitarian aid. Thousands of displaced people were flooding into the area. I've left till last a description of one of the linked feminist projects in Belgrade, specially significant for its work with refugees. It's the Autonomous Women's Centre against Sexual Violence, now known simply as the Autonomous Women's Centre (AWC). There was overlapping membership and continual interaction between this centre, Women in Black (Žene u Crnom) and the Women's Studies Centre. With the particular attention it gave to refugees and to women survivors of rape and its emphasis on individual relationship and care, the AWC was well placed to implement in very practical ways the principle driving all these organizations – the refusal to differentiate between people on the basis of ethno-national 'name'.

The AWC was founded in 1993 by women who had already (in 1990) started an SOS phone line for women and children victims of violence and would later go on to create a Women's Shelter and a Girls' Centre. Lepa Mladjenović and Slavica Stojanović were involved. Central to the analysis of the AWC was that domestic violence and war rapes are connected. They were not saying that the violence of war and the violence of peace are identical, but that there is, as Lepa wrote, a 'logic of violence that is rooted in patriarchy': 'Serb perpetrators got up from the beaches and their coffee bars: the voice of the nation asked [them] to raise their heads and show what they have learned so far. They were to roll up their sleeves and show that the skills of torturing, raping, threatening women can be used against the enemy' (Mladjenović 1993).

So the AWC became a place of feminist consciousness-raising and skilled individual counselling and care, especially for refugee women and their children. Just as attending a course at the Women's Studies Centre, getting involved in the AWC or the Shelter was often a first step for women into Žene u Crnom, where you would take the harder step on to the street, 'outing' yourself as a feminist and antimilitarist.

The women of the AWC began visiting five refugee camps on a regular basis. One of them was the Belgrade mosque where hundreds of now perilously isolated Muslims were being sheltered. At first they simply helped out the refugees with food, medicine and clothing, helping women individually and through group work to regain self-confidence and re-establish their lives as best they could within the hellish conditions of the camps. They were sensitive to tensions, for example between those from ethnically 'pure' and 'mixed' marriages and families. They gradually deepened their connections with refugees through a project they called 'I Remember' in which women were encouraged to talk and write about their experiences (ŽuC 1994).

Maja Korac is a feminist sociologist, a resident of Belgrade who during the war took refuge in London and later in Canada. She went back to Belgrade in 1997 to interview women refugees and activists. She wrote of the latter:

> the acute, everyday problems of women they have been working with have become the 'spaces' of these women's productive co-operation and exchange ... Through this kind of communication they have been able to accept their diverse positionings as a site of 'unfinished knowledge', the knowledge that is continuously redefined in relation to women's different life situations and their differentiated relations to power. (Korac 1998: 60)

The activists also worked hard to maintain links with women in the other former Yugoslav republics, especially those now cast as 'the enemy'. Keeping connected wasn't easy. The postal service didn't function and the phone lines were continually inaccessible. It was a great gain when the Zamir (For Peace) Internet server was opened and email became a possibility. In the meantime from the Serb capital from which war was being launched, they for their part launched parcels to their Muslim friends under attack in Sarajevo. At times this became obsessive. The commitment meant, Lepa wrote:

> thinking about the packets in the supermarket, or on any trip through town. It meant thinking about the packets when foreign women came and asked what we needed, or when they brought us a gift which we left in the closet for the packets. It meant that every time I went home, I would look in front of the store to see if they had thrown out cardboard boxes which we could use for the packets. Then I would drag them in. In my home there were always empty cardboard boxes piled on top of each other to the ceiling, just in case. We traded cardboard boxes.

Jadranka showed her how to fill every little space in the boxes with beans. 'From my life in Belgrade,' said Lepa, 'it was not easy to imagine what one bean meant to an address of hunger' (ŽuC 1997: 109).

Through email, and through the medium of 'international' women who could travel with less restriction and risk, good connections were built between the Belgrade feminists and those women's projects in Bosnia and Croatia that clearly shared their politics, including the Centre for Women War Victims in Zagreb and Medica Women's Therapy Centre in Zenica which was responding to the needs of women raped and traumatized in the war. Eventually a small number of these women were able to travel to meet each other. Sometimes they met at events organized in other European countries specifically for that purpose by Women in Black and other groups. In August 1993 Žene u Crnom itself organized, in the northern Serb city of Novi Sad, the first of what would become annual Women in Black international encounters, the core of a 'network of women's solidarity against war'. Among the women from Serbia and Montenegro and many 'international' women who came to Novi Sad, were a number of women uprooted from other spaces of the former Yugoslavia.

In the later years of the Bosnian war these annual encounters continued, but more direct contact also became possible. In March 1995 ten women from Belgrade and ten from Zagreb met at Istria on the (once Yugoslav, now exclusively Croatian) holiday coast. In April and October that year, groups travelled from Belgrade to the Bosnian towns of Sarajevo and Tuzla. Also in 1995, in a particularly important and characteristic move, women from Belgrade and Zagreb accompanied women of the Muslim and Serb areas of a bitterly divided Bosnia to a seminal meeting in Banja Luka. In 1996, in the uneasy interval between the Bosnian and Kosovan wars, a landmark conference was held in Zagreb on Women and the Politics of Peace (Centre for Women's Studies 1997). In that year, too, women from the AWC went to Bosnia to help Medica train volunteers for an SOS line for women experiencing violence in the family.

Lepa later wrote of that moment: 'There were women who had survived sexual torture and the death of their men. And there were we, coming from the places the torturers came from. And we all knew these facts about each other' (ŽuC 1999: 21). But this kind of delight in 'finding' each other again on the basis of shared values was sometimes short-lived. They quickly learned that positionality counts for a great deal, and the war had been precisely intended to fix people's position. For some of those labelled with the name of an aggressor group it was relatively easy to reject the ethnic name, refuse the label, and claim an undifferentiated woman's identity. But those suffering ethnic cleansing as a named group often reacted by affirming that belonging, turning what may once have been a mere census category into a chosen identity and even a source of pride. Ultimately the connection they sought to establish had to be a political one, through a feminist understanding and rejection of nationalism. And it always began and ended in a valuing of individual experience and an ethic of care, 'caring for oneself and the other equally'. They didn't always succeed. Rape, for example, became an inflammatory issue between women, a bitter dispute dividing on the one hand those who condemned all rapes including those committed by 'their own' men, on the other those who considered this disloyal and would condemn only the 'enemy' rapist. Again it was feminist theory that helped them cut through this tangled thicket – the understanding that rape of women in war is a way one group of men 'send a message' of scorn and humiliation to the other (Seifert 1995).

When the conflict intensified in Kosovo/a, not so many miles to the south in 'their own' republic, Žene u Crnom turned their weekly actions in Republic Square, their leaflets and their public statements, to condemnation of 'the massive and brutal violations of individual and collective human rights of the citizens of Albanian nationality'. They called on Serb soldiers and police to refuse service in Kosovo/a; they supported Albanian nonviolent responses. They meanwhile tried in every way possible to maintain connection with Albanian women.

The 1998 volume of *Women for Peace* is full of discussion and analysis of the deepening crisis and carries several articles by Albanian women, including Nora Ahmetaj and Nazlie Bala, the coordinator of ELENA Priština, a women's human rights centre, and mentions visits made to Kosovo/a by the Belgrade women (ŽuC 1998).

When the NATO bombs started falling on Belgrade in March 1999, the Autonomous Women's Centre consciously addressed the fear that threatened to paralyse them. They set up what they called a 'fear counselling team', using the phone lines intensively to keep contact with women elsewhere, helping each other overcome the panic awoken by the bombardments. In the first twenty-five days, five telephone counsellors had 378 phone sessions with women in thirty-four towns. But it was now exceedingly difficult to maintain contact with women in Kosovo/a (ŽuC 1999: 222). *Their* fear was less of the new reality of the NATO intervention than of the old reality of Serb officials, army, police and local extremists. One Belgrade woman wrote at this time: 'My moral and emotional imperative (no matter how pathetic it sounds) is to spend hours and hours trying to get a phone line to Priština' (ibid.: 183). Žene u Crnom, now banned from demonstrating, caught between 'Milosević on the ground, NATO in the air', refused to condemn the NATO bombing. They told the rest of us, anxiously reading their emails, so long as we can't condemn our regime we won't condemn NATO. By all means do this for us! (ibid.: 27).

The personal is international

The history of Žene u Crnom and the wider movement of women against militarism, nationalism and war in the former Yugoslavia is inseparable from the history of the women's anti-war movement in Western Europe, and further afield. There was intensive contact in these years between women across the line that separated an apparently peaceful Europe from a zone of full-scale war. For Žene u Crnom, this international contact was no mere luxury but something they felt necessary for survival. They saw themselves as extending the feminist slogan 'the personal is political' to 'the personal is international' (ŽuC 1994: 1).[4]

Italian women had already started to make international links with war-afflicted countries in the late 1980s, with visits to Lebanon, the Palestinian territories and Israel. Women of Torino, Rome and Bologna were involved. Elisabetta Donini told me: 'We were trying to take the first step on the ground, contacting women on both sides.' In the summer of 1988 they organized a women's peace camp in Jerusalem, attended by sixty-eight women from several Italian towns. This travelling group would soon take the name Women Visiting Difficult Places (Visitare Luoghi Difficili). When in Israel, many Italian women joined the Women in Black vigils and eventually, as mentioned in chapter 2, the various groups across Italy began to take this name, Donne in Nero.

In the summer of 1991 some of these same women and members of the mainstream Italian Peace Association (Associazione per la Pace) went to make contact with Serbian and Croatian women and consult on ways they could all oppose the impending war in Yugoslavia. Mariarosa Guandalini from Verona was one of them. She told me how in Belgrade they met Staša Zajovic, Lepa Mladjenović, Neda Bozinović and others. 'They greeted us and hugged us warmly. Nobody knew how to react at that time, how to be ready for the war that was coming.' Women like Mariarosa, living in the northern Italian cities, not far from Italy's common border with Slovenia, felt the threat of war in Yugoslavia acutely. In September that year they organized a peace caravan which attempted to cross the new ethnic borders in the disintegrating Yugoslavia. Throughout the 1990s, and even until today, there would be continuous crossings by feminist women between Italian and Yugoslav space.

A parallel movement was happening in the case of Spain. Indeed, in an important sense it was the women activists of the former Yugoslavia that brought into being a distinct feminist antimilitarist current there. In 1992, as the fighting shifted from Croatia to Bosnia, a group of men from the Movimiento de Objeción de Conciencia (MOC) travelled to the region to make contact with Yugoslav war resisters. They were warmly received in Belgrade by Žene u Crnom who greatly impressed them with their analysis and activism. On their return, women members of Madrid MOC, in collaboration with groups in other cities, invited ŽuC's Staša Zajović to come to Spain for a speaking tour.

While they remained engaged in the antimilitarist work of the mixed group, the MOC women were developing a specifically feminist critique and activism. A member of Madrid Women in Black, María del Mar Rodríguez Gimena, when I met her in 2004, told me how their experience inside the mixed movement had been 'a double militancy, as it usually is'. Eventually, as Almudena Izquierdo put it, they found 'there wasn't enough space in MOC to explore our ideology ... We needed a specific space to discuss women, nationalism and militarism.' Several of these Madrid women created a group independent of MOC. Soon they were aware of similar feminist antimilitarist groups elsewhere in Spain. Later that year a women's antimilitarist encounter was held in Merida, attended by women from ŽuC Belgrade, for whom by now an extensive support project was being organized in Spain. Concha Martin Sánchez, in interview, explained that at this stage they had been

> a diffusion group primarily, distributing their output. Our aim was to give voice to women in a war situation who were offering alternatives to war, to make people here aware ... The [financial] help we gave them was not seen as humanitarian. It was an exchange, because we were learning from them – working against war and militarism at both local and global level.

These solidarity actions built a considerable awareness throughout Spain of the work of Women in Black in Belgrade so that, as feminist antimilitarist initiatives sprang up around the country, many took that name. By the mid-1990s groups of 'Mujeres de Negro' existed in Madrid, Castellon, Palma de Mallorca, Seville, Valencia and Zaragoza among other places. Many were helping fund women's projects in the former Yugoslavia, inviting women over for rest and recuperation and getting them media attention. In turn their members were visiting the Yugoslav region and participating in the annual encounters in Novi Sad.

A particularly 'internationalist' element in this growing Women in Black network was in Cataluña. Their contacts were less with the Serb capital Belgrade than with women in Croatia and Bosnia. When a group of women got together in Barcelona early in 1993 one of their first activities was to visit the Centre for Women War Victims in Zagreb. On return they began to seek contact with women refugees from Bosnia, who were scattered in various reception areas in Cataluña. They visited them, offered support and provided a context in which they could meet each other. This Barcelona group didn't choose to call themselves Women in Black but (in Catalan) 'Dones per Dones', by which they meant, in effect, 'women here for women there'. Their work of contact and co-operation would soon involve them with women's organizations in Palestine/Israel, Colombia, Afghanistan, Russia and Chechnya.

ACE
ŽENE U
RAT
POČELE S
9. OKTOBRA
1991

Žene u Crnom, the Women in Black group in Serbia, demonstrate in Republic Square Belgrade with multicoloured silk peace flags brought by women from Italy.

Žene u Crnom sustain their public opposition to the militarism and nationalism that still deform Serbian society long after the end of the Yugoslav wars. They continue to work together as women emerging from nationalist wars, addressing issues of guilt and responsibility.

In Spain as in Italy, the connection with Žene u Crnom and its sister initiatives in Belgrade prompted women to think more deeply and more analytically about the nature and purpose of their activism. As we saw, far from closing down on feminist theoretical analysis, war had stimulated it. From the praxis of activism in Belgrade there was emerging, albeit in a sporadic flow of short articles, discussion notes, leaflets and scraps of rhetoric, a startlingly clear and explicit conceptualization of nationalist and militarist ideologies and social structures as vehicles of patriarchy, and of women's bodies as pawns in these interlocked power relations. So, Concha said: 'they contributed to our thinking by what they told us of the "social militarization" of the Balkans. They enabled us to see the Yugoslav wars from a particular perspective, differently from the way the media and the international community were representing things.'

Theory, though, was travellling in both directions. In September 1992 the Italian women of Visitare Luoghi Difficili organized a conference in Bologna with the title 'Many Women, One Planet'. Recently published work by Floya Anthias, Nira Yuval-Davis and Cynthia Enloe was a significant input, providing a common gendered understanding of the basic themes of fundamentalism, nationalism and militarism (Anthias and Yuval-Davis 1989; Enloe 1989). The participants on this occasion, in addition to the Italian women and a handful from elsewhere in Europe, were women from Palestine and Israel. However, there was a ready application of the ideas also to the current war between Serbs and Croats, just then extending to engulf all Yugoslavia. It was through mechanisms such as the Bologna conference that feminist theory moved to and fro between women in the war-torn spaces of Yugoslavia and Israel/Palestine and the Western European countries.

The Many Women, One Planet conference was organized by Bologna's Centro di Documentazione delle Donne, in which a key actor was Raffaella Lamberti. She and Elisabetta Donini had both been thinking and writing about gender and identity. The concept of identity just then becoming current, in Italy as elsewhere, involved an understanding that identity is not something you're born with and grow to fulfil. Rather it's fluid, multi-layered, changing and constructed, allowing for a degree of individual agency.[5] Many women present at the conference were, due to the nationalist conflicts they were caught up in, deeply uncomfortable with their own 'received' national identities. But they realized too that they could not rely on finding a shared politics in the common identity of 'woman'. They were aware of positionality: women stood in different places in relation to structures of power. They were conscious of intersectionality: each woman had an individual relationship with other identifiers such as race, nation, ethnicity and religion. If identities were so complex and unpredictable, then any one person's sense of self could not be read off from her ascribed 'name' but must be explored, tested and negotiated. The ground on which we would find each other and act politically together could only, ultimately, be shared *values*. In the Bologna conference that common ground was identified as the commitment 'to finding a fair solution' of the conflicts.

Around this time the Italian women were bringing into play in their trans-border activism terms they would describe as 'among our key words as Italian feminists': *rooting* and *shifting*. They meant 'that each of us brings with her the rooting in her own memberships and identity, but at the same time tries to shift in order to put herself in a situation of exchange with women who have different memberships and identity'. They had begun to evolve the notion of 'politica trasversale', something Nira Yuval-Davis, and later I too, would go on to elaborate as 'transversal politics' (Yuval-Davis 1997 and 1999; Cockburn 1998; and Cockburn and Hunter 1999). In the long and painstaking process described above, of refusing inimical nationalist 'names' and negotiating difference and belonging on their own terms, it will be clear that the women in Yugoslavia were inventing transversal politics throughout the war. I discuss it further in chapter 7. Below, bringing up to date the account of Žene u Crnom, we can see it at work today in their postwar activities.

After war: from guilt to responsibility

When I visited Žene u Crnom in October 2004 for purposes of this study, it was specifically to attend a two-day seminar on Women's Peace Politics at which the Belgrade women were joined by women from other towns in Serbia, and also from Bosnia-Herzegovina. But first I spent a few days at the apartment in Jug Bogdanova meeting and interviewing individuals. Just down the road from the market and bus station in old Belgrade, this office is a busy place, the hub of activities that extend to women in other Serbian towns, to Croatia, Bosnia-Herzegovina and other parts of the former Yugoslavia, and to many other countries of the world. Staša is the coordinator, but responsibility and work in Žene u Crnom is widely shared. At any one time they'll be planning a workshop, preparing for a demonstration, answering emails, writing a news mailing to the international WiB network, editing a publication, dealing with a print order, receiving a visitor, getting ready for a journey, writing a funding proposal, keeping the accounts. They publish prolifically, bringing out a handsome diary each year, and an annual volume titled *Women for Peace* in Serbian, English and sometimes other languages.

From the seminar on Women's Peace Politics I learned about ŽuC's recent work and current thinking. For a start, I began to understand the scale and intensity of their activity since the wars ended. They've long since overcome the restrictions on internal travel and communication imposed by the war. Mainly funded by a five-year grant from the Heinrich-Böll Stiftung, they've organized several series of workshops on feminist, antinationalist and antimilitarist issues in five locations in Serbia. As a result of these and other activities (ŽuC 2005), they are no longer just 'Women in Black Belgrade', as WiB worldwide tends to know them. They now comprise a network with members in many other places in Serbia and Montenegro for whom, as Staša puts it, 'the Belgrade office is our common house, a common place of solidarity'.

There were around thirty of us at this October workshop. Staša facilitated the event in partnership with Zibija Šarenkapić, of the Cultural Centre Damad, an NGO from the predominantly Muslim town of Novi Pazar in the Sanžak region of Serbia. Staša set the scene. She didn't stress, and didn't need to, that the participants came from both Serbia and Montenegro *and* Bosnia-Herzegovina, that the Bosnian women were from both the Muslim-Croat Federation and the Republika Srpska, and they were thus all bearers of 'names' constructed as bitter enemies by nationalist forces in the recent wars. The purpose of the workshop, she simply said, was to build 'women's solidarity and friendship, trust and confidence as a tool in resisting militarism'. She asked women to remember to speak and address each other as individuals, rather than in the name of some collective identity. She reminded us that patriarchal society assigns the role of nurture to women and ascribes certain values to them, such as being 'peaceful', but these are social constructions. We all know of women war criminals. It's not on the basis of being women but only by political work, knowledge and choices that we can act together as women against militarism and nationalism, she said.

As women began to speak I quickly picked up their feeling of living in menacing times. Milosević was defeated in elections on 24 September 2000, and forced out of power by popular demonstrations on 5 October. He had been replaced as president by Vojislav Koštunica. However, since 2000, when Prime Minister Zoran Djindjić was murdered, with the Kosovo/a question unresolved and trials of war criminals scarcely begun, Serb 'clerical' nationalism was resurgent, the Radical Party commanded a large proportion of the vote and the prospects for lasting democracy had deteriorated. Though militarization had decreased slightly, this had been offset by an increase in the malign political influence of the Orthodox Church. There was no sign of a recovery of truly shared living and co-operation between 'Muslims' and 'Orthodox' in either Bosnia or Kosovo/a.

I asked both Zibija and Staša what they hoped for from this seminar. The women who were present, Zibija told me, came from local communities where women's roles are still traditional and where, besides, any solidarity between women of one community and the 'other', is deeply suspect. In such circumstances the meeting would be valuable were it only to give participants the sense that 'there are like-minded women you can count on'. At best, they might be able to plan some shared activity for the future. Staša explained that ŽuC do not think in terms of 'reconciliation', a notion that 'suggests we are different peoples who have to resolve a dispute'. On the contrary, they were all Yugoslavs who had been named and divided by nationalist politicians and militarists intent on erasing every indication of similarity and shared existence. It was not a question of 'reconciling', therefore, but of refusing the arbitrary barriers placed between people, re-establishing connection and seeking political grounds for solidarity.

A description of the circumstances from which some women came to the workshop may help indicate the significance of the discussions. Present at the meeting were women from the Bosnian towns of Srebrenica and Bratunac. They are only 11 kilometres apart, in what, at the end of the war, became the Republika Srpska. Before the war, Srebrenica's population numbered 37,000 (80 per cent Muslim, 20 per cent Serb). Bratunac had 32,000 inhabitants (68 per cent Muslim, 32 per cent Serb). In an incident in 1992 the

Bosnian Army had killed numerous Serbs in this area. Now, as the Serb nationalist forces approached, many Muslims fled from Bratunac and other places, swelling the population of Srebrenica, an area supposedly protected by the UN forces. But, in spite of the UN presence, Serb extremists massacred an estimated 10,000 Muslims on 11 July 1995. The victims were mainly men and boys, though 700 women are also unaccounted for. Almost all surviving Muslims left the area, to reside (for shorter and longer periods) in the Muslim-controlled part of Bosnia or abroad. In these years many Bosnian Serbs were also killed by Croat and Muslim fighters. There is some co-operation today between survivor associations of all three communities (and Kosovans) with the support of the International Institution of Exhumation and Identification.

Two groups of Muslim survivors of Srebrenica and Bratunac were represented at our seminar: one organization which favours the return of Muslims to live in what is now in effect a Bosnian Serb mini-state; one which does not favour return. Some thousands of Muslims have returned but they are living with little organizational support in lonely and threatening circumstances among their former 'enemies'. Also at the meeting were women from three Bosnian Serb organizations from the town of Bratunac and the neighbouring village of Kravica. Many thousand Bosnian Serb refugees fleeing from Central Bosnia settled here during the war so that today the area is predominantly Serb, with enclaves of Muslim returners. There's virtually no contact of a constructive kind between the Bosnian Serb and Bosniak (Muslim) communities, save that which these few women's organizations have contrived. One woman from Bratunac said: 'There's a hidden border round our town. A few brave women have crossed it.' Their presence here at the seminar, together with women of the Muslim 'survivor' associations, hosted and supported by women of Serbia (including Sanžak) was thus very significant, and characteristic of Žene u Crnom.

A central issue in the discussions I listened to at the workshop was the relationship between responsibility and guilt. ŽuC are firm in the belief that it's unhelpful for an individual to take on collective guilt. Women are conditioned to feel guilty, and it leads to self-hatred, anger and ultimately to more violence. Better to say, 'I take responsibility but I don't feel guilty'. The realities the women faced together weren't easy. I heard one woman say, 'We must find the criminals who still go free in our cities and get promoted in the police because they were good killers and rapists, and burned a lot of houses.' It took my breath away to hear another reply: 'My brother is one. I hope he will be punished.' 'Serb' women in particular are vulnerable to deep feelings of guilt for crimes that Serb nationalist forces committed in their name, for not having seen what was happening in time, for not having taken a stand against it. But crimes were committed on all sides, and this should be acknowledged without falling into a 'hierarchy of victims' ('we suffered more than you'). The alternative is to increase our detailed knowledge of the past, acknowledge the crimes that have been done 'in our name' and take responsibility for them through our own choices and actions for the future.

Notes

1 The state was called Serbia and Montenegro at the time I visited Belgrade for this research in October 2004. Montenegro, however, seceded during 2006.

2 The dominance of Serbian, Croatian and Bosnian Muslim identities, fostered not only by political leaders in the region but also by 'the international community' in its attempts to resolve the conflict, obscures the fact that Yugoslavia actually comprised twenty-two ethnic groups with twenty languages between them.

3 The name is Kosovo in Serbo-Croat, Kosova in Albanian language. For political reasons the women of Žene u Crnom choose to combine the spellings this way.

4 The most concrete value of the international connection was funding. The sustained work of all the projects mentioned here was only possible because of the money collected and donated by groups in other countries (the Italian women were a particularly generous and reliable source), or contributed directly by feminist-friendly funding organizations, such as the Global Fund for Women and the Urgent Action Fund (USA), Mama Cash (Netherlands) and Kvinna til Kvinna (Sweden). Women's organizations in other countries gave them the chance to inform a European and world public about women's experience in the Yugoslav wars and the feminist mobilization against the war-makers. Also important in reducing their isolation was the presence in Belgrade, even in the darkest days of the war, of supporters from other countries willing to volunteer their labour power until expelled by the Serb authorities.

5 The following account is drawn from correspondence of this period exchanged between those planning the conference, and information from Elisabetta Donini in interview.

FOUR

A refusal of othering: Palestinian and Israeli women

§ In this chapter I turn to another geographical space in which another ethno-nationalist political project has brought immense suffering and many years of armed conflict. Here, too, there are women enacting disloyalty by refusing an enmity proclaimed by politicians and militarists. There are differences, however. The women in this case represent three identity groups. Some are Israeli Jews, some are Palestinians living in the Occupied Territories and some are Palestinian citizens of Israel. I look at two organizations, Bat Shalom (Daughter of Peace) in Israel and the Jerusalem Center for Women (JCW) in occupied East Jerusalem, connected in a process known as the Jerusalem Link. The existence of these three social actors, Israeli Jews and Palestinians inside and outside Israel's 1967 borders, is the product of a long history, of which, necessarily, there's no agreed version. For purposes of this brief historical background I have made reference to both Zionist and anti-Zionist sources. (They include Davis 1987; Said 1995; Stasiulis and Yuval-Davis 1995; and Sachar 1996.)

The creation of Israel: 'independence' and 'catastrophe'

The Israeli state came into being in 1948. From the late nineteenth century a Zionist movement among Jewish communities in many countries had encouraged Jews to migrate to the land containing the holy places of the Jewish religion. The movement had erroneously represented Palestine as a territory more or less empty of people. In reality it contained a substantial population, mainly of Arabs, both Christian and Muslim. From the end of the First World War the area was governed by Britain under mandate. By the end of the Second, the genocidal acts of Nazi Germany, added to the Jews' centuries-long subjection to persecution in the diaspora, had increased international support for the project of a Jewish state in Palestine.

United Nations General Assembly Resolution 181 of 29 November 1947 partitioned Palestine for two potential states. The Jewish state was to be created on 57 per cent of Mandatory Palestine, an Arab state on the remaining 43 per cent. Despite many decades of Jewish inward migration, the total Jewish population at this time was no more than half a million. Even inside the territory designated by the UN for Israel, the Jewish population was slightly smaller than the Arab (Davis 1987: 22). In the fighting that accompanied the establishment of the Zionist state, however, the Israelis seized 24 per cent more than their UN-designated land. Of an estimated Palestinian population of just under a million, 750,000 were ejected from these de facto Israeli borders, many to live in nearby refugee camps in Lebanon and Jordan, while approximately 150,000 remained under military rule within Israel, many of them displaced from their homes and lands. The year 1948 is celebrated by Israeli Jews as the moment of 'independence'. By Palestinians everywhere it's mourned as the moment of their catastrophe, the 'Nakhba'.

In the next two decades there was sporadic fighting between Israel and neighbouring Arab states. A Palestine Liberation Organization (PLO) was founded in 1964 that did not recognize the Israeli state and engaged in exchange of armed attacks with Israeli forces. In 1967 Israel seized territory from the state of Jordan (the West Bank of the Jordan river), from Egypt (Gaza and the Sinai peninsula) and from Syria (the Golan Heights). Although Sinai was later returned to Egypt under a peace deal, the other three territories are still occupied by Israel and in this way a considerable Palestinian population has come under Israeli rule.

In 1987, twenty years after the occupation, a relatively nonviolent resistance movement, the intifada, began in the territories. Successive peace initiatives were prompted by Western governments. In particular, the Oslo Accords of 1993 achieved mutual recognition of Israel and the PLO, and provided for creation in the West Bank and Gaza of the long-promised Palestinian state. The Israeli government, however, failed to implement the Accords, meanwhile fostering Jewish settlement in the territories and further restricting Palestinian movement by closures.

In 2000, new peace negotiations took place at Camp David in the USA, but did not succeed. On 28 September, Ariel Sharon, then Israeli leader of the opposition, staged a highly publicized visit to the Al-Aqsa mosque in Jerusalem. It was particularly provocative to Palestinian opinion as appearing to claim this Muslim holy place for Jews. Angry protests by Palestinians ensued, not only in the Occupied Territories but also, unusually, among Palestinians living in Israel. They evoked bloody repression by forces of the Israeli state. Thirteen Israeli Palestinians were killed by police. The period of Palestinian uprising that has continued since then is known as 'the second intifada'. An Amnesty International report summarized the Israeli actions following the events of October 2000:

> From the first days the Israeli army abandoned policing and law enforcement tactics and adopted military measures generally used in armed conflict, routinely using excessive and disproportionate force against civilians, including frequent air-strikes and tank shelling in densely populated Palestinian residential areas, large-scale destruction of Palestinian homes, land and infrastructure, and the imposition of military blockades and prolonged curfews which kept the Palestinian population imprisoned within their homes. (Amnesty International 2005)

In retaliation, in addition to the armed resistance inside the Occupied Territories, there have been attacks by Hamas and Islamic Jihad suicide bombers on civilian targets inside Israel. The Amnesty report counted the deaths and injuries in the four and a half years following the outbreak of the second intifada in October 2000. More than 3,200 Palestinians had been killed by Israeli forces, including more than 600 children and more than 150 women. More than 1,000 Israelis, including more than 100 children and some 300 women, were killed by Palestinian armed groups. Thousands more had been injured. Most of the victims were unarmed civilians who were not taking part in any armed confrontations (ibid.).

The report also emphasizes the serious impact of the occupation on many aspects of Palestinian women's lives and presents individual women's testimonies:

> Palestinian women in the West Bank and Gaza Strip have lived for most of their lives under Israeli occupation and have been facing a triple challenge to establish their rights: as Palestinians living under Israeli military occupation which controls every aspect of their lives, as women living in a society governed by patriarchal customs, and as unequal members of society subject to discriminatory laws. Living under decades of Israeli occupation has dramatically curtailed development opportunities for the Palestinian population

in general and has increased violence and discrimination against Palestinian women in particular. (ibid.)

The government of the USA, which deems the security of Israel vital to its interests in the Middle East, supplies an estimated $3 billion a year in aid, most of it military. While successive US administrations have called for Israel to fulfil its obligations to Palestinians, they have never threatened withdrawal of this economic and military support. Since the events of October 2000 there has been no official peace process between Israel and the Palestinian Authority.

'Facts on the ground': unilateral Israeli moves

In 2002 the Israeli government began construction of a continuous 26-feet-high concrete wall inside the West Bank, eventually to be 420 miles long. The government term this partition the 'Defence Fence', while opponents call it the 'separation Wall' or 'Apartheid Wall'. Its proclaimed intention is to prevent potential suicide bombers from entering Israel. Its construction has been accompanied by the building of new roads, banned to Palestinians, and the increased use of military checkpoints inside the West Bank.

Critics of this new Israeli strategy point out that its real aim is not security, which it cannot achieve. It's designed, on the contrary, to surround, connect and protect Jewish settlements, to carve out land for future settlements, and enfeeble any future Palestinian state. Since the route of the Wall is not on the Green Line but in many cases well within it, its construction, they suggest, is a bid to redraw Israel's borders so as to permanently incorporate parts of the West Bank in defiance of UN Resolution 242. The map of the intended wall shows it circling East Jerusalem, cutting off its Palestinian population from that of the West Bank. It will virtually sever the north and south of the West Bank at its narrowest point (McGreal 2005).

The building of the Wall is having an extremely disruptive and impoverishing effect on Palestinian life, further restricting movement and separating many villages from their fields and olive trees. Its construction has been condemned by the International Criminal Court and the UN General Assembly. Palestinian communities have been engaging in nonviolent direct action against the Wall, supported by Israeli and international activists. They've been met with stun grenades, tear gas and rubber bullets.

In the summer of 2005, Israeli Prime Minister Ariel Sharon

abruptly took an initiative to 'disengage' Israel from the Gaza Strip, withdrawing all the Jewish settlers residing there. It was a startling move that resulted in highly emotional scenes, widely shown on television, in which reluctant soldiers carried away weeping settlers, who portrayed themselves as the victims of Israeli defeatism. The borders between Gaza and Israel and Egypt were subsequently sealed. Though there were military and economic gains to Israel in the move, it was interpreted as a gesture towards peace, and Sharon was internationally applauded for 'disengagement'. Even many leftwingers and peace activists in Israel gave him the benefit of their doubts. But it soon became apparent that Jewish settlement was still being expedited in the West Bank. So – more sceptical opinion on the Israeli left sees Sharon's unilateral move (it was not even presented to, let alone discussed with, the Palestinian Authority) as part of a plan to proceed independently to 'bury' the Palestinians, turning Gaza into a prison, while splitting up the population of the West Bank in a series of disconnected 'bantustans'. He is reported as having told his rightwing supporters: 'My plan is difficult for the Palestinians, a fatal blow. There's no Palestinian state in a unilateral move' (Shlaim 2005: 30). Sharon subsequently fell seriously ill, but the Kadima ('Forward') Party that he founded to pursue his policy won the national elections in March 2006.

Israeli activism against the occupation

The second intifada has greatly changed the nature of the anti-occupation movement in Israel. The groups that were formerly important – Shalom Achshav (Peace Now) and Gush Shalom (the Peace Bloc) – have shrunk and are less in evidence, while relatively new organizations have come to the fore. Although few in numbers, these are lively and engage in nonviolent direct action. One is Ta'ayush (Life in Common), formed in 2000, a grassroots movement of Arabs and Jews working to break down the walls of racism and segregation and to end the occupation by constructing a genuine Arab–Jewish partnership. Another is Anarchistim neged Hagader (Anarchists against the Wall), an anti-authoritarian group of around one hundred people, who organize regular demonstrations against the Separation Wall.

Israeli anti-occupation activism, like the mainstream anti-war movement in other countries, has tended to be male-dominated and masculine in style – indeed, at worst positively militaristic

– and has ignored the gender significance of Israeli militarism and the occupation. This has been one reason for the evolution since 1987 of a lively Israeli women's anti-occupation movement. Many women's groups and networks sprang to life at different times after the first intifada began in 1987. We know from chapter 2 that one of them was Women in Black.

Today WiB and seven other women's organizations are allied in the Coalition of Women for Peace.[1] The Coalition employs a general co-ordinator, Yana Ziferblat-Knopova, and a fund-raiser and international coordinator, Gila Svirsky. Apart from supporting its member groups in many different ways, the Coalition itself engages in advocacy, campaigning and outreach. It tries to influence 'middle-of-the-road' Israeli opinion through programmes such as the one they call Reality Tours. Groups are taken on an advertised coach trip to see 'parts of the conflict they have never seen before', the Separation Wall, military checkpoints, refugee camps and Palestinian homes. The 'tourists' meet local people, hear a talk before the trip and have an opportunity to discuss it afterwards. Four thousand Israelis have now been on these tours, Gila told me.

The Coalition, more than any of its member groups, maintains international connectedness for the Israeli women's peace movement. They've constructed and now manage an active website in three languages (<www.coalitionofwomen.org>). They also run an email list of 4,000 addresses worldwide, which reaches tens of thousands more. Of the member groups, Women in Black is the most international. Gila is a long-time member of WiB's Jerusalem vigil. In a way it is now the Coalition that 'do' internationalism 'as' Women in Black, since WiB themselves have no permanent organizational structure. For instance, when WiB decided to hold the conference in Jerusalem in August 2005, it was the Coalition of Women for Peace that provided the organizational infrastructure and staff to make it possible.

Of the other eight organizations allied in the Coalition, four are particularly active. New Profile, a feminist organization of women and men, has a fine reputation for its articulate opposition to the militarism of the Israeli state and its practical support for those, including an increasing number of school-leavers, who refuse to serve in the Israeli Defence Forces. (It will appear again in chapter 8.) Second, Machsom Watch organizes groups of women to position themselves at checkpoints on a daily basis to monitor the behaviour towards Palestinians of Israeli soldiers and police, recording and reporting abuses. A third organization, TANDI, the Movement of Democratic Women for Israel, is socialist in origin and works for the empowerment of women. A majority of its members are Palestinian citizens of Israel; a minority are Jews. Among other things they run courses in democracy and gender issues, act in solidarity with women of the Occupied Territories, work for democracy in Israel and support women survivors of domestic violence. However, it is to the fourth organization that I devote the remainder of this chapter: Bat Shalom and its Palestinian partner organization, the Jerusalem Center for Women.[2] Among the Coalition's eight member groups, it's Bat Shalom who do the most connective work between Jews and Palestinians. This doesn't mean they don't actively and directly oppose the occupation – as we shall see, they do that too. But when they take actions of that kind it's always, so far as possible, as a partnership of Palestinians and Jews. And that, of course, is itself a fundamental challenge to the Israeli state.

Bat Shalom, the Jerusalem Center for Women and the Jerusalem Link

In 1989, a meeting was convened in Brussels between prominent Israeli and Palestinian women peace activists, supported by European women. The meeting initiated an on-going dialogue that in 1994 resulted in the establishment of the Jerusalem Link comprising two women's organizations, Bat Shalom on the Israeli side, and the Jerusalem Center for Women on the Palestinian side. The two organizations 'share a set of political principles, which serve as the foundation for a co-operative model of co-existence between the Israeli and Palestinian peoples' (see <www.batshalom.org>).

Bat Shalom (Daughter of Peace) Bat Shalom has its principal office in Jerusalem and a second in Afula, in northern Israel. It has several paid staff and a twenty-five-strong governing board that includes a number of former Knesset members and other women of public standing. The majority of the board are Jews, while approximately a quarter at any one time are Palestinian citizens of Israel. The board and staff span rather a wide range of political opinion, from Zionist to non-Zionist and anti-Zionist. (Each of those terms of course has many different and contested meanings.) There's also quite a range of opinion in Bat Shalom on another dimension: women, gender and feminism. While some have thought of it as a 'women's organization with some feminist members', a recent board decision affirms it as 'a feminist organization'.

Bat Shalom has two parts – the all-Israel organization based in West Jerusalem and a regional element specific to northern Israel, which as we shall see differs from it in important ways. The West Jerusalem office is the main site of Bat Shalom's international relations and political publishing, as well as local projects in and near the city. It's also the place from which Bat Shalom carry on the careful work of contact and correspondence with the women of the Jerusalem Center for Women, their partners in the Jerusalem Link. I was able to interview Molly Malekar, the director; Lily Traubmann, political coordinator; Manal Massalha, a former staff member in the Jerusalem office; and Aida Shibli and Khulood Badawi, board members.[3] Molly and Lily are of Jewish background, while Manal, Aida and Khulood are all Palestinian citizens of Israel.

In Jerusalem the occupation is felt very strongly and continuously. It's always a fundamental fact of life in the city, impossible to forget for a moment. So, Bat Shalom's practical projects centre on opposing the programme of Jewish settlement and the construction of the Wall, and keeping alive the notion that the city will one day be fully shared, and become side-by-side capitals for Israel and the eventual state of Palestine. For example, it has been active in Silwan, a Palestinian district in the old part of East Jerusalem, where the municipality has a programme of house demolitions. Khulood Badawi explained this as a strategy of Judaization, 'cleansing' the area of Palestinians by land-use planning policy. She said:

> They've declared a green area, a kind of park, and issued hundreds of demolition orders. They don't offer re-housing. The municipality won't even give building permits to Palestinians in East Jerusalem. Either they must build illegally or go to the West Bank. This is transfer by land-use planning. They don't actually take you forcibly, but induce a kind of self-transfer.

Bat Shalom has also built links to neighbouring Palestinian villages. Here the Israeli state is applying a different policy, cutting off the communities from each other and from Jerusalem. Bat Shalom joined local women of Bidou and Aram in demonstrating against the Wall as its route approached these villages. They'd hoped, against all odds, that their partnership might somehow stop the Wall. But the Israeli state is relentless in creating its concrete 'facts on the ground'. Molly told me how more and more difficult cross-Line work is becoming. She said: 'I've worked with Palestinians for twelve years. For the first time now I'm afraid of crossing the Wall. But I do it. For me it's an act of protest, saying "no" to attempts to wall us off. As women and as feminists we know what it is to be kept behind closed walls.'

The Jerusalem Center for Women Palestinian East Jerusalem is not far from Bat Shalom as the crow flies, but it's in another poltical universe. Here the Markaz al-Quds li l-Nissah (Jerusalem Center for Women, JCW) has its office. It employs seven full-time staff members and a part-time accountant and is governed by a board of trustees, comprised in the main of women who are well situated in Palestinian institutions (see <www.j-c-w.org>). The various members are associated with a range of political parties in what was, till March 2006, the ruling Palestinian coalition, but serve on the board as individuals rather than representatives. The JCW holds annual general assemblies of the membership, involving around eighty women, activists from all parties, human rights and women's organizations, as well as independents.

It was Natasha Khalidi, the director, and Amal Kreishe Barghouti, a board member, who told me about the Center's work. Since the start the main activity has been among Palestinian women in Jerusalem, in projects of empowerment, consciousness-raising and the encouragement of political participation. For instance they've run: capacity-building for young women; educational programmes for housewives on human rights and democracy; legal advice and counselling for families whose houses have been demolished by the Israeli authorities; support for women political prisoners in Israel; a conflict resolution training project for university students and young activists; and have offered support to women running for elections, while also campaigning for quotas in local elections.

The Jerusalem Link The JCW is Bat Shalom's partner in the Jerusalem Link. The two organizations are autonomous, each taking its own national constituency as its primary responsibility, but together they 'promote a joint vision of a just peace, democracy, human rights, and women's leadership'. Mandated to advocate for peace and justice between Israel and Palestine, they've agreed a set of political principles, which they say 'serve as the foundation for a co-operative model of coexistence between our respective peoples' (JCW 2005). The principles include recognition of the right of the Palestinian people to self-determination and an independent state alongside the state of Israel within the pre-1967 borders, Jerusalem as the shared capital of both states, and a final settlement of all relevant issues based on international law.

In their periods of contact, Bat Shalom and the JCW have tackled some tough issues. The most bitterly disputed is the 'right of return' of Palestinians to their former homes in Israel. Their agreed principles state: 'a just solution to the Palestinian refugee question is an essential requirement for a stable and durable peace. This solution must honour the right of return of the Palestinian refugees in accordance with UN resolution 194' (ibid.). It's a cautious formulation, but an achievement none the less. Lily Traubmann, Bat Shalom's political coordinator, emphasized that the 'right of return' 'is an important demand on the Palestinian side, and the JCW must put it to us clearly if they are to maintain credibility with their own people. There's no public discussion of this at all in Israel, except for scare-mongering. It's as though the problem will disappear. But it's absolutely necessary to raise the issue. It opens up questions that go beyond the return to pre-1967 borders. It's implicitly about a return to the borders originally laid down by the United Nations in 1948.'

Not long ago the two organizations were close to agreeing a stronger and more explicit statement. A political committee of six women, three from Bat Shalom, three from the JCW, worked hard to reach agreement on it. But, Natasha told me, two years into the intifada, with the isolation of Arafat, with collective punishment going on and the silence of the international community, they had been set back. At such times the more conservative element in Bat Shalom and in the Israeli peace movement as a whole are able to 'lower the ceiling', she said, and offer fewer concessions. All the same the two organizations have developed an interesting methodology over recent years. They've engaged in what they call a 'public political correspondence', an exchange of letters published in Palestinian and Israeli newspapers simultaneously. The letters are carefully discussed on the individual sides, and then together, before publication. Through this kind of work they are gradually updating and strengthening the founding principles, and plan to republish them soon.

Problems of dialogue: Palestinian perspectives

For Palestinian women of the Jerusalem Center for Women, it remains a continually open question whether and when the contact with Israeli women is beneficial and advisable. The Link has fallen into inactivity for several periods in its ten-year life. The events of 2000 caused a rupture. Looking back to that time Natasha, director of the JCW, said she'd felt '*Yani*, we're kidding ourselves. What has this relationship brought us? We're back to convincing the world and Israel that the Occupation is unjust. Just that after thirty-eight years! We've got nowhere. The brutality of the IDF in October 2000, the helicopters bombing, assassinations, attacks on peaceful demonstrations – it was very shocking to us.'

For a while they'd ceased contact with Bat Shalom. But a couple of years later women were beginning to feel 'let's have another attempt'. So they reopened the dialogue. However, Palestinian reasons for talking are very different from those of Israelis. Amal Kreishe Barghouti, JCW board member, said, 'It's a method of survival for us, for me. For the Israelis it's more an ethical issue, an expression of political commitment.' Amal herself firmly believes, despite the recent adverse developments, that a two-state solution remains the only practicable future. Dialogue is necessary, she says, to help Israeli women like those of Bat Shalom, who are a minority in their society, to 'market' this solution in Israel. At the present moment too, they try to motivate the Israeli women to work within their community to expose 'the big lie on disengagement'.

Nevertheless the JCW women have to be very careful in defining the terms of their contact with Bat Shalom. Amal Kreishe said: 'What we have with Bat Shalom in the Link is emphatically *not* co-operation or co-existence.' While Palestinian society supports dialogue with Israel, they are against anything that could be considered 'normalization' of the situation, she continued. So JCW tread a careful line. They shun the 'people-to-people' projects that are pressed on them by foreign funders. She said: 'We have the Jerusalem Link principles to reassure Palestinians, and our own guarantees that we are only in dialogue, not in negotiation.' On the other hand, it's not all Palestinian women who would wish to be part of the Link. Natasha agreed: 'You would only have a special category of women who would want to be in the JCW. All Palestinian women want peace, but not many continue to believe that negotiation, dialogue, even just speaking to the Israeli public, is worth the effort. So you need women who see it as a valid strategy alongside the intifada and alongside official negotiations – when these happen.'

I had the opportunity of interviewing three women who did *not* see dialogue as a valid strategy in present circumstances. Nadia Naser-Najjab and Raja Rantisi both teach at Birzeit University in the West Bank; Nadia in education and psychology, Raja in languages. Rana Nashashibi directs the Palestinian Counselling Center in East Jerusalem, a community-based mental health organization. Though they have been involved in contact activities in the past, and still occasionally meet Israelis in their professional lives, they don't see dialogue as useful at present. Nadia Najjab said: 'The problem is, meeting with Israelis as Palestinians, we have one hope: to influence them, to try and change the negative perception of Palestinians that exists in Israel – and it exists even within the peace movement itself. It's us who are desperate to change the status quo ... For the Israelis there's time for a long process, for us there's not.'

Raja Rantisi wanted Palestinian voices to be heard by Israelis, but experience showed her that 'even if you become the best of friends, the situation itself hasn't changed'. Dialogue can't meet Palestinian expectations. 'Lots of Palestinians think the Israeli peace activists haven't done enough during the second intifada. There are various views on the reasons for the weakness of the movement. The struggle has become defined around specific issues, among which are: the rights of the refugees; borders; the legitimacy of suicide bombers; and the status of Jerusalem. Because the Israeli peace movement isn't a unitary voice, a lot of disputes come up between them on these things. For most Israelis now they are fundamentally threatening issues. It puts the peace movement, who would otherwise be open to talking about them, in a difficult position internally – they're seen as traitors.'

In talking with these three women I saw clearly how the profound asymmetry between Israelis and Palestinians, those who have a state and 'rights' and those whom they deprive of both, undermine projects of co-operation. They feel Israeli activists too often want Palestinians to step into their shoes and understand their difficulties within Israeli society, but are unwilling to step into Palestinian shoes and understand what *they* need to hear – an admission of shame for 1948, for 1967, for present aggression. Nadia said: 'A few do. But there are others who have always got "exclusions" in their heads. They'll say "No to the Occupation", but "Don't talk to us about the right of return!" They pick and choose the agenda. Israelis want dialogue with us so they can sleep well at night. If Palestinians want dialogue, it's so that Israelis *can't* sleep well at night.' And Raja added: 'And we're winning. They don't sleep at night!' One effect produced by the asymmetry is that some Israelis (not Bat Shalom, it's important to add) speak of themselves as a 'peace movement'. For Palestinians such a concept, of course, makes no sense. Rana said, 'What does it mean to be a "peace" activist in Palestine? We can only *resist oppression*. Justice necessarily comes first. Peace is a second step.'

Problems of dialogue: Israeli perspectives

On the Israeli side of the Green Line, too, the legitimacy and value of contact and dialogue are contested. Underlying that fact, however, is the unpalatable reality that most Jewish people pass their lives without ever getting to know 'an Arab' as a person. At most they may be aware of one (usually a man) as a nameless manual worker. (Palestinians for their part know Jews better. Nadia Najjab reminded me: the oppressed always know the oppressor better than the oppressor knows the oppressed – they need to.) Even among those Jews who wish to overcome the separation, there can be nothing routine or 'normal' about it. Yehudit Keshet told me: 'You have to make an effort to meet Palestinians. It's always somehow artificial. You say to yourself, "I *will* go and meet Palestinians".' When they do make contact, friendship between Jews and Palestinians is continually undermined by the fundamental inequality. Relative to Palestinians, Jews are always privileged, and, more specifically, are the beneficiaries of injustice, so 'when you do meet it's always a careful dance around each other's feelings, each taking care not to tread on the other's toes', as Yehudit said. Consequently, only those Jews who are deeply committed to political change seek contact with Palestinians.

Even in the context of Bat Shalom and the Jerusalem Link, the Jewish women sometimes feel ambivalence and hesitation. Some have to deal with a suspicion that women of the 'other' organization are less interested in contact with ordinary Israeli women than with elite Israeli women who have some purchase on the political system. 'Women who can make a difference, who are close to power – that's who they want to be working with.' At the same time they have to acknowledge there's some truth in Palestinian suspicions that Israeli women need the contact to make *themselves* feel better, to assuage their feelings of guilt and to show that some Israelis 'aren't that bad'. As Molly Malekar put it, Palestinians might well complain, 'You occupy us and then want our sympathy for your bleeding hearts!' It's important, she stressed, that Israeli women be very clear in their own minds, and to Palestinian women, that they have their own political interest in contact. This isn't just a patronizing kind of 'support' or 'solidarity'. 'I wouldn't dare to say to Palestinians that I'm doing what I do *in solidarity* with them. In any case it's not true. I'm part of the conflict, and I have my political interests in the contact with them.' On the basis of such realism, she was optimistic about the future of the Link: 'It's true you can't count on it, that it'll be sustained. But there are certain women on both sides who have political trust in each other, trust that they aren't in it for their careers but are genuine about dialogue. Most women know that we have a lot to lose if we split apart, not just as Israelis and Palestinians, but as feminist women.'

The presence in Bat Shalom of Palestinian Israelis aids the cross-Line link. Whichever side of the Line they live, Palestinians share the trauma of the Nakhba. Families were split up at this time, so that many are kin. Despite the half-century living apart and the huge difficulties of communication put in their way, they retain a strong sense of being one people. There have been times when relations between the two groups were not wholly trusting and untroubled. In the early years when Palestinians in Israel were experiencing the misery of military control, those in the Occupied Territories could feel they shared an oppression. But in the first intifada, Israeli Palestinians weren't actively involved. And as some Israeli Palestinians managed to benefit from Israel's overall prosperity, their continuing inequality with Jews notwithstanding, those in the Territories felt a gap opening up between the two communities. As Aida Shibli put it, Palestinians living in the territories 'may feel a bit that we "don't know how the other half lives". They would think: you have the Israeli standard of living, lucky you! They think it's easier living here than under the occupation, and of course it is.' But the second intifada has engaged Palestinians on both sides of the Green Line, and the threat of 'transfer' voiced by rightwing Israeli politicians clearly identifies Palestinian Israelis with the external 'enemy'. So today there's a greater confidence in solidarity.

Khulood Badawi is a Palestinian Israeli who, as a board member of Bat Shalom, feels positive about the Jerusalem Link. But she pointed to the inevitable inequality between an organization positioned in Jewish West Jerusalem and one in occupied East Jerusalem. The inequality is reproduced, what's more, inside Bat Shalom itself. The organization in Jerusalem is predominantly Jewish, with no Palestinian staff and, as we saw, only around 25 per cent of the board are Palestinian. Despite this, Khulood feels the Link is worthwhile because 'we do address the hard questions: Jerusalem, settlements, the '67 borders and – most difficult of all, the "right of return". We don't just choose the things on which there's easy agreement. There has been a huge process of gradual gains in agreement'.

'Being women': a basis for dialogue?

The question then remains: what exactly does 'being women' achieve in the case of the Jerusalem Link? Women are disadvantaged and marginalized in Israel and the Occupied Territories, whether in Jewish, Christian or Muslim cultures. They all experience the armed conflict in a gender-specific way. Is this enough to validate dialogue? Not necessarily. Women resist in their own, differing, ways. There are substantial inequalities in the price Jewish and Palestinian women pay for breaking gender norms. Women differ too in how much their political circumstances make it feasible or desirable to seek common ground in 'being women'.

Of the Jerusalem Link, Natasha claimed no more than 'We're sending messages to the two peoples. That we're women, with a number of principles, discussing critical issues and demands with each other. We have an opinion.' But she went on to suggest that women can find common ground in the life experiences they share: 'As women we see things differently. There's something women understand more and are able to contribute to mainstream discussions. We understand the repercussions of the occupation on everyday life, on families, on the future. We understand racism, oppression and the abuse of power. Because of our experiences of oppression in our societies, we can affiliate with each other across cultures. But be careful! The relationship hasn't been easy. Being women hasn't enabled us to bypass obstacles. On both sides we were brought up in conventional societies.'

While women's experiences could be a motivation for dialogue, it was not necessarily the case that they would be a subject of *direct* discussion between Israeli and Palestinian women in the Link.

Natasha went on to explain: 'Although it would be relevant from a social point of view, we can't talk about "family law" with the Israeli women – with Bat Shalom, for instance. I could talk to an Italian or another woman about it, but it's forbidden for me to be a bridge between Jewish and Arab women on such an issue.'

I asked Raja, Rana and Nadia what they felt about this. Rana felt cautious about the kind of feminism that shaped the thinking of some Jewish women activists. Western feminists had failed to recognize that Palestinian women 'start from a different place' and their priorities should be respected. 'We didn't get that tolerance from the West.' They had raised issues of undoubted importance to women, she said, such as equal pay for equal work, and the perception that 'the personal is political' (especially vital in areas where the patriarch l family is still the norm). But problems arose when moving from concepts to action:

> What issues get priority? Whom should we target? At what level? This is complicated. I do believe that in principle all oppression should be seen as being at the same level, there should be no 'hierarchy of oppression'. But in the case of Palestine, can you really talk about domestic violence before you talk about the occupation? The more urgent thing, the thing that creates the conditions for violence, is the occupation. This is a major divergence between us. Western feminists can condemn rape, but when it comes to occupation there's a certain ambivalence. In my view, if you condemn rape you have to condemn the occupation, which is itself a rape. Rape and occupation both attempt to debilitate, to annihilate our identity, to reduce us to submission. (Nashashibi 2003)

It was a wonder to them that Israeli or foreign feminists could say in all seriousness, as they often do, 'Tell me, how do you suffer *as women* under the occupation?' Nadia said: 'I can't be so feminist when I see the checkpoints. I see Israeli soldiers treating men and women alike. I see it from a national perspective. We're suffering here, men and women both. How can I say those Israeli women soldiers at the checkpoint are my sisters?'

Talking feminism with Israeli women, they felt, is bound to be superficial because in the most important matters Palestinian women have more in common with Palestinian men than with Israeli women. They may very well have a critique of Palestinian men and talk to each other about how their society is male-dominated, but in the present circumstances that critique has to remain within their own community.

Rana, Raja and Nadia are from the left and, though not now active in political parties, are still informed by ideas they bring with them from student days in the Communist Party of Palestine. So when talking to Israeli women, as Nadia put it, 'what I want to discuss with them is political. I want to know what's their position on the occupation and how they plan to work with us against that.' Whether the dialogue is to be about politics or women's issues, it's the same. 'I ask are they willing to apologize for what Israel's done and what it's doing now. If they are, then we can talk.' Likewise, from her standpoint in Bat Shalom, Molly Malekar said: 'Even if we agree on women's issues, feminism won't necessarily bring us to the same side of the table, because the national issue will remain to be resolved between us.'

Within Israel: Palestinians in a Jewish state

If in Jerusalem it's impossible to forget the occupation, in the north of Israel, where Palestinian towns and villages are located within the wide agricultural landscapes of the Jewish kibbutzim and moshavim, what you can't forget is the basic inequality of Palestinians and Jews inside Israel. Palestinian citizens of Israel are in theory just that – citizens. But in a state that's formally and officially Jewish they necessarily in practice lack the status of full citizens. There are several aspects to the massive discrimination against Israeli Palestinians. One concerns property. Having been, in many cases, displaced and/or dispossessed in 1948, they are not permitted to reclaim their property or to buy land or buildings outside designated areas. Most have been obliged to adopt an urban way of life. Once independent farmers, their economic opportunities are now severely restricted and many are now hired hands for Jews. The land laws result in a high degree of physical concentration – Arab hamlets have become villages, villages have become towns, all densely packed.

Another aspect of Palestinians' second-class citizenship derives from the fact that they may not serve in the Israeli Defence Forces. Few Palestinians, of course, would wish to do so. Nevertheless, for Jews such service is a recognized rite of passage to citizenship from which Palestinians are excluded. Palestinians also experience cultural marginalization in Israel. Although Arabic is one of the two official languages of the Israeli state, its use is not promoted. Jewish children emerge from school with no more than a few words. Television programmes barely recognize the presence of an Arabic culture in the country. Aida Shibli told me of her surprise and delight when one day a message flashed on to the screen saying 'Have a good day' in Arabic. It turned out to be an advertisement by an NGO working for equal rights in Israel. 'But just the fact of seeing Arabic on the screen – that was amazing. It never happens. Usually there's no mention of us, nothing about us. Zero.'

There's economic discrimination, too. In the few institutions where Palestinians and Jews do mix, Palestinians' experience is something like that of women in male-dominated organizations. You have the qualifications, but you are overlooked. You do the work, but somebody else gets the credit. Even in left and feminist organizations, Manal Massalha told me, you have to be alert to the way power works. 'Even Bat Shalom reproduces the power relations of Israeli society in microcosm. For example, you have to ask, who decides the agenda? Who takes what for granted? It's an Ashkenazi Jewish hegemony. For things to be equal you have to *specifically* include me, the collectivity I belong to, my different experience.'

As a result of the incomplete citizenship of Palestinians in Israel, Khulood Badawi said: 'We're always seeking rights and laws that guarantee equality, challenging the state on its duty toward us. They always turn the question round and remind us of our duties to the state, challenging us on our loyalty.'

As well as the structural racism inherent in the state as a Jewish state, there is a great deal of deeply imbued personal racism. Khulood said: 'There's great ignorance about us among the Jewish majority. They think of us only as "Arabs" and believe they know everything there is to know about *them*. They don't recognize us in the way they recognize other Arabs – as "Egyptians" or "Jordanians", for instance. We're just "Arabs" with no roots, as if we were created along with the Israeli state. The only kind of relations Israeli Jews have with "Arabs" is as their boss. It's embedded in Jewish consciousness that dirty work is for Arabs. So the relation isn't based on acknowledgement of equality, even at the human level. It's always from above looking down.'

Palestinians are considered by many Jews to be *less than* human. Yehudit Keshet told me that she and other women in Machsom-Watch are often told by soldiers at the checkpoints, depriving Palestinians of water, food and toilets, 'Don't worry about them, they don't feel it the way you or I do.' They are also considered *inhuman*. Sharon Dolev said, 'A lot of Jews consider racism to be realism. They'll say, "We know one thing about Arabs: they're people who don't value life."' Aida Shibli works as head nurse of a hospital emergency room. This skill and status don't protect her from a patient who feels free to shout at her and insult her, 'You Arab!' Mariam Yusuf Abu Husein, an activist in Northern Bat Shalom, put it this way: 'Arabs and Jews are Semites, so they are not supposed to hate each other. But due to the crisis there is a fertile environment for hatred between the two peoples. However, I think that most Jews *hate Arabs*, while most Arabs *hate what Jews do*. I work with Jews in the hope that things will be different for my son than for my father. My father, whatever his abilities, felt put down by Jews, and hated them. I want my son to look at those people my father hated, and see them not from below but from the height that his abilities deserve.'

Khulood told me a personal story to illustrate the existential gap between Palestinian and Jewish people in Israel. The story is important, she said, because it is indicative of a wider reality. As a child she took part in one of the 'people-to-people' contacts that were current after the Oslo Accords. Children of her Palestinian high school (education is ethnically segregated in Israel) were taken to a Jewish school to meet local Jewish children. 'The first shock was seeing the school – so grand and well-equipped compared with ours, it might have been a university! The next shock was to find we had no common needs in the encounter. Their need was to test the stereotype, check out if we were human beings. The kind of question they asked us was, "Do you have sex before marriage?" We didn't even know there was such a thing! For our part, our need was to talk about our nationality, our identity, the Nakhba, the occupation. Then again, of course they didn't know Arabic, and our Hebrew was not so good as theirs, so our capacities in the meeting were totally unequal. I realized later that I had been *used* by the Ministry of Education. We were part of a programme. It was an experience that did me personal and lasting damage.'

Northern Bat Shalom's main contribution to ending the conflict in Palestine/Israel, their 'anti-war' activism, is challenging this Jewish racism towards the Palestinians who live among them. As long as the racism prevails, so will armed conflict. The oppression of Palestinians in the Occupied Territories will continue to seem legitimate to many Jews, and the threat of expulsion will hang over Palestinian citizens of Israel.

Northern Bat Shalom was formed in 1993 by Jewish and Palestinian women living in 'Megiddo, Nazareth and The Valleys'. It's in the region known as the Triangle and Lower Galilee, a part of Israel much of which was wrongfully seized in 1948 and has a large population of Palestinians. As mentioned above, they have an office in the Jewish town of Afula, and two part-time paid programme coordinators. One is Yehudit Zaidenberg, a Jewish woman who was born and has lived most of her life on a kibbutz. The other, until recently, was Nizreen Mazzawi, a Palestinian from Nazareth. A Palestinian replacement for Nizreen is being sought because it's felt to be important to share the work equally between a Palestinian and a Jew. Lily Traubmann, also Jewish, is Bat Shalom's political coordinator. She lives in Megiddo kibbutz and is active in Northern Bat Shalom as well as in Jerusalem. The remainder of this chapter is based mainly on interviews with Yehudit and Lily, and with Samira Khoury and Mariam Abu Husein (already mentioned above), Palestinian Israelis living respectively in the towns of Nazareth and Umm el-Fahm, and both active members of Northern Bat Shalom.[4]

Moving beyond dialogue

For its first five or six years, the main activity of Northern Bat Shalom was 'dialogue workshops', bringing together Palestinian Israeli women of the Arab towns and villages and Jewish women of the kibbutzim and moshavim of the Wadi Ara, Lower Galilee and The Valleys. Yehudit Zaidenberg explains: 'It was a process of "getting to know each other". We believed that, with acquaintance and knowledge, the huge fear each felt of the other would lessen and relationships would form. And that did happen.' Once confidence was gained, social and cultural activity no longer seemed enough. They felt ready to deal with political issues. The aim then shifted and became, Yehudit explained, 'to effect change in the political thinking among the people around us – ultimately to effect change in political reality'.

The events of October 2000 were a turning point for Bat Shalom as for many leftists in Israel. Local Palestinians were very aroused. Whereas many Jews on the left felt disappointed by the new radicalism of the Palestinians, Yehudit and other Jewish women in Bat Shalom felt a profound solidarity with it. She says: 'To me what happened wasn't a surprise. We'd known that Palestinians couldn't endure such inequality and injustice for ever. What astonished me was that my friends in the kibbutz felt so betrayed.' At that moment she felt alienated from the latter. So October 2000 resulted in a drawing apart within some of the membership of Northern Bat Shalom. It could no longer be taken for granted that Jews and Palestinian members were completely in accord. The numbers of actively engaged women fell off. Fewer came to participate in their events.

Among those who remained, there was a radicalization. The choice of themes for discussion began to take more risks with conventional Jewish opinion, which in this rural region is conservative Zionism. Since 1996, a major event in the calendar of Northern Bat Shalom has been Sukkot, a Jewish festival, when they set up a sukkah, or tent, and invite women and men for a programme of talks and discussions, and a hold a roadside demonstration. In 2002 the theme they chose for the sukkah was 'racism'. It was a bold and controversial move. Yehudit said, 'We need a radical change in Israeli thinking. There are solutions. But for them to become possible we need first to see Palestinians as human beings.' It dismayed some of the more Zionist members, including Vera Jordan, a former board member and still today a committed activist in Northern Bat Shalom. She felt: 'Introducing racism is provocative. Humanist Jews can't accept that nationalism is racism. For them racism is "what the Nazis did". They can't see themselves as that bad. And they are not. They won't be able to identify.'

None the less, 'little by little we became more anti-Zionist', Yehudit said. Some Jewish women did indeed withdraw. Some Palestinian women pulled out too, but for a different reason. In the political conditions after October 2000 they no longer felt it productive to work with Jewish women. For both Palestinian and Jewish women, the price paid in their communities for working with each other had become greater. Bat Shalom was reduced to an active core in which both the numbers and relationships of Palestinians and Jews were more equal. The emphasis of the group's activities shifted away from cultural co-existence work, such as celebrating Christmas, Hanukah and Ramadan together. They started a series of 'political cafés', looking for instance at the effect on women of globalization and economic trends. At election time they exposed speakers from different political parties to women's questions. They showed films on Palestinian and women's issues, and invited their directors to discuss them with the audience. They organized bus tours to 'unrecognized' and 'vanished' Palestinian villages, particularly disturbing to Jews who saw for the first time the extraordinary deprivation of some Palestinian communities and were obliged to face the reality that under the lush grass of many kibbutzim lie the foundation stones of destroyed Palestinian villages.

I learned about these more recent developments from Mariam Yusuf Abu Husein, a nurse responsible for children's health in a school in Umm el Fahm. She first encountered Bat Shalom in 2001 when she saw the sukkah at Megiddo crossroads and went in, curious to find out what was going on in the tent. She was attracted to the organization by two things. These were feminist women who saw Arabs as a partner in a common struggle; and they were opposing the occupation and active on 'all the burning issues'. She became one of a new 'generation' of Palestinian activists that have brought a challenging presence to Northern Bat Shalom. She's clear that Palestinians give as much as they get from being part of it. Her reply evoked 'positionality' for me with wonderful clarity. 'If you were to ask me why I'm in Bat Shalom, it's because Lily, Yehudit and the other Jewish women are *like* me, but they are *not* me. They don't live in my skin. They can't do it without me.' Lily, who overheard this, said, 'I agree utterly!'

In relating to her Jewish partners, Mariam has certain conditions. 'I want Jews first to acknowledge all this land they live on was Palestinian – after that we can talk. I would have preferred they'd never come. Now they're here, and we live with that. But I want the wrong confessed. Only then can we talk about a solution.' That having been said, she finds a valuable quality in Bat Shalom: they can and do discuss anything. No issues are too sensitive to tackle. 'It's not that we expect necessarily to resolve all our differences, but at least we can talk about them.' In few situations where Jews and Palestinians meet is the talk so honest.

Although she liked the principles of Bat Shalom, Mariam felt she could contribute new ideas and directions. She wondered, for instance, why the group's main annual event was at Sukkot. Although the event had always been organized by Bat Shalom's Palestinian and Jewish members together, the date is associated with the Jewish calendar. It had been chosen because mothers would be on holiday at that time. But which mothers? She pointed out that this Jewish Feast of Tabernacles is not a holiday for Palestinian women. She suggested Bat Shalom might think of a day that could be more generally relevant.

After the first dispossession of Palestinians in the creation of the Israeli state, land seizures continued. In particular, Israeli Palestinians commemorate 30 March as Yom al Ard (Land Day). On this date in 1976 the Israeli state, in its programme of 'Judaization' of the Galilee, expropriated land from the villages of Arraba, Sakhnin and Deir Hanna. Here for the first time the villagers rose up in opposition. Six people, including one woman, were killed in the resulting police violence. The commemoration of Land Day had always been essentially a Palestinian event. When the Israeli Jewish left recognized the day it had been to support Palestinians. Now Mariam and the other Palestinian women of Bat Shalom suggested to the Jewish women that this day should be seen as 'not just our problem but yours too'. Land Day had been lived by both communities, the oppressor and oppressed. Now they needed to remember those events together. She said: 'It was very important to me and other Palestinians in the organization that all Bat Shalom women should take on Yom al Ard as their own issue.' Lily Traubman adds, 'This was a very radical step – to recognize that Yom al Ard is an Israeli concern, not just a Palestinian one. That we all have to take responsibility for it.'

The step was radical in another way, too. In their Land Day activity, Bat Shalom represented the theft of the land as a women's issue. Yom al Ard activities had always been led by men, with women following behind in the demonstrations, but never part of the leadership. Mariam said: 'Bat Shalom presents itself as a feminist organization. Failing to understand this is the very opposite of feminist. Women have a special relation to the land. Women work the land, they plant the seeds, they carry the water from the wells. The well or spring is a feminine symbol, it is protective, containing, and gives people water to live. Palestinian women used to meet each other at the well or at the spring. It was a rare thing, a legitimate public space for women. When Palestinian communities were displaced from their land and forced to be town dwellers, women suffered in a particular way. Yom al Ard marks a significant loss for women.'

Now Bat Shalom commemorates Land Day annually, in Umm el-Fahm, Nazareth or another Palestinian location, the first women's organization to do so. They mount a two-day event, at which the older Palestinian women recount the events of the Nakhba and

Land Day from their perspective, visits are made to local villages, and there are invited speakers. Up to a hundred women attend these occasions, including many Jews. The younger Palestinian women who attend are often hearing this history for the first time.

Northern Bat Shalom work as much as possible in both the Hebrew and the Arabic language. They've gathered and published testimonies of older women, seeing this careful listening to women as 'a feminist way of working'. A current project involves young people in nearby Palestinian and Jewish communities being trained in interview method so they can record older women relatives remembering 'what they did in 1948'. The two groups of children will join up to prepare a piece of theatre based on the testimonies. Lily emphasizes that this memory work is not about 'victimhood', but about how women actively struggled and resisted the brutal processes to which the Israeli state subjected the Palestinian population. 'We want to bring to view an alternative kind of heroism – a heroism that's not militaristic.'

We saw earlier in the chapter how Bat Shalom and the JCW, women's organizations both, come together in the Jerusalem Link in implicit awareness that they share something as women. The Link principles state that 'women are committed to a peaceful solution of our conflict' and that 'women must be central partners in the peace process' (JCW 2005). But the focus of the principles is the search for a just resolution of the conflict, without further mention of gender relations or women's rights. As we've seen, in present political circumstances it's impossible for women from the two sides of the Green Line explicitly to make women's oppression the basis of their dialogue. The same applies to Jewish–Palestinian relations *inside* Israel. It's not that the patriarchal oppression inherent in 'one's own' national and family structures is in any sense denied. Indeed, all Northern Bat Shalom's practical work together is predicated on it. It's just that the overt and public critique is carried on elsewhere, separately.[5] The Jewish and Palestinian partners in Northern Bat Shalom each implicitly support the other in their critique, but the historic injustice and present imbalance of power make it politically tactless to be more explicit.

On the other hand, it's clear, even if barely articulated, that women in their everyday lives feel a connection between the racist construction of enmity and the sexist construction of women as other. In seeking each other out as women they turn the connection to political advantage. New Profile, the Israeli feminist antimilitarist organization, writes of Israeli militarization that it's a process that revolves around 'othering'.

> It turns on maintaining the image of a fearful enemy thought to 'understand only force' and on projecting the image of defenceless, passive 'women-and-children' whose need for protection justifies state violence. The enemy, on the one hand, and 'women-and-children', on the other, are militarism's 'others' – each serving to sanction the practice of war and the continued supremacy of a masculine elite of fighters. (New Profile 2005)

Though they would not have presumed to do so, New Profile could easily in these words about Israel have been describing Palestinian society too, with its cornered, embattled and increasingly militant men, and the women and children whose safety and honour they feel obliged to protect.

The connection between sexism and racist enmity became very clear to me when I was in Jerusalem, listening to Aida Shibli, Bat Shalom board member and Palestinian citizen of Israel. She has no doubt that the oppression of women, the oppression of Palestinians and, more widely, the effects of past and present imperialism are intimately linked. She said: 'If you de-legitimate one section of the population, the 20 per cent that's Palestinians, then you can easily de-legitimate the 50 per cent that's women. When you say anybody is other you legitimate every othering process and exclusion. We have to insist that it's the same mechanism working against women, against Palestinians and in the violence of war worldwide. We must work against all three simultaneously.'

Notes

1 For the names and details of those to whom I am indebted for the material on which this chapter is based, please see Acknowledgements.

2 Other members of Coalition of Women for Peace are the Fifth Mother; *Noga – a Feminist Journal*; NELED (Women for Co-existence); and the Women's International League for Peace and Freedom, Israel chapter.

3 Amira Gelblum, Judy Blanc and Debby Lerman, whom I interviewed in other contexts, are also board members of Bat Shalom.

4 In 1996 I made a study of Jewish–Palestinian relationships in Northern Bat Shalom, see Cockburn (1998).

5 There are Israeli feminist organizations concerned with issues such as discrimination and violence against women. One is Isha l'Isha

in Haifa, another is Kol Ha-Isha in West Jerusalem. There are also women's organizations in the Palestinian communities that address women's issues. For example, Al Zahraa, based in Sakhnin and active more widely in Palestinian northern Israel, writes in its introductory leaflet: 'Arab women are the most disadvantaged sector of the population, facing double discrimination, as Arabs within the Jewish state, and as women within an Arab patriarchal society, dominated by men.'

FIVE

Achievements and contradictions: WILPF and the UN

§ It's time to return to transnational networks. In chapter 2 we met Women in Black, Code Pink: Women for Peace and the East Asia–US–Puerto Rico Women against Militarism Network. But these are small and new transnational phenomena in comparison with the venerable Women's International League for Peace and Freedom (WILPF), which has its origins in the turmoil of the First World War and has thrived to become today a substantial NGO with an office in Geneva, consultative status at the United Nations and branches in thirty-seven countries.

The peace-activist women of WILPF had their forerunners. Jill Liddington recounts how a Quaker-led peace movement in Britain started as early as 1816, in the aftermath of the Napoleonic Wars. From the beginning, many of the members were women, and by 1820 Female Auxiliary Peace Societies existed in several towns in Britain. In the 1840s peace-minded women also formed Olive Leaf Circles of which there were 150, with an estimated 3,000 members, by the early 1850s (Liddington 1989). Joyce Berkman credits a Swedish feminist, Frederika Bremer, with being the first to put forward the idea of a woman-only international alliance dedicated to peace. It was 1854, the year the Crimean War began. Some years later, in Geneva in 1867, soon after the American Civil War with its massive death toll, Eugenie Niboyet founded just such an autonomous organization of women for peace: the Ligue Internationale de la Paix et de la Liberté. France's WILPF section still carries this name today. Niboyet considered the struggle for international peace as 'inseparable from economic and social justice', a conviction that would persist in WILPF (Berkman 1990: 145). In Britain in 1872, at the close of the Franco-Prussian war which cost Europe a quarter of a million military casualties and half a million civilian dead and wounded, a Women's Peace and Arbitration Auxiliary of the British Peace Society was set up, and many Quaker women continued to be active around the peace issue into the 1880s (Liddington 1989).

Berkman concludes: 'As founders of all-female peace societies and active members of peace groups including men, women enjoyed more presence and influence on the peace movement in the 19th century than on any other reform movement, save perhaps Abolition' (ibid.).

However, the rise of the suffrage movement in the later years of the nineteenth century deflected women's attention from international relations. The turn of the century saw the Spanish–American War bringing death and destruction in the Pacific and Caribbean, and the Boer War inflicting atrocities in South Africa. Individually, many women continued to be preoccupied by these events, but the momentum was now in the suffrage movement. Many women believed that winning the vote and getting women represented in political decision-making was the best hope of bringing an end to war. The onset of the First World War heightened the tension between these two concerns and forced a split among suffragists in France, Britain and the USA. The majority chose to support their governments in pursuit of the war. The minority, brave enough to withstand the surge of patriotism, continued to link the refusal of war with women's right to representation (ibid.).

The Women's International League for Peace and Freedom

In February 1915 a small group of such women living in the Netherlands, Belgium, Germany and Britain called an international congress of women of the belligerent countries to protest against the war and seek the means for ending it. It would take place in The Hague, in neutral Netherlands (Bussey and Tims 1981). They enlisted the participation of women of the United States' Women's Peace Party, and on 13 April 1915, forty-seven women sailed from New York. The following day in London a National Conference on Women was held at Central Hall, Westminster, to discuss a peace settlement. Of the women attending, 180 enrolled for the Hague congress, though British government intervention prevented all but three, who happened to be outside Britain at the time, from attending (Liddington 1989).

The four-day International Congress of Women opened on 28 April 1915, attended by 1,136 delegates from twelve countries, including Germany and Austria, with more than 2,000 women present at the final session. The event seems in retrospect, and perhaps appeared at the time, an all but unbelievable achievement. Just across the border, Belgium was already occupied by German forces. Only a hundred miles to the south the two armies were dug into the trenches of Ypres. It was agreed that the congress would not address the question of relative responsibility for the war. Instead, the focus was on the democratic control of foreign policy, the practicalities of a negotiated peace and women's suffrage, still high on the women's agenda. Interestingly, one of the resolutions adopted at The Hague foreshadowed UN Security Council Resolution 1325, to be discussed below, in calling for the inclusion of women's voices in the peace settlement (Bussey and Tims 1981).

The congress established an International Women's Committee for Permanent Peace and committed two groups of envoys, one in Europe and one in the USA, to carry its resolutions in person to the heads of state of both warring and neutral countries. The envoys were received with respect, but there was no response to their call for a conference of neutral nations to mediate between the belligerent states (Liddington 1989). In May 1919, not long after the armistice, women from both the winning and losing side in the war held a second congress to coincide with the meeting of statesmen at Versailles to draft the peace treaty. As the details of the post-war settlement emerged from Versailles, the women's congress issued resolutions strongly criticizing its punitive terms, which they correctly foresaw would lead to poverty and starvation in the defeated countries and give rise to more national hatred and a renewal of war. It was clear now that a continuing organization was needed to advocate for a women's peace and a people's peace. It took the name, the Women's International League for Peace and Freedom.

Harriet Alonso picks up the story of post-war WILPF. Soon after the Zurich conference an office was opened in Geneva. By the mid-1920s the organization had 50,000 members in forty countries. In the USA WILPF was already reaching out to women in Latin American countries and protesting against US military interference in the region, as they have had cause to continue doing to the present day. In Europe, WILPF was active, particularly on disarmament and the strengthening of the League of Nations as an instrument for peace. The 1930s, however, brought serious dilemmas, not only for WILPF, but for the peace movement generally. It was a struggle to maintain unity and coherence in the face of Japan's aggression in Asia, Mussolini's invasion of Abyssinia, Franco's troops destroying democracy in Spain and the arrival of Jewish refugees fleeing

German Nazism. WILPF's members and branches were divided, with some continuing the call for universal disarmament while more left-leaning women stressed social and economic revolution and resistance to fascism, even at the cost of war (Alonso 1993; Bussey and Tims 1980). I shall return to this painful tension between 'justice' and 'peace' in chapter 7.

No sooner had the Second World War war ended than the Cold War began. WILPF were in an uneasy position. With their campaign against nuclear weapons and a slogan of 'peace and freedom', many saw them not as neutral but as aligned with the Soviet Union. In the USA they were harassed in the McCarthyite purge of communists (Swerdlow 1990). On the other hand, ironically, with the rise of the new left in the 1960s, WILPF was deserted by some women who saw it as too *anti*-communist (and too hierarchical, too conservative in style with its meetings, petititions and lectures). A new international organization now formed to the left of WILPF, with strong representation in the USA. Called the Women's Strike for Peace (WSP), it opposed bomb tests and the draft for the Vietnam War. Some delegates even flew to Indonesia in July 1965 to meet Vietnamese women of the National Liberation Front and communist government of North Vietnam, signing a statement opposing the US presence there (Alonso 1993).

Second-wave feminism was born in these same years. The United Nations responded to the movement, proclaiming a global Decade for Women from 1975 to 1985. 'Women' began to get a profile, worldwide. While WILPF and WSP were active in this movement, 1970s feminists in Europe and the USA were less concerned with peace than the struggle for reproductive rights and sexual autonomy. But then, on 17 November 1980, a signal event occurred in the USA. Two thousand women marched on the Pentagon in opposition to the Cold War, the arms race and nuclear testing, among them many WILPF women. They dramatized their action with giant puppets. They made a 'cemetery' commemorating unknown women, victims of the war machine. Their banners read 'Take the Toys from the Boys'. This Women's Pentagon Action was repeated the following year (ibid.).

In 1981, when it was learned in the UK that the British government had agreed to the basing of US cruise and Pershing missiles there, some women walked in protest from Wales to the Royal Airforce Base at Greenham Common in Berkshire, one of the sites proposed for their location. Like the US women, they stated that as men traditionally left their homes to march to war, now women were doing the same in the interests of peace. As we shall see in chapter 6, this was the beginning of a mass movement of British women against US–UK war policy, involving an encampment at Greenham that would endure for more than a decade despite continual efforts, verbal, legal and physical, to remove it. US women set up a women's peace camp at Seneca Falls, and the US WILPF section raised money to buy a farmhouse there to serve as back-up to the camp (ibid.). There would soon be massive protests in Europe, culminating in a day of action on 22 October 1983 that saw big street demonstrations in many cities. WILPF collected a million signatures in the course of one year and delivered them to NATO. None of this stopped the first shipment of missiles, which arrived on 12 November.

Thus, campaigning for an end to enmity with the Soviet Union, the arms race and the nuclear threat during the 1980s was a strengthening experience for women's peace activism, overcoming apathy and healing former divisions. WILPF emerged into the 1990s in strength, campaigning against the Gulf War, the continuing aggression and sanctions against Iraq, the Yugoslav nationalist wars and the Rwandan genocide. Today, in a new millennium, like the anti-war movement worldwide, it is preoccupied with resisting the 'war on terror'.

WILPF's organization and scope

WILPF is organized as a pyramid, on a base of national sections and their local groups. The principal decision-making body is a three-yearly international congress of members, to which national sections send a number of elected delegates, proportional to membership size. Their implementation is promoted in the intervening years by an annual International Executive Committee meeting comprised of members elected by national sections to act on behalf of International WILPF. Each of these, too, has its open annual general meeting, its elected president and treasurer and its executive group. International committees carry forward work on themes agreed in each three-year forward plan. WILPF is thus much more formal, as well as larger and more widely known and recognized, than Women in Black or Code Pink.

The League is administered from an office in Geneva which implements the IEC's decisions, ensures the flow of information to and from national sections and supports the agreed programme of activity. It publishes a periodic newsletter, *International Peace Update*, and liaises with WILPF's UN offices. The League has had consultative status at the UN through the Economic and Social Council since 1948, and in addition has special consultative relations with the Food and Agricultural Organization in Rome, the International Labour Organization in Geneva and the UN Children's Fund in New York. As well as pressing the UN on issues relating to peace and security and their other substantive concerns, WILPF persistently lobby for reform and democratization of the UN itself (WILPF 2006a).

WILPF is remarkable, too, for the breadth of its concerns. Even in 1915 the founding women understood, and WILPF still organizes on the understanding, 'that all the problems that lead countries to domestic and international violence are connected and all need to be solved in order to achieve sustainable peace' (WILPF 2006b). This means in practice that the organization does not limit itself to campaigning on issues of war and peace, militarization and disarmament, although those concerns remain central. Its Program and Plan of Action 2004–2007 includes major campaigns on environmental sustainability, and on global economic and social justice. Under the former heading they take on the right to clean water and a healthy environment; the rights of indigenous peoples; education for sustainable development; the implementation of the Kyoto Protocol on climate change and other international conventions; and a critique of 'the UN global compact with transnational corporations'. They oppose privatization and commodification of essential common resources; campaign to cancel the debts of poor nations; support fair trade and the elimination of poverty; and work for human rights and democracy. They see the three programme areas as overlapping and reinforcing each other, and are active in the broad-based World Social Forum movement (WILPF 2006c).

Another strong feature of WILPF is its commitment to anti-racism. Soon after its formation in 1915 there were African American women activists in the Women's Peace Party, forerunner of WILPF in the USA. But they were few, and the reasons would be familiar to WILPF women today: on the one hand racism was prevalent among white Americans, and on the other for most black American women peace was not the priority. The white leadership of WILPF established an Interracial Committee, but it proved controversial and had little success in improving the ethnic balance (Blackwell 2004). After the Second World War some fresh African American faces appeared in WILPF. They brought a distinctive understanding of peace, rooting it soundly in racial justice. As Mary Church Terrell had said to an all-white audience at the International Congress of the Women's Peace Party in 1919: 'White people might talk about permanent peace until doomsday, but they could never have it till the dark races were treated fair and square' (ibid.: 188). It is certainly due to the African American pioneers in WILPF that the organization today makes anti-racism central to its campaigning.

Carrying 'women, peace and security' into the UN[1]

WILPF today reaches women far beyond its membership, not only through its websites (<www.wilpf.org>, <www.wilpf.int.ch> and various local sites) but particularly through hosting 'PeaceWomen'. This widely read web portal (<www.peacewomen.org>) is an outcome of another phase in WILPF's life and work to which I now turn. It's the most remarkable institutional achievement of women's anti-war movements to date: the acquisition of United Nations Security Council (UNSC) Resolution 1325 of 31 October 2000, on Women, Peace and Security.

From the global perspective on women's movements against militarism and war that I'm bringing to this book, the resolution is significant in several ways. It came about through the efforts of women of many countries, some thinking of themselves as feminists, some not. It entailed co-operation between women very differently positioned in relation to structures of power as well as differently located in relation to wars, and successful handling of the mechanisms of an international institution – and the UN Security Council might be considered the most influential one of all. It involved a wide, nameless, ad hoc transnational network, very different in kind from those considered in earlier chapters. It has been, and remains, an informal, unnamed but highly productive alliance, in the interests of a specific project, of women in local and international non-governmental organizations, governments, many departments of the United Nations and in universities.

How much of the network's achievement is due to individual women and how much to the institutions in which they were located is difficult to say. Tracing the history it's possible to see a certain serendipity – it just so happened that 'so-and-so' was there at the right moment. But she, or he, could scarcely have been effective as a lone individual without organizational backing. Personally, I believe both are important and for this reason I mention many individual women's names below. The reader should not suppose, though, that these were the only women involved. A full list would run to hundreds, perhaps thousands, and would include a web of women spreading from the United Nations Plaza in New York to the killing fields of many war-afflicted countries.

United Nations Security Council Resolution 1325 is brief and easily grasped.[2] Its preamble acknowledges both the specific effect of armed conflict on women and women's role in preventing and resolving conflict, setting these in the context of the Security Council's responsibility for the maintenance of international peace and security. It has eighteen brief points covering, broadly speaking, three principal themes. One is *protection*, including the recognition of women's rights, a clearer understanding of gender-specific needs in time of war, the protection of women and girls from gender-based violence, particularly rape and other forms of sexual abuse, and an end to impunity for these crimes. A second is *participation*. Women's work for peace must be recognized, they must be included in decision-making at all levels in national and regional institutions, including in significant posts in the UN itself, in mechanisms for the prevention and management of conflict, and in negotiations for peace. A third theme is the insertion of a *gender perspective* into UN peacekeeping operations, and in measures of demobilization, reintegration and reconstruction after war. The adoption of the resolution was the culmination of a two-day debate. It was the first time since the foundation of the United Nations that the Security Council, the peak of the UN structure, the body vested with responsibility for the world's security, had devoted an entire session to debating women's experiences in conflict and post-conflict situations (Cohn et al. 2004).

How did this come about? The groundwork was laid by women attending the United Nations sequence of World Conferences on Women. The issue of women in relation to war and peace was addressed with particular energy at the third conference in Nairobi in 1985. Resulting from the fourth, in Beijing in 1995, the Platform for Action featured 'Women and Armed Conflict' as one of twelve 'critical areas of concern'. The Commission on the Status of Women (CSW), a functional commission of the UN Economic and Social

Council, subsequently reviewed, chapter by chapter, the Beijing document, debating the 'Women and Armed Conflict' chapter in its conference of 1998. How could these proposals be operationalized? At the two-week-long meeting, among hundreds of women were thirty or forty from local women's organizations in conflict zones around the world. A group of international NGOs calling themselves the Women and Armed Conflict Caucus, coordinated by WILPF, led the process of drafting an outcome document. It was at this meeting that the emphasis of the activists shifted subtly from getting armed conflict on to the UN 'woman agenda' to getting 'women and armed conflict' on to the main agenda. They set their sights on the Security Council, the power centre of the UN, responsible for the maintenance of international peace and security.

In the year 2000, at the UN General Assembly 23rd Special Session, government delegations examined further initiatives needed to implement the Beijing Declaration and Platform for Action. The event was termed Beijing Plus Five. It resulted in a political declaration with sections on women and armed conflict. More importantly the CSW conference in March that year proved to be a turning point. Anwarul Chowdhury, Ambassador of Bangladesh to the United Nations, was currently president of the Security Council. On 8 March, International Women's Day, which occurred during the conference, he made a powerful speech, stressing the importance of examining the intersections between gender, peace and security. He prompted the issue of a Security Council press statement on the same theme, and continued to be supportive of the caucus in their pursuit of a Security Council open session.

At this point, warmly mandated by the many outspoken women coming to the CSW from war-zones, the caucus became the NGO Working Group on Women and Armed Conflict. Its members were: Amnesty International (Florence Martin was their enthusiast in New York, and Barbara Lochbihler would soon leave WILPF for Amnesty); International Alert (often represented by Eugenia Piza-Lopez and Sanam Naraghi-Anderlini); the Hague Appeal for Peace (Cora Weiss); the Women's Commission for Refugee Women and Children (Maha Muna); and the International Peace Research Association (represented by Betty Reardon). Later, the Women's Caucus for Gender Justice (Rhonda Copelon) would be involved. Finally, there was WILPF. Edith Ballantyne, secretary general of the League for twenty-six years, had now become WILPF's Special

Adviser on UN Matters. Since Nairobi and before, she had been pressing for the recognition of women as actors for peace. Felicity Hill was director of the WILPF office at the UN. She continued to convene and coordinate the efforts of the NGOs. In my interview with her I learned about the intensive lobbying and diplomacy of the next few months.

The NGO women were by now, in terms of UN mores, stepping well out of line. This was a piece of feminist chutzpah. Resolution 1325 may well be the only Security Council resolution for which the groundwork, the diplomacy and lobbying, the drafting and redrafting, was almost entirely the work of civil society, and certainly the first in which the actors were almost all women. But the NGOs needed allies inside the system. They intensified their cultivation of the women's advocates in the UN structures, particularly the Department for the Advancement of Women (DAW), the Secretary General's Special Adviser on Gender Issues (Angela King), and the United Nations Development Fund for Women (UNIFEM) where Noeleen Heyzer, director, and Jennifer Klot, peace and security adviser, were key actors. Initially sceptical about the NGOs' prospect of getting a Security Council session, they gradually warmed to the task of supporting them.

The presidency of the UNSC rotates between countries on a monthly basis. Each president may, if she or he wishes, initiate a thematic debate. They needed one of the ambassadors to pick up 'Women and Armed Conflict'. Who could it be? 'We certainly didn't want it to be one of the "permanent five". They've all fuelled conflict and participated in arms races,' Felicity Hill recalled. 'We didn't really want it to be a Western country. Ideally we wanted a country that had experienced conflict and could speak authoritatively to lead on this.' So they approached the Namibian Ambassador, Martin Andjaba. It happened that the Namibian delegation were already alert to gender issues in armed conflict. Earlier that year Windhoek had hosted a meeting of a review panel on Mainstreaming a Gender Perspective in Multidimensional Peace Support Operations, organized by the UN Department of Peacekeeping Operations. It had produced a comprehensive review of gender issues in peacekeeping and made concrete recommendations. Ambassador Andjaba's presidency of the Security Council was coming up in October. He agreed to sponsor an open session on Women, Peace and Security. 'Wilpfers were jubilant,' Felicity said. 'That was a great day!'

The NGO Working Group, however, didn't just want an open thematic session of the Security Council. They wanted a resolution to come out of this, the strongest expression the Council can give, stronger even than a presidential statement. Despite the adoption of 'gender mainstreaming' in the UN in 1997, the Security Council remained a highly masculine and masculinist entity. Among the fifteen members there was one woman at that time – Patricia Durrant, the Jamaican Ambassador. She would prove valuable as a dignified female presence guaranteeing that her male colleagues could not diminish the seriousness of this women's issue. But the men needed educating. The Working Group ensured that each mission received a bundle of key feminist books on the subject, their arguments carefully summarized – crib sheets for reluctant students. They supplied a list of experts for them to consult. They compiled every reference to gender and conflict issues in UN documents to provide examples of agreed text that would support their agenda and helpfully give the ambassadors a familiar UN language in which to discuss women, peace and security. They learned the protocol for getting the ear of Council members and their delegations, and they urged local NGOs back home in member-state capitals to nurture relationships with relevant departments of government. Meantime they were drafting and redrafting a resolution. They gave it to Ambassador Andjaba, who passed it to UNIFEM, and thereafter to Security Council members for prior discussion. At each step modifications were made.

On 23 October, the day before the Security Council session was due to be held, the Working Group mounted what is known as an 'Arria formula' meeting, an event at which Security Council members can meet representatives of civil society. On this occasion the NGO guests were Inonge Mbikusita-Lewanika from the Organization of African Unity, Isha Dyfan from the Sierra Leone section of WILPF, Luz Mendez from the National Union of Guatemalan Women, and Somali delegate Faiza Jama Mohamed from the Africa Office of Equality Now in Kenya (Hill et al. 2003). They described graphically the experiences of women and girls in the conflicts of their war-ridden countries and illustrated the peace-building work of grassroots women. It was a primer for the Security Council Open Session that followed on 24 and 25 October, at which representatives from forty member-states spoke on the issue. It was the first time in the UN's half-century of life that the Security Council had given the full weight of its attention to women. And the public gallery was full of them, now and then clapping enthusiastically. No such thing had been seen before in this hallowed chamber. The following week, on 31 October 2000 (Hallowe'en, festival of witches) UNSC Resolution 1325 was adopted. The 'last bastion of gender-free thinking in the UN' (in Felicity Hill's words) had fallen.

Implementation: the hard road from rhetoric to practice

Now the question was: how to move from resolution to reality? To the regret of the NGOs, 'women, peace and security' was not designated a regular annual recurrence on the UNSC calendar. Keeping the issue live in the UN was going to mean unremitting work. But UNSC 1325 was unusual, perhaps unique, in having a civil society movement behind it. As Felicity Hill put it: 'This is a live document; this is a document with a constituency, because it resonates with the women who experience war on a daily basis.' Since Resolution 1325 had no designated institutional location in the UN, the NGO Working Group stayed in existence to sustain the momentum. They obtained funding from the Ford Foundation for a coordinator so that Felicity could return her attention to her work in WILPF. Ford also funded WILPF to employ a small team at their UN office, enthusiastic and skilled young women, to set up the PeaceWomen portal mentioned above (<www.peacewomen.org>). When mapping this actor-network that produced 1325 we should certainly include funders, chipping in support along the road, and especially the Ford Foundation and Mahnaz Ispahani, the officer there who recognized the importance of backing the active NGOs with funds.

The PeaceWomen portal was launched a year to the day after the adoption of the resolution, a repository of information culled from women in war-zones, including bibliographies, lists of contacts, a guide to the UN system, tools and materials from campaigning organizations. It continues to be an important resource for women's anti-war movements worldwide, fostering exchange of news and views, and publishing a fortnightly e-newsletter. Two years later UNIFEM launched a complementary web portal on Women, War and Peace (<www.womenwarpeace.org>) to provide national and international actors with up-to-date information in 'gender profiles' of countries in conflict, documenting the impact of conflict on women and their peace-building activities. It would be a prompt to the UN system to include gender awareness in all its security work, and particularly in the reports generated by the UN that are submitted in the name of the Secretary General to inform the Security Council's decision-making. Each of the NGO Working Group member-organizations also took individual action in support of implementation. For instance, International Alert devised a monitoring framework with measurable indicators for the core issues of 1325 (International Alert 2002).

Of course, the main implementers had to be UN agencies and national governments. An Inter-agency Task Force on Women, Peace and Security was set up to coordinate a system-wide strategy in the UN structures. The women's most notable success was with the Department of Disarmament Affairs, where the supportive Under Secretary General, Jayantha Dhanapala, commissioned consultants to produce a gender action plan, in which important connections were made between gender and the department's work on landmines and small weapons. Their most depressing failure was in the crucially important Department of Peacekeeping Operations, where instead of the well-staffed gender unit they had been led to hope for, it took nearly four years before one low-grade post was created to deal with gender for the entire department. Comfort Lamptey was recruited for this all but impossible job. Fortunately, some peacekeeping field operations had already pioneered gender officers and gender units. At the mission in East Timor (UNTAET), for example, Sherrill Whittington had done exemplary work. She and other gender officers in the field fed back valuable experience and motivation into UNDPKO in New York.

There was action, too, at governmental level. The Canadian government had been a positive force throughout. Indeed, before the women initiated 1325, the Canadian mission had introduced the notion of people-centred 'human security' to the military-minded Security Council. Now, in the person of Béatrice Maillé, Canada prompted the formation of a group of governmental supporters called Friends of UNSC Resolution 1325, which grew to include twenty-even governments. The idea (though it seldom materialized) was that the governments, working as a bloc, would influence developments in the UN. For example, they could seek budget allocations in support of 1325.

The NGO Working Group meanwhile chased and chivvied. They distributed 20,000 copies of the resolution. They prompted its translation into scores of languages. They wrote annual reviews of implementation. They held regional consultations in Africa, South Asia and Europe, developing new information-sharing networks. On the first anniversary of 31 October 2000, they achieved a second presidential press statement and a second Arria-formula meeting at which Security Council members met Natercia Godinho-Adams of East Timor, Haxhere Veseli from Kosovo and Jamila, an activist from Afghanistan (she uses only the one name). Women by now were beginning to use 1325 locally. Reports came from Kosovo/a, Melanesia, Iraq, Russia and other countries of women acting on the resolution; and women in the Democratic Republic of Congo demanded (and got) the gender office and gender perspective that the UN peacekeeping mission there had failed to think of bringing with it.

Other members of this complex network were individual feminist academics in universities. Some, like Betty Reardon, located at Columbia University and active in the International Peace Research Association, had been pressing the case since Beijing. She, Cynthia Enloe of Clark University, Ann Tickner of the University of Southern California and others, had written the books that the NGOs used to brief the Security Council members. Some of them had attended a dialogue between academics, activists and UN officials organized by PeaceWomen in April 2002. Present that day, too, were Iris Marion Young of the University of Chicago and Carol Cohn, then at Wellesley College. Carol is a researcher who had studied gender mainstreaming in international peace and security organizations. She was now instrumental in founding a group of researchers, the Boston Consortium on Gender, Security and Human Rights, again funded by the same key programme officer at the Ford Foundation. The idea behind the consortium was to attempt to strengthen the interaction between the universities, the UN and NGOs, and get more relevant research into the hands of policy-makers. One discipline that badly needed a make-over, as we shall see in chapter 9, was international relations. In IR, as Carol understated it: 'To take on the issue of women or gender is not generally seen as a smart career move!'

Academics were also important as wordsmiths. The process of obtaining the resolution unleashed an avalanche of books and papers. Scores were produced between 1995 and 2005 on the theme of women and gender in relation to war and peace, security and peacekeeping. Some were published commercially (see, for instance,

Whitworth 2004; Mazurana et al. 2005). Some were published by NGOs such as International Alert, employing feminist academics on a consultancy basis (e.g. El-Bushra 2003). But two major reports sprang directly from the resolution. The first was the Secretary General's official report pursuant to 1325. Titled *Women, Peace and Security*, it was drafted by Dyan Mazurana of Tufts University and Sandra Whitworth of York University Toronto (United Nations 2002). The second, published simultaneously by UNIFEM, was an 'independent experts' report'. More field-based, this was drafted by Jennifer Klot, Pam DeLargy, Aina Iiyambo, Sumie Nakaya, Saudamini Siegrist and Felicity Hill, while the formal authors were Elizabeth Rehn and Ellen Johnson Sirleaf (Rehn and Sirleaf 2002).

Real-life women of course are difficult to categorize and, besides, in this story, they often shifted from one box to another. Thus those two 'independent experts' fielded by UNIFEM to write its report had migrated for this purpose from the political world, where they are rare female figures. Elizabeth Rehn had been the world's only female minister of defence (in Finland), while Ellen Johnson Sirleaf was a unique female minister of finance (in Liberia). In 2006 Sirleaf would be elected president of that country, the first African woman head of state. Another mixed identity is that of Felicity Hill, who resigned from her NGO, WILPF, in late 2001 and became an international civil servant, a peace and security adviser in UNIFEM. Aina Iiyambo, who had actively supported the NGO Working Group from within the Namibian mission, was also drawn into UNIFEM. Sheri Gibbings started as an intern in WILPF and ended in the academic sphere, writing a master's thesis analysing WILPF's engagement with the UN over 1325 (Gibbings 2004). Felicity Hill also subsequently wrote a master's thesis, on the impact of 1325 beyond the Security Council (Hill 2005).

So this transnational advocacy network (the term was popularized by Margaret Keck and Kathryn Sikkink 1998) was a complex and shifting set of women and institutions. WILPF was at the core, but would not have seen itself as leader. Felicity Hill said: 'There were so many involved. It's difficult to say who was a driver, who was a passenger. Everybody played the driver role at different times ... Some people in this actor-network were invisible and needed to be invisible – people within the Namibian delegation and the Jamaican delegation, for instance, working quietly with UNIFEM and with us in the NGOs. The NGOs did shine! We really got ourselves together. We looked for support, we knocked on doors and everywhere we found someone who was interested. But we were all links in a chain. We all fed each other's enthusiasm. It was really moving and uplifting.'

Limitations of the institutional route

While WILPF celebrated the passage of 1325, many women in the organization nevertheless felt that something had been lost along the way. WILPF tends more to feminism than the other five organizations in the Working Group and, like the Hague Appeal for Peace, but unlike the others, they are explicitly antimilitarist. Amnesty focus mainly on human rights, the Women's Caucus for Gender Justice on international law. The Women's Commission for Refugee Women and Children are clearly humanitarian in their concerns, while International Alert are mainly about peace-building. They could all be satisfied that 1325 responded pretty well to their intentions. WILPF, however, regretted the absence of two major themes in the resolution. It spoke only fleetingly of women's role in preventing war, and made no mention of *ending war itself*, which, after all, was the main reason the United Nations was established and precisely the Security Council's brief. Nor did the resolution say anything about the gender regime that causes women's victimization in war and their exclusion from peace processes.

As it was, lacking antimilitarist clauses, the resolution could be seen as co-optative. We've seen that two of its main themes were the protection of women, and their representation. You could say that 'protection' emphasizes women's passivity, their victimhood. In the absence of a strong statement against war, this could be seen as simply trying to 'make war safer for women'. Worse, states could cite the protection of women (as they did when invading Afghanistan) as a spurious legitimation of their militarist goals. Certainly, the second theme, that of getting women better represented at all levels of decision-making, recognizing their aptitude for negotiation and their peace-building skills, helpfully heightens women's profile as doers, as having agency. On the other hand, it could be taken as a sign that the United Nations had woken up to the idea that women could be a useful resource in helping them do their job. The third theme of the resolution, gender-mainstreaming in the various UN and member-state departments responsible for handling war situations, was essentially calling for an alertness to women. It was hardly a call for revolution in the gender order.

The fact was, WILPF's feminist and antimilitarist message had become muted as it adapted to the needs of other members of the Working Group. In turn, the message of the Working Group as a whole had been diluted in the process of working in coalition with United Nations bureaucrats, albeit women, and the officials of member-states who, at every stage, pressed realism on the activists, stressing the limits to what the Security Council was likely, at best, to take on board. And if a resolution was what was wanted, they were no doubt right. It is, and everyone knew it, very easy to alienate Security Council members by introducing emotional demands or appeals on issues they see as outside their remit. So, as Felicity Hill wrote in her thesis, the NGOs succeeded only by being self-effacing and self-censoring, using information, persuasion and 'rhetorical entrapment' to bring along the UN personnel, civil servants and diplomats concerned (Hill 2005). Four years later, in a lecture at the University of Warwick, Carol Cohn neatly summarized what had been happening then. She said:

> Protecting women *in* war, and insisting that they have an equal right to participate in the processes and negotiations that *end* particular wars, both leave *war* itself in place ... [1325 is not] an intervention that tries either to prevent war, or to contest the legitimacy of the systems that produce war – that is, 'to put an end to war'. In this sense it fits comfortably into the already extant concepts and discursive practices of the Security Council, where the dominant paradigm holds a world made up of states that 'defend' *state* security through *military* means ... Letting (some) women into decision-making positions seems a small price to pay for leaving the war system essentially undisturbed. (Cohn forthcoming)

The second dimension in which the resolution was deficient was in its rendering of gender. As Felicity Hill told me in interview, the text dwelt on 'the under-representation of women. It did not mention or explain the over-representation of men. It was very far from being a resolution dealing with men and masculinity as causes of women's insecurity.' In a round-table discussion published in the *International Feminist Journal of Politics* she said: '1325 is potentially revolutionary as it could transform ways of understanding how security is conceived, protected and enforced. It could make photos of only male leaders at peace negotiating tables starkly outdated. But for this to happen, the focus has to move from women to men, and it still hasn't happened' (Cohn et al. 2004).

Carol Cohn illustrated this point. To have an effect you have to address 'the pernicious, pervasive complexities of the gender regimes that undergird not only individual wars but the entire war system'. Take rape, for example.

> You can ... hope that through defining rape as a war crime rather than as 'natural' ... there may be some deterrent effect. But without addressing the intersection of gender and ethnicity, and the gender regime that makes a physical, sexual attack on a woman a blow against the 'honour' of a man and his community, how likely is it that rape will stop being used as a weapon? Or [in the case of military prostitution] you can write a Code of Conduct for peacekeeping troops that has a strict prohibition against 'fraternization' with local women – but without addressing the nexus of militarized power/constructions of masculinities/gendered inequalities in access to paid work/and global economic inequality, how likely is it that that Code of Conduct will make a significant difference? (ibid.)

The fact is that just as the UN is unable to criticize the USA, capitalism and militarization, so is it quite unable to make any critique of masculinity. Sandra Whitworth would later write in her post-1325 study of UN peacekeeping: 'There is ... no discussion within UN documents of militarism or militarized masculinities or, for that matter, of masculinities more generally' (Whitworth 2004: 137).

In June 2005, Carol Cohn and Felicity Hill were invited to address the Sweden-sponsored Commission on Weapons of Mass Destruction, the 'Blix Commission'. They picked up this issue that had been excluded from the 1325 process. Their message to the commission was 'take note of masculinity'. One of the successes of the '1325 movement', after the passage of the resolution, had been in the field of small arms and light weapons. This was partly due to the existence of an excellent NGO, the International Action Network on Small Arms (IANSA) with a woman director, Rebecca Peters, who had set up a women's portal on their website and fostered the activities of women opposing gun culture and collecting weapons in countries as far apart as Brazil, Africa and the Pacific. But it was also due to the fact that, in the field, there is simply no escaping

The link between gun ownership and masculinity is widely recognized. Women in London (above) demonstrate against the biennial international arms 'fair' where small arms and light weapons are fast-selling export commodities.

The possession of nuclear weapons also evokes masculine posturing. Women's protests in Britain have often focused on the Atomic Weapons Establishment at Aldermaston (above, 1987) and sites of missile silos such as RAF Greenham Common (below, 1983).

the connection between guns and men. 'The attachment of men to their weapons, the link between masculine identities and men's unwillingness to give up their weapons, is recognized in the disarmament, demobilization and reintegration process as one of the biggest obstacles to peace,' Felicity told me in interview. Now, addressing the Blix Commission, this is where the two women began. Starting with hand-guns they stepped neatly to nuclear devices and the Non-Proliferation Treaty, a field where gender is never mentioned, as though, Felicity said, 'the devastatingly indiscriminate nature of nuclear weapons exceeds a threshhold beyond which gender ceases to be relevant'.

Carol had done research as a participant observer among nuclear intellectuals and scientists. She had shown how masculine symbolism is central to professional and intellectual discourse about nuclear weapons (Cohn 1987). Nuke-talk is man-talk, even lad-talk. As a result, 'the emotional, the concrete, the particular, human bodies and their vulnerability, human lives and their subjectivity – all of which are marked as feminine in the primary dichotomies of gender discourse' are left out of nuclear and national security considerations (Cohn et al. 2005). The two feminists told the Blix Commission:

> Governments and international institutions are increasingly accepting that small arms and light weapons (SALW) are practically associated with masculinity in many cultures, with men as the vast majority of the buyers, owners and users ... it would be naive to assume that this association suddenly becomes meaningless when we are talking about larger, more massively destructive weapons. And more naive still to think that it doesn't matter. (Cohn et al. 2005)

A valuable lever for women anti-war activists

So UNSC 1325 has its weaknesses, but it was an achievement for all that. After fifty-five years and 4,213 sessions of the Security Council, here at last was a public acknowledgement at the highest possible level of the gender-specific, deliberately inflicted torment of women in warfare. Here women's agency and capability were brought to view, and governments and international bodies authorized to increase support of women's work for peace. It was proof that the demands of women's movements and the thoughts of feminist theorists are capable of influencing global governance.

Some activist and feminist women were able to inhabit, or step momentarily into, academic spaces whence they could make a valuable analysis and critique of the '1325 process'. Meanwhile, women all over the world have been gladly making use of its existence as a lever to other gains. Two examples drawn from my research visits to widely separated countries can illustrate the point.

In Colombia, while La Ruta Pacifica, as we saw, were mobilizing women from the grassroots in high-profile incursions into public space, another women's organization, the Alianza Iniciativa de Mujeres Colombianas por la Paz (IMP, Alliance Initiative of Colombian Women for Peace) was dedicating itself to 'negotiating with power', carrying a women's agenda into formal peace processes on just the lines envisaged in UNSC 1325 clauses 1 and 2.[3] With the support of Swedish women and their trade unions, backed by a Swedish funding organization, they prepared themselves for an intervention in any peace negotiations the Colombian government might enter in future, be it with the guerrillas or the paramilitaries. IMP consulted women in seven regions of the country in seven social sectors, including young women, peasant women, indigenous women, trade union women, Afro-Colombian women, academics, public servants and feminists. In the course of a year they assembled 600 demands covering five categories of exclusion: economic, political, cultural, territorial and social. At a four-day consultative assembly of 230 women chosen by direct voting by sector and region, these demands were consolidated into a twelve-point basic negotiating agenda. 'This was our suitcase,' Rocío Pineda told me. It was women's baggage, that they could carry with them into any peace process to which they might gain access. First they used it to lobby mayoral and local candidates in the elections. Then, in 2003, when the government announced its intention to pursue peace negotiations with the high command of the Autodefensas Unidas Colombianas (AUC), the principal paramilitary force, the IMP eight-woman political committee decided to write to the government, stating their concern about a possible impunity deal and their interest in achieving some mechanism of intervention for women. They made clear certain requirements: that civil society must have an adequate presence at the talks; victims of paramilitary crimes should be represented; and a Truth Commission must be on the agenda. Ultimately the women gained a place as observers at the peace talks, a first in the long history of Colombia's many negotiations.

Resolution 1325 has been taken seriously by women in Israel and Palestine. When UNIFEM produced a 'basket of tools' – a glossary of terms, guidance on how to organize groups to carry the resolution forward, and on how to mobilize parliament to legislate for it – Isha l'Isha (Women for Women) in Haifa picked it up and ran with it, translating it into local languages. The most substantial move, however, has been the establishment of an International Women's Commission (IWC) which would be capable of an intervention in any future Israeli/Palestinian peace negotiations. It aims to bring a civil society perspective to negotiations, together with a gender perspective, and the actual inclusion of women at the table.[4] Its birthplace was the Jerusalem Link, and the founding duo were Maha Abu-Dayyeh Shamas, on the Palestinian side, and Terry Greenblatt, at that time director of Bat Shalom, on the Israeli side (we met these organizations in chapter 4). Later, Terry was replaced by Knesset member Naomi Chazan. In May 2002 Terry and Maha went to New York to address the Security Council in a meeting initiated by the NGO Equality Now, and in August that year they address an appeal to the 'Quartet', made up of the EU, the UN, Russia and the USA. They shared with them their ideas

> on how we might contribute to the elevation of the discourse on the Middle East to a different level away from the military escalation and the insane violence ... by enabling the insights, perspectives and concerns of Palestinian and Israeli civil society, and especially women, to inform the political dialogue and negotiations that will have to be re-launched at the political level to achieve a just and durable peace. (Equality Now 2002)

Later, Maha Shamas described to me the structure that has evolved. The commissioners will be 'prominent politicians and feminists' and include twenty Israelis, twenty Palestinians and twenty international women. The latter will come from both the global North and global South, and their role will be to put pressure on their own governments. In August 2005 there was a meeting in Istanbul of ten Palestinian and ten Israeli women under the auspices of UNIFEM to carry the IWC project forwards. In Israel, using an amendment to the law on Equal Rights for Women, passed by the Knesset in June, the preparatory group have actually succeeded in establishing the International Women's Commission as a legal Israeli entity. The commission has also been recognized in Palestinian law and by a presidential directive. Maha told me at the beginning of November 2005, 'We have a charter now. It's still under wraps, but will be published soon with an official launch.' She emphasized that 'We don't just envision the management of the conflict – we're seeking a sustainable solution. And we're not looking for a parallel peace process – our aim is actually to access negotiations.'

These two, and other, interventions by women in peace processes are not without risk. They can be criticized for idealism. After all, at the time of writing, peace talks are the last thing on military and militant minds in Israel and Palestine. They can be criticized for co-optation. In the case of Colombia, the women of IMP themselves recognized the danger that the collusion of the rightwing Colombian government would see the paramilitaries let off with token punishments, extending their malign power into the political arena. Nevertheless it's clear that many women believe we have to risk getting our hands dirty if we are to make a contribution to resolving armed conflicts and ending war itself.

Notes

1 This section is based on interviews with Felicity Hill and Carol Cohn, for whose details please refer to the Acknowledgements. I also benefited from numerous ephemeral papers with which they supplied me. The main published resources are referenced.

2 The text of UNSC Resolution 1325 can be accessed at <www.un.org/Docs/scres/2000/sc2000.htm>. A useful point-by-point annotation has been produced by the United Nations Development Fund for Women, see 'Security Council Resolution 1325 Annotated and Explained' at <www.womenwarpeace.org/toolbox/annot1325.htm>, accessed 23 January 2006.

3 For information on IMP I am indebted to Rocío Pineda, a founding member and key activist, please see Acknowledgements.

4 For information about the Women's Commission I draw on conversations with Maha Abu-Dayyeh Shamas and Terry Greenblatt. For details please see Acknowledgements.

SIX
Methodology of women's protest

§ Women featured in this book strongly believe that their way of organizing, processes of relating, style of action and wording of messages, are different from those of the mainstream anti-war movement. They base the view on evidence, since most have dealings with the latter. If you asked the many and varied women I met in my travels of 2004–05 'What is it you are most sure you have in common?', the chances are they would say '*How* we do it'. In a way, organizing *as women* is itself a distinctive approach within the range of methods of anti-war protest. It implies a choice – choosing the context in which you think you can work best and be most effective. There's the comfort factor. And besides, as women you're noticed in a particular way by the public, something that can be exploited to good effect.

Many of the women I met had begun their political lives in the left. The women of Vimochana, in Bangalore, for instance, told me how as leftists in the 1970s they'd come to see the movement as an authoritarian structure, dogmatic, subsuming all struggle into itself. While they shared its politics of social justice and equality, they began to feel it was hardly different from the Indian elite in uncritically adopting Western notions of 'progress' and 'development', inappropriate in Asia. Together with male comrades, they developed an alternative philosophy that set store by local and regional discourses, and collective responsibility combined with individual autonomy and creativeness. By 1979 some of the women were calling themselves 'socialist feminists' but later they would say 'we crossed beyond the left', 'we draw from it but don't take it as our own'. Scarcely yet knowing it, they were helping found an autonomous feminist movement in India. Today Vimochana are a complex and successful women's organization focusing on violence in Indian society, including individual patriarchal violence against women, communal violence, the Indian state's militarization, its nuclear rivalry with Pakistan and brutal suppression of resistance movements. (See photos pp. 30–1.)

Responsible process, minimal structure

The women I met in Italian Women in Black (Donne in Nero) used the term 'modalità' (way, manner) of relating. Ada Cinato of Torino DiN, for instance, contrasted their group today with 'the aggressive modality of patriarchy' they'd experienced on the left. She said: 'In the old politics it was difficult to be "different". We couldn't use our ordinary way of behaving, as women – in the trade unions for example. They didn't take account of "difference", or accept it. We give importance to relationship, to being directly responsible, each one of us. [In Donne in Nero] the way we discuss, the way we speak with others, is comfortable for me.'

Ada used the term, women's 'ordinary way of behaving'. Other women represent this same 'way' as a consciously feminist approach. Certainly, this is how the group Collectif Femmes en Noir in Brussels describe their practice. Unlike other Women in Black groups, they've chosen not to demonstrate against war but instead to work with survivors of war, women seeking asylum in Belgium. They attach great value to an explicitly feminist ethics, by which they mean creating a responsible and inclusive workgroup, without hierarchy. Because they are conscious of the 'universality of patriarchal power', and the dangers of a patronizing 'humanitarianism', they assert absolute equality between themselves and the women 'sans papiers' (undocumented, 'illegal') they might otherwise be seen as 'helping'. They say simply: 'We are a collective of *women with and without papers*.'

I found that, although all the groups I met aspired to shared work and skills, consensual decision-making, transparent processes and responsibility in relationships, it was the smaller groups with rather consistent membership who were best able to sustain a level of practice that satisfied them. Bay Area Women in Black, in San Francisco, are thirteen women, mainly Jewish, uniquely focused on influencing local Jewish opinion on Israeli injustices towards Palestinians. They've been a closed group for some time, and would think very hard before opening to new members because, they said: 'To remain motivated we need to be able to talk shorthand between ourselves, easily understand and trust each other.' Sandy Butler is someone with a deep spiritual life and practice, struggling with patriarchy in her religion and feeling acutely what she calls the 'deep shame inherent in being a Jew today, and an American'. She said: 'It's only possible for me to do my political activism with women who engage one another personally, politically, spiritually. The fullness of our interaction, the ability to bring all of who we are to the group, makes the work possible in such hard times.'

Working in explicit recognition of community doesn't mean groups are always amiable and non-conflictual. On the contrary, the approach imposes an obligation to recognize and deal constructively with disagreement. As Celine Sugana said of their experience in Vimochana: 'We share, we fight. We feel free to do that. It's our birthright. But we don't walk away. We don't leave each other – or only for a little while. We try to put people back together.'

As a consequence of prioritizing quality of relationships and spontaneity in action, most of the groups I met had chosen to have minimal structure and little division of labour. An example of this simplicity would be Women in Black (Vrouwen in 'T Zwart) in Leuven, Belgium. Ten or eleven women who are part of a 'feminist antimilitarist lesbian activist' friendship network meet in their lunch-hour each Wednesday and stand in a vigil near the entrance to the City Hall. When their half-hour 'stille wake' against war is over, they share a meal in a nearby café, discuss future actions, solidarity work and networking, and then disperse back to work. The rest is left to email. (Note, however, that their off-street work is super-effective, since one of their number, Lieve Snellings, is the key e-list manager for WiB worldwide, keeping women in touch across the continents.) At the other extreme in terms of structure is the Women's International League for Peace and Freedom with its worldwide system of national branches and delegate conferences. But it's not always a question of scale necessitating structure. As we saw, Code Pink, on the way to becoming a worldwide movement, has so far retained a marked casualness about organization. In Italy there are strong feelings both for retaining the total autonomy of the forty-four local Donne in Nero groups and conversely for introducing some degree of overall co-ordination that might increase their national impact. Such examples show how women respond to the demands of organization in the way that suits them best, but are unable to evade the inherent contradictions. Each solution brings with it a cost.

Žene u Crnom in Belgrade is one of rather few women's anti-war groups that have their own office space. Some other WiB groups, characteristically in Spain and Italy, share a corner in a Women's House (Casa de la Mujer, Casa delle Donne). In some cases women in an organization with wider goals are organizing antimilitarist activity from the base of an office which houses their activities as a whole. Vimochana is one. Another is Amargi (Amargi Kadın Akademisi) in Istanbul that works from a centre for which the rent is paid by individual subscription. Here they run courses of feminist criticism and gender studies, do local consciousness-raising among women and work in support of survivors of male violence. Simultaneously they engage with Turkish militarism and address the Turkish–Kurdish conflict, working for connection between Kurdish and Turkish women. They organized an initiative they called the Women's Peace Table, taking it to several towns and cities and finally to the Kurdish south-east, with the aim of 'substituting talk for patriarchal violence politics towards the Kurds'. Pinar Selek stressed: 'We don't just oppose militarism at moments of threatened war. It's intrinsic and continual for us. Violence against women, *and* the ongoing war with the Kurds, are central matters for us.'

In the eight countries in which I came across Women in Black groups, I found most of them mounting their vigils and carrying on their other activities with minimal organization. Most groups exist as little more than a phone tree or an e-list of women among whom decision-making is shared and informal. There are small variations. In the Union Square group in New York a disagreement had erupted due to the informality of their decision-making process. As other women before them, they were encountering the hazards of structurelessness. So they set up a five-woman steering group (albeit fully open and with rotating membership) delegated to make decisions. In Bologna they'd found it practical to appoint one of their members a group coordinator. Most WiB groups seem to have only occasional meetings for discussion and decision-making. Torino are exceptional in their regular weekly meeting. But it depends a lot on the tasks that are current. From time to time there are bursts of organized activity around, let's say, group visits to or from another country, International Women's Day, or a new threat of war.

If minimal organization is characteristic of Women in Black, other kinds of women's anti-war activism necessarily call for more administration. This is particularly the case when complex and sustained activities involve interaction between organizations and across borders. Take, for example, Winpeace (Women's Initiative for Peace in Greece and Turkey). I knew them first and foremost for their political campaigning. Greece and Turkey have been in a state of enmity since the two nations were founded. Winpeace call on their two governments to reduce military budgets, especially those parts of military programmes that have been directed specifically against each other's country. But I found they also have several practical projects: a 'literature exchange', translating children's and adult books between the two languages; programmes of peace education, including a curriculum for use in schools; youth camps in which Turkish, Greek and Cypriot students can get to know each other and share courses on conflict resolution; and a project of 'agro-tourism', involving co-operation between rural women of three Turkish villages and a Greek Aegean island. This sort of activism is a far cry, in its administrative demands, from simply getting a weekly vigil on to the street.

Vigilling and other street work

Women in Black are best known as vigillers, although as we've seen that's not all they do. WiB vigils vary in regularity, frequency and size. A tradition has grown up whereby each vigil group is entirely autonomous. The WiB international website invites women anywhere to start their own, offering simple guidelines. Usually vigillers choose a public place with plenty of passers-by, like San Francisco WiB, in their downtown financial district. Some groups have a local military base to picket. Gulf Coast WiB can hardly ignore their overbearing neighbour, the MacDill Air Force Base, site of US Central Command which directs military operations in the Middle East. The smallest vigil I heard of was in Berkeley, California, where for seven years the group was reduced to two women. Neither felt able to take a week off because two were needed to hold the banner. The largest have been the one-off assemblies of thousands of women at huge international events, such as the UN Fourth World Conference on Women in Beijing in 1995, and more recently at World Social Forums in many cities of the world, organized by Corinne Kumar and other women of the Indian feminist organization Vimochana, the Asian Women's Human Rights Council and El Taller International. Everywhere women carefully word their placards to show why they're there and get across the message in a very few words. Often leaflets are handed out, to give more information.

In my travels I stood with women in New York, sharing their dripping brollies; in the shade of a banyan tree in Tampa Bay, Florida;

in mellow evening sunshine in the historic centre of Verona; and on the steps of the city hall in Bangalore as the daylight faded, the parakeets and black kites circled overhead, and the crowds returned from work. And each experience felt very much like home, our London vigil. Everywhere I went, women told me pretty much the same about their intentions in vigilling. The methodology is based on the idea that people welcome good information and are capable of thinking, changing their minds, and being inspired to act on their own account. It implies a model in which the effect on any given person in the street can ripple outwards as people influence each other. Who knows, maybe voting patterns could be affected, and political behaviour. Those who already share your ideas can be encouraged and strengthened by seeing you taking a public stand on them. People often say, 'Thank you for doing this for me'. But expressions of doubt and opposition are welcome too. Chiara Gattullo in Bologna said: 'It's a good chance for me to meet people who don't agree with me. I don't try to convince anyone, but I hope they'll stop and think for themselves.' Then again, women say they also stand there, in a sense, for their own benefit. Chiara added: 'It helps us to pay attention, it's renewing a personal commitment that we act on elsewhere.' A lot of women told me it satisfies them in some deep way just to stand there with a placard that expresses *exactly* what they feel. 'Io Donna Contro la Guerra' ('I, a woman, against war').

If, for some women, the vigil is a kind of spiritual practice, something they miss if they absent themselves for a while, for others it's more of a task. It can be depressing. 'It's heavy! An hour seems very long,' Margherita Granero (Torino) said. 'I feel our lack of connection with the public. It's as though we come from another world. It drives home to me how distant we are from the majority, and I suffer from that.' Some women find vigilling boring, but in some circumstances it can be frightening. It took a lot of courage to go out and stand in Republic Square in nationalist Belgrade, a city full of armed and hyped-up men, launching wars of nationalist aggression. Jasmina Tešanović said of their initial vigil: 'We did it first and thought about it afterwards. Standing on the street we all thought: what are we doing?! It was like having sex for the first time. It hurts, but you think, OK, next time I'll enjoy it!'

Some vigil groups have felt the need to vary the formula. Belgrade ŽuC is one of them. When I was with them in October 2004 they

Women tend to choose methods of protest that avoid abuse of people or environment. Here on London's South Bank women 'paint' a powdery message that will quickly disperse underfoot and wash away with the first rain.

NEVER
AGAIN

NEVER
AGAIN
NO TO
ARMS TRADE

were using a huge swathe of rainbow-coloured silk and translucent banners for visual effect (see photos on pp. 96–7). In Tokyo women walked through the city rather than standing still, and wore artistic black hats and costumes. Mujeres de Negro in Madrid have sometimes done street drama. They've stripped naked and painted themselves red, poured 'blood' into the city fountains.

From the schools to the law courts

Taken overall, women's anti-war groups use a wide range of methods. Many of them are not, of themselves, unique to women, although the modalità, the process by which they are carried out, may be. In chapter 1 I mentioned the mass mobilizations of La Ruta Pacifica in Colombia, and in chapter 2 Code Pink's worldwide 100,000-signature petition. We saw that Code Pink have also done shareholder interventions in US companies involved in post-war Iraq. Some women in Spain organize 'objeción fiscal', withholding taxes that will be spent on the military. In certain countries women are doing work on the gathering and decommissioning of small arms. For some groups it feels important to be well embedded in their own local community, working on local issues that connect to militarism and war, such as instances of racism against migrants or violence against women. Others by contrast, or as well, travel widely to learn about and give support to women in other countries. By their name, as we saw, Dones per Dones in Barcelona mean 'women here for women there'. They keep in touch with Colombian, Afghan and Russian women as well as Palestinian and Israeli women. Jennifer Beach of San Francisco Women in Black told me about their connections with women of the Philippine women's organization Gabriela, both locally in California and in the Philippines. She said: 'Visits like this have an immeasurable effect. Activists need to travel. Maybe like artists, they need inspiration. It's fantastic for us to meet feminists who are opposing US dominance out there in the world. It's important for us to understand how imperialism has specific effects on women. To see that there's no safe zone. It impacts on all of us.'

In India I met Syeda Hameed of WIPSA, the Women's Initiative for Peace in South Asia, who told me about the reciprocal visits they'd made between women in India, Pakistan and Bangladesh. Travelling by bus, they'd made difficult journeys across tense borders at times when it seemed 'nothing short of madness' to visit people deemed 'the enemy'. After one of these journeys they wrote:

> As women we felt we were beginning a new way of relating, a new way of bringing the ordinary people of our two countries together ... We are against violence which is perpetuated as a means of resolving disputes in the family, the community and between countries ... If women of the South Asian region are united, they can pressurize the governments to stop destructive political power games. The borders and boundaries are insignificant when hearts and minds meet. (WIPSA 2003: 30)

Three other methods stand out in the repertoire of women activists: working the political system; education; and use of the law. Again, these approaches are not uniquely those of women's organizations, but their modalità, in practice, often is.

Political lobbying We saw that cornering heads of state was Marwopnet's speciality in Sierra Leone. I found other groups lobbying lesser politicians and parliaments. Most seem to do this political work because practicalities dictate it, not because it's something they particularly enjoy. When the 2004 presidential election approached in the USA, offering a chance to displace George W. Bush, even Bay Area Women in Black decided they had to get out on the stump. They identified single women as a potentially anti-Bush segment of the electorate. Frances Reid made a five-minute video designed to get them to register for the poll and, when the election came, the whole group doorstepped and car-pooled to get women into the voting booths. Sandy Butler said, ruefully: 'For the first time in my life I'm doing electoral politics. What melancholy pragmatism!'

Elsewhere and at other times women have actually stood for election to get a platform for their views. Some, while active at the Greenham Common Women's Peace Camp in the 1980s (see below), stood in the parliamentary elections as Women for Life on Earth, contesting the seats of the Secretary of State for Defence and other Conservative Party ministers. In 2004, Women Act against Military Violence in Okinawa worked hard, but failed, to get their coordinator Takazato Suzuyo elected as mayor of Naha City, from which position she could have contested US militarization of the island.

Information and education Most of the women's groups and organizations I met do some writing and leafleting, and try to get the attention of the media, particularly local radio. Some speak of what they do as counter-information. Some do it more intensively and consistently than others. The Women's Peace Camp at Aldermaston in Berkshire, UK, as we shall see, have maintained their presence outside the Atomic Weapons Establishment for over twenty years and are currently monitoring the building of new facilities that will enable the development of a new generation of nuclear weapons. In September 2005 the UK Secretary of State for Defence promised a public debate on renewal of the current UK Trident missile system. Popular concern had been woken by the women of the peace camp, among other organizations, researching and publishing the facts and keeping the issue in the public eye.

Certain Mujeres de Negro groups in Spain and Italy carry out peace education in local schools. We saw that Winpeace have produced a peace curriculum for Greek and Turkish schoolchildren. In Oregon, USA, I met Carol van Houten who told me about the work of CALC, Community Alliance Lane County. In September 2001 the Bush administration passed a new education law which, among other things, obliged school administrators to allow military recruiters into schools and to release the names and contact details of students, unless withheld by the specific request of individual parents. CALC 'sat in' at the local school board until they, like the military, were assured access to schools and the right to notify parents that they could refuse to release the children's details. Carol described her visits to address both boys and girls of school-leaving age. She said 'The recruiters are so clever. They listen to what a child wants and promises they'll get it. They say, "You can study any subject, electronics, whatever you like", "You can go to training with your best friend", "You can just be in the police". But when they get you in, you're sent to do whatever they decide. Our aim in CALC is to lay before students the facts the recruiters leave out – for instance, that you're signing up to an eight-year commitment.' This is the kind of work that requires not only a gender perspective but co-operation between women and men. Carol goes to schools accompanied by a male veteran who can speak convincingly to boys from his experience of combat service.

Uses of the law I found women had used, broadly speaking, three juridical strategies in their activism against militarism and war. One was to invoke the law to bring politicians to account under international law. The second was to break the law with political intent. A third was to use the law rhetorically and symbolically to publicize wrongs.

We saw in chapter 1 how the women of the International Initiative for Justice in Gujarat chose to make legal arguments to get justice for the women raped in the pogrom of 2002. Since the Indian government had refused to acknowledge the jurisdiction of the International Criminal Court, the women instead invoked the 1948 International Convention on the Prevention and Punishment of the Crime of Genocide. The Indian government had ratified this in 1959 but had never introduced the legislation needed to give it effect. Their report recommended that the international community declare a genocidal alert with regard to Gujarat and call for the extradition of those chargeable with crimes against humanity.

Rebecca Johnson told me the story of how, in the autumn of 1984, she and twelve other women of the Greenham Common Women's Peace Camp and their seventeen children had gone to New York to bring a case in the Supreme Court against President Ronald Reagan, Defense Secretary Caspar Weinberger and the US military chiefs of staff. With the support of two US congressmen, the Center for Constitutional Rights and US women activists, they made the case that the nuclear-armed cruise missile, a first-strike weapon, was illegal under the US Constitution and international law, and sought an injunction to prevent deployment in Britain. They failed, but the case was a source of valuable publicity for the anti-cruise movement.

It was Helen John, who has served several terms in prison for her activism, who illustrated for me the second strategy, of breaking the law or alternatively pushing it to its limits. A lot of energy in the peace camp at Greenham went into contesting the laws – for instance, the local by-laws governing use of common land, under which the state tried to get the camp removed. The women also happily broke the law because, as Helen put it: 'It's a basic principle of democracy that it's justified to break the law if the law's upholding something bad.' A lot of women involved in Greenham and at other military bases in the UK in the 1980s repeatedly broke the law by entering the bases, embarrassing the authorities and sometimes damaging equipment. They used the resulting court hearings to publicize the case against nuclear weapons and their delivery systems, and to show their disrespect for the court's authority on this issue.

If found guilty, many women refused to pay the fines imposed on them and were consequently sentenced to short terms in prison.

Helen acknowledges that British women, now as then, are lucky to live in a country where law-breaking is a viable activist strategy, where it's unlikely to get you killed, tortured or locked up for years, and where prisons could be seen as relatively comfortable, warm places, indeed five-star hotels to women who have been camping under plastic in midwinter. Helen herself found going to prison 'massively politicizing': 'A lot of the prisoners come from very impoverished backgrounds, they're there for all sorts of crimes, but often it's because of lack of opportunity. A lot of them are taking the rap for a man. You have the opportunity to talk to them, reach out to them. They could understand what we were doing in our protests and that the changes we were calling for would improve their children's chances.'

The third use I found women making of the law was dramaturgical. Sometimes they had set up simulated tribunals of war leaders or criminals. Among the most sustained and politically thoughtful enactments have been a series of Courts of Women, mounted by the Asian Women's Human Rights Council. The AWHRC describes its concern as 'the escalating violence against women in the context of the growing militarization and nuclearization of the nation states in Asia and the Pacific, and the wars, fundamentalism, communal and ethnic conflicts that are enveloping the region' (unpublished leaflet).

Between 1993 and 2004 they've organized twenty-two courts, in the Asia-Pacific region, the Arab world, Africa, Central America and the Mediterranean, and the series continues. A panel of judges hears testimony from women who travel from many different countries to tell their stories. Madhu Bhushan of the AWHRC explained to me that the purpose of these courts is 'to create alternative political spaces. They spring from a vision rooted in a critique of the dominant human rights discourse and its ideological underpinning in Enlightenment values, such as possessive individualism, rationality and objectivity.' The courts therefore don't involve a prosecution and defence. The witnesses aren't cross-examined, they're believed. The jury, composed of women chosen for their wisdom and experience, doesn't find guilt or innocence, but rather listens, understands, reflects and synthesizes what it hears. Corinne Kumar is a key actor in the AWHRC and also in El Taller International in Tunis, an NGO working in the global South. A motivating spirit behind the courts, she writes:

> The Courts of Women seek to weave together the objective reality (through analyses of the issues) with the subjective testimonies of the women; the personal with the political; the logical with the lyrical (through video testimonies, artistic images and poetry) … [they are] sacred spaces where women, speaking in a language of suffering, name the crimes, seeking redress, even reparation. (unpublished leaflet)

Of course, the borders one places around 'women's movements against militarism and war', the activities one defines as inside and outside this phenomenon, are arbitrary. I've chosen not to include the hundreds of projects of reconciliation, focused and long-term work involving professional skills in healing the hatreds exacerbated by war. I've also chosen to exclude from review the thousands of humanitarian projects concerned with war victims and survivors, valuable as these are. Anti-war activist women I spoke with, such as the Collectif Femmes en Noir in Brussels, are reluctant to term the work they do with asylum-seekers 'humanitarian', preferring to frame it as political, a natural corollary of anti-war work.

However, the intensity of conflict in some countries means that humanitarian work sometimes has to stand in for peace activism. In Kashmir, for instance, the Indian Army is deployed against a Muslim insurgency under some highly illiberal legislation, the Armed Forces (Special Powers) Acts of 1958 and 1972, the Disturbed Areas law, and since 2002 the Prevention of Terrorism Act. Inside Kashmir the conflict makes it too dangerous for women to be openly, politically active against the brutal Indian military presence on the one hand, and the violent strategies of insurgents on the other. Concerned Indian citizens can protest from outside the troubled region against the atrocities committed by the state in their name. But in Kashmir itself, the best recourse is humanitarian projects. A good example of a response to this dilemma is the work of the Delhi-based NGO Aman (Peace). The organization's aims include reduction of violent conflict as well as humanitarian work with survivors. But in Kashmir, Sahba Husain, a feminist psychologist and Aman trustee, does what is pragmatically possible. She runs a project on 'gender, mental health and conflict', among women in the villages. She says: 'Death on the scale experienced in Kashmir produces catastrophic trauma. Mental ill-health is an epidemic there.' The only hospital mental health department had 48,000 registered outpatients in 2003.

Ritual and symbolism

A distinctive feature of women's peace activism is the creative use of ritual and symbolism. Sometimes it's a genuine expression of current spiritual practices in a given culture, or a revival of such practices. More often it's a reinvention of culture, based on vaguer notions of a past when people lived closer to nature, or when women and women's knowledge were more valued. Greenham women sometimes used witch symbolism – spectacularly in the Hallowe'en mass action of 1983 when women, dressed as witches, used the sheer weight of numbers to bring down four miles of the perimeter fence. Greenham witchery commemorated a historical event: one of the last witches in Britain is believed to have been executed on the Common. It also reclaimed the traditional knowledge and power of women, remembering that those persecuted and burned in the medieval witch-hunts were women healers and seers. At another level it simply put to good political effect the festive witch imagery of children's Hallowe'en parties.

Women in Black's vigils use drama (deploying themselves iconically in urban spaces), ritual (silence) and symbolism (choosing to wear black, the colour of mourning in many cultures). Code Pink use the colour pink symbolically too, cheerfully mixing their metaphors. They're parodying the commercially hyped 'pink for a girl', the colour code for the feminine. The words 'Code Pink' are a spoof of the military system of security alerts: 'Code Red', etc. As we saw above, the women also neatly translate for their own political purposes the trope of the 'pink slip' – the employment dismissal notice. 'Slip' was then reinvented in a play of words as a woman's silky undergarment, which again unrepentantly exploits the present-day commercialization of the feminine.

Whether the symbolism is ancient or modern, at international meetings I've seen women happily join the small ceremonies that each group offers. For example, at the meeting in Manila of the Women's Network against Militarism, Terri Keko'olani, an indigenous Hawai'ian woman, opened sessions with a prayer for ancestors to be with us in the meeting. The Korean women one evening led a ceremony with traditional paper costumes, bells and candles. We decorated trees with messages, and enjoyed the multiplicity-in-unity expressed by the Puerto Rican women's huge and colourful quilt (see photo p. 72).

Bay Area WiB draw on current religious ritual, inventively adapting Jewish practice in place of the standard Women in Black vigil. For instance, they've twice celebrated the new year festival of Tashlich by attracting a crowd on the beach around huge puppets (see photo p. 55). In 2003 they made tall cardboard partitions to simulate the Israeli separation wall. The people were invited to rip pieces off the wall, write messages on them and take them to the puppets who in exchange gave them pieces of bread to cast into the water. Traditionally, Penny Rosenwasser explained, this symbolizes 'letting go of ways we missed the mark' in the year gone by. Sandy Butler said: 'We're inventing a new liturgy. People are hungry for a place to be political using ritual form rather than words. To feel and express how tormenting, painful, complex, outraged, committed we are as Jews – while the Israeli government is doing what it is … For me our rituals – these shapes and forms that creative feminists conceptualize – are a way of honouring the spiritual and political dimensions of being a Jew. Everything about my spiritual and political life that feels important is there.'

I found a conscious and persistent use of symbolism in La Ruta Pacífica in Colombia, where they have a deft way of mixing hard-headed economic and political analysis with an evocation of women's ancestral traditions and spirituality. A whole section of their impressive 185-page book (*La Ruta Pacífica* 2003) is devoted to symbolism, which they list as one of their principal strategies. Their aim is 'the deconstruction of the pervasive symbolism of violence and war and the substitution of a new visual and textual language and creative rituals and other practices that "recover what women have brought to the world"'. La Ruta's use of symbolism isn't about abandoning rationality but combining it with intuition and emotion to invent expressions that are surprising, clear and powerful enough to interrupt and contradict patriarchy, militarism, authoritarian masculinity and exclusion. It's about using non-verbal images in a world in which we are bombarded by wordy politics to such an extent that words are felt to have lost their sense. It's about excavating and recovering a feminine knowledge that's been subordinated, silenced and buried. It's also about crossing the borders between Christian traditions in Colombia and surviving pagan traditions, both native American and African in origin.

La Ruta's main themes concern countering violence and death, affirming life and renewal, and asserting connectedness and sisterhood (sororidad). They use rhyme, rhythm and music in chanting and singing, drumming and dance. They make reference to the elements: earth (planting, seeds), fire (use of light and torches) and water (bathing together in the river). They use colours symbolically – yellow for truth; white for justice; green for hope; blue for making amends. They use clothing, white and black. They ritualize hands and touch. They stitch and sew quilts and banners with words and images. Above all, the trope of weaving (tejer, tejido) recurs. On the one hand this represents connectedness – they sometimes use the visual image of a spider's web. On the other hand the notion of weaving, unravelling and weaving anew, symbolizes the creative cycle of life, death and renewal; and perhaps most importantly the deconstruction and reconstruction of meaning.

It may be that the very varied women who comprise La Ruta Pacífica react in differing ways to the symbolic dimension of the organization's strategy, some ascribing it more validity, some less. Sometimes the symbolism itself, but even more the words used to describe it, border on the essentializing and romanticizing of 'woman'. But undeniably the organization's inventive use of symbolism and ritual has great value in drawing together women of different regions and different traditions in Colombia. In each of their countrywide mobilizations, from the first in Urabá to the most recent in Choco, symbolism has been powerfully effective in generating a sense of shared lives and sisterhood, and in converting a protest against the very negative phenomena of militarism, violence and death into an experience (even if only lived for brief moments) of their very opposites.

The political use of silence

Women in Black groups aren't the only ones that use silence as a political medium, but they are helpfully explicit about it. In India the women came to the idea out of exasperation with the political scene around them. 'No more shouting and screaming,' Celine Sugana said. 'Nobody was listening to all the rhetoric.' Their vocal silence contrasts with the powerful visual message conveyed through placards and leaflets. In Gulf Coast Women in Black, in Florida, USA, the women start their vigils by reading aloud a statement about silence. They feel it sums up their whole message, and makes other words redundant.

> The silenced ones who cannot talk for themselves are: the women, the children, the mothers, the fathers, the sisters, the brothers, the

> aunts and nieces ... all the humans deprived of their capacity to say: 'enough of this already – enough!'
>
> Our silence provides an opportunity for the birds, the crickets, the squirrels, the lizards to express themselves, letting us hear their sounds and music of peace. Our silence lets them all show us all the peripheral beauty we are destroying everyday.
>
> Our silence lets the land resonate by herself – making us more aware that all the noise we make as humans is covering up our deeds of destruction pursued by greed while creating great distraction. A distraction that victimizes everyone. A distraction that allows us to omit the forgotten ones.
>
> We maintain silence as a loud sound addressed to all the misguided leaders of this planet.

So strongly do they believe in the political effectiveness of silence that when 3,000 anti-war protesters assembled at the gates of MacDill Air Base, and Gulf Coast Women in Black were offered an opportunity to speak from the public platform, they accepted – and used their five minutes to maintain absolute silence. Silence in that place confronted sounds of terrible import. When the invasion of Iraq began you could hear roaring planes, they told me, taking off from the runways. 'We heard the very sounds Iraqi women would hear a few hours later. From one Gulf to another!'

Not all women, however, agree about silence. While the Public Library WiB group adhere strongly to silence, their neighbours in Union Square WiB feel differently. Sherry Gorelick wrote to me: 'There's so much ignorance about Israel and Palestine that to be silent would be to have the meaning of our vigils supplied by the ignorance created by the media. Silence is complicity unless the void is filled by communication.' Besides, they feel the chattiness of their vigil opens a door to passers-by. Helen John, too, is someone with strong feelings about this. She says: 'Why should we silence ourselves? Men have silenced us for years. I understand using silence when there's nothing meaningful left to say. But unspeakable things should be spoken about and explained to those who don't yet understand. Silence can disempower you.'

Women's peace camps

I draw on Britain for my examples of the practice of 'camping', but not because this is the only place the strategy has been used.

There have been sustained women's peace camps in the USA, at Seneca Falls, in Australia at Pine Gap and other places too. But the women's peace camp at Greenham Common, Berkshire, between 1981 and 1994 was surely the longest-lived and most widely known. It was followed by more intermittent women's camps outside the Atomic Weapons Establishment at Aldermaston from 1985, and at the US intelligence facility at Menwith Hill in Yorkshire from 1994. In these paragraphs on camping and nonviolent direct action, I draw on interviews with three women, Helen John, Rebecca Johnson and Sian Jones, who've all had extensive experience of these camps and associated activities.

On 12 December 1979, Prime Minister Margaret Thatcher announced that the US government would be basing cruise missiles in the UK. Many people were shocked that such a decision could have been taken by the Cabinet without discussion in Parliament. In August 1981, as I mentioned in chapter 5, women living in Cardiff, Wales, feeling that conventional means of protest through the political system had failed them, decided as a last resort to walk the 125 miles to the Royal Air Force base at Greenham Common where the first missiles would be located. They intended simply to hand in a petition to the base commander requesting a TV debate. When refused, some of the women chained themselves to the fence. Helen John was one of them. She remembers how the US officer eventually came out and belittled their protest, saying petulantly: 'You can stay there as long as you like as far as I'm concerned.' Some of them decided to take him at his word. Helen, despite having a husband and children back in Wales, thought, 'All right. This is where it makes sense to be.' It was a moment that radically changed the course of her life.

Women came from all over the country to join the Cardiff women. There were a few men present at the start. But there were problems with drugs and alcohol. And, besides, women soon observed that, while they were the ones maintaining everyday life at the camp, it was often men who annoyingly stepped forward as spokespeople. A decision was made, after much painful debate, to be a women-only camp. Thereafter, for thirteen years, there would be a unique women's space on the Common, shoulder to shoulder with the masculine world of the military. Repeatedly evicted, their tents and possessions confiscated, they learned to make 'benders' of slender branches tied together and covered with plastic sheeting that could easily be built anew when the bailiffs had gone. At the height of the camp there were scores of women permanently settled in five camps outside different gates in the nine-mile perimeter fence. Inside the base, builders began to prepare the silos to receive the missiles. The campers called for a mass demonstration to 'Embrace the Base' and blockade its gates. On 12 December 1982, 35,000 women responded. Joining hands they encircled the entire base. Next day and intermittently for years thereafter women would lie down and block the entrances and exits (see photo pp. 218–19). Roaring over their heads the massive transport planes brought in the missiles, and many of the same women were still there to see them flown back to the USA after Gorbachev and Reagan signed a treaty for the removal of intermediate-range missiles from Europe.

Camping is a form of nonviolent direct action against the military system. Sian Jones says, of camping: 'It's to do with physical proximity, it's about placing ourselves right there on Ministry of Defence land. It's about taking their space, inhabiting their space.' But it's not an easy option. Quite apart from the rigours of living out of doors, year-round, in primitive conditions, you can get seriously hurt at the hands of police, bailiffs, soldiers and angry local men. Rebecca Johnson spent a lot of time at the Greenham camp and was often a speaker, informing audiences at home and abroad about the campaign. She helped me think through just what this methodology achieved. For a start, having a resident camp at Greenham Common enabled many women from all over Britain to participate in the campaign: 'It needed some of us to commit on a long-term basis, to deal with the evictions day after day. But also so that other women could dip in and out, come and stay for periods of time, for weekends or whatever. They could do their jobs, have their families and at the same time be part of Greenham.'

The visitors brought provisions and fresh energy for other nonviolent forms of direct action, such as cutting or climbing into the base, dancing on the silos and runways, taking and driving vehicles, occupying buildings, doing occasional damage and taking up police and magistrates' time in the ensuing court cases. A camp, Sian added, is 'a thread that holds us together and gives us the capacity to think, to act, and then to persist in our actions'. There is a valuable sociality inherent in the camping process. Around a campfire, in direct contrast to the silent vigil, you *talk*. And plot and plan.

Camping is also about *seeing and being seen*: bearing witness to what the people in the base are doing, observing their activity, finding out exactly what it means and making the base equally visible to as wide a public as possible. 'It was us watching them, but also making them see us,' Rebecca said. The women wanted to be in the face of the military. They wanted the American servicemen and their wives and children, driving in and out of their homes in the base, to see and understand the protest. Third, a camp is about learning and counter-information. 'At Greenham, we got good at *reading* the base,' she went on. They exposed just how insecure military 'security' really is. The purpose of the mobile cruise missile, launched from a road vehicle, is secret deployment to hidden sites around the country. But the women learned to detect indications that the missile launchers were to be taken out on exercises. They would alert Cruisewatch (a mixed organization of women and men) so that from the moment it left the base the convoy would be followed and impeded at every step of the way. Eventually there was nothing secret about cruise missiles. The entire British public (and the Soviet Union) could know where they were at any given moment.

Anne Lee, Helen John and others have similarly carried out intensive research inside and outside RAF Menwith Hill. This US field station with its huge white golf-ball globes is part of the United States' early warning system and missile defence 'Star Wars' programme. An occasional women's camp began here in 1994. The women work closely with the local group Citizens for Peace in Space, and make good use of information from the Global Network against Weapons and Nuclear Power in Space, of which Helen is one of the nine global directors. As with Greenham and Aldermaston, communications with the public through radio and other media have been important resources for the Menwith Hill women intent on getting the eyes of the world to focus on the true meaning of what's going on, in secrecy behind barbed wire, and what it signifies for our safety.

Nonviolent direct action: putting the body into play

I didn't meet any women's organization addressing militarism and war whose members had any disagreement on the principle of nonviolence. But how *active* that nonviolence should be, and how *direct* the action, are always under discussion. The male storm-troopers of the left dismiss nonviolent direct action (NVDA) as soft, elitist and middle-class, while some pacifist-minded women on the contrary feel it flirts with violence. A vigil is nonviolent action, but it's not direct. A 'die-in' at a military air display, while direct, and pleasingly dramatic, is relatively passive. Some women find it disturbingly evocative of women's victimhood. By contrast, blockading a road or a gate where you seriously mean to stop something happening is a more active form of NVDA. NVDA has to be prompted by a very real anger or a very real fear, because it is often physically and emotionally costly. As Sian Jones points out, in the 1980s during the Cold War many people were afraid that a nuclear war was imminent. At the same time it was characteristic of women's groups to stress that nobody should be induced to take part in NVDA just because others wished to do it. Each one should think independently and do what she felt comfortable with. Helen says of her many years of camping and NVDA: 'It's for myself I'm doing it, for me as an individual. Because I really do mean "not in my name". What I do has to be for me the correct thing to do. For me it's to try and obstruct the path of this big force that threatens to run right over the top of me. I don't know quite how I arrived at this, but I just can't compromise with them.'

NVDA is a demanding methodology, and requires preparedness, training and support. Sian believes it should be dovetailed intelligently with other approaches. In addition to taking NVDA, the Aldermaston women are currently contesting the proposed building developments in the base through the planning committee of the local council and by other means. She said: 'You need to know when it's most productive to argue the case in a meeting, and when the process is so disreputable it's better to show it up by lying across their threshold inside a plastic body bag.'

Whether it's men or women, putting your body on the line for politics is an effective, if perilous, strategy. But for women, because of the way women are often reduced to the body and routinely sexualized, putting the body in play has a special meaning. Just before I arrived in India in 2004 an incident took place in the state of Manipur. Men of the Indian Army came at night and killed a woman, Thangjam Manorama, they wrongly believed to be active in the armed struggle for Metei independence. Her body, raped, mutilated and half naked, was found in the morning. She had been shot six times, including through the genitals. On 15 July, twelve women of the Meira Paibi women's movement, whose aim is violence reduction in Manipur, went to the headquarters of the

Assam Rifles, in the historic Kangla Fort. They stripped naked. They shook the gates. Mainly elderly women, they held placards saying, 'We are all Manorama's mothers', 'Indian Army rape us!' There were photographers and reporters present and the images that circulated next day in newspapers and on television, first locally and then India-wide, caused shock and concern about the Indian military's activities in north-east India.

Sian Jones said of women's political use of their own bodies: 'It's powerful because it uses incongruity. It challenges inhibition and politeness.' Reflecting on women's NVDA, she added: 'There's a definite feeling of you being up against it, of personally putting yourself in a very physical relationship with male power. At Greenham initially you had fully armed soldiers. We were in direct opposition to the people who were plotting to blow up the world. And it's especially interesting doing this as women, using our bodies to prevent men using their power. I know it's odd that in order to resist nuclear war, the ultimate form of violence that men threaten, women are prepared to put ourselves into a situation where men can hurt us. You can't do it alone, but you can with other women in a very tightly supported way. Then you can feel even while you're lying on the ground that actually we're the ones who have the power – and it's a very collective feeling.'

Prefigurative struggle

If there's one principle underpinning women's anti-war activism it's what the Spanish women call 'coherencia entre fines y medios' – literally, coherence between ends and means, or making sure that your activist practice reflects the kind of society your movement aims to build. 'Prefigurative struggle', it was called on the left in the 1960s and '70s. This subsumes nonviolence, but goes further. One thing it implies is that relationships between yourselves as protesters and the soldiers and police officers who represent the state or the military, even if they are sometimes necessarily antagonistic, are at least respectful and whenever possible involve conversing with them about what you and they are doing.

Another thing the principle requires is that relationships between women and men in the movement be equal, sensitive to the oppressions and injustices women often experience at the hands of men. I can best illustrate this by the following account. I had interesting interviews with two women in Barcelona, Elena Grau and Isabel Ribera, and two in Zaragoza, Carmen Magallón Portolés and Montse Reclusa, who had been part of a group that for fifteen years published a well-respected antimilitarist journal *En Pie de Paz* (roughly translatable as 'On Foot for Peace'). The paper was produced by a 'collective of collectives', small groups in eight cities. Editorial work was done in one place, design in a second, production in a third, distribution from somewhere else again. Individuals came together from these groups in two meetings for each issue of the journal. There would usually be fifteen or more at these production meetings, and usually more than half would be women. Sometimes there were babies. Elena and Isabel both gave birth to daughters during the *En Pie de Paz* years. They would be breastfeeding, discussing, writing, all at once. 'We believed that any project of transformation must be reflected in the social relations,' Carmen said. So the women continually interrogated the structure and the process in which the journal was created. Some of the men wanted a hierarchy, with a director and an editorial board. Others, and certainly the women, wanted a horizontal organization, with no specialization, all co-producers, working by consensus. 'Some men simply didn't know *how* to do this.'

Women insisted on a peace culture in the group itself (Greenham Common had been influential on them). At one moment there was a fierce and bitter fight between two groups of men over Basque nationalism. 'At that moment,' said Carmen, 'we women put our foot down. Without having agreed it in advance we said clearly and trenchantly, "We don't want to work like this."' In this group, they insisted to the men, the point is not to win an argument. Any thought should be thinkable here. It should be acceptable to be uncertain, to not have an answer. The men were giving priority to decisiveness, speed, order. Women were prioritizing relationships. 'We wanted to do everything differently. Elena wrote one article in which she said "We produce the journal because we love one another." This was too much for some of the men. They thought it was sissy! They simply didn't understand what we wanted to say: that the strength of the project derived from the love and friendship there was between us' (Carmen).

So the women, Isabel said, 'became hegemonic' in the journal. Eventually some of the men left. Those who stayed joined fully in the childcare and the cooking. At first they said, 'We can't think and look after babies at the same time.' But they learned to do their part. The childcare had to be shared because the women were so central to the work of the journal. 'They were very different from us. They doubted our choices at first. But they liked the way we were and acted, and were very respectful. We were able to build bridges between women and men, and warm friendships. In the end we could discuss difficult issues between us' (Elena).

Women's cultural hegemony was visible in the journal itself, too. 'From the start we wanted the publication to look beautiful,' Carmen said. 'We were the ones who cared very much about the form. We were careful in choosing words and images. We thought, *everything* communicates.'

So 'working for peace', for these women, meant nonviolence in private life and in collective groups as well as in international politics. Montse said: 'In political history there are two currents. One's about life, the other's about power.' Putting together what she and Carmen subsequently said, I get the following sense of where the women's politics of prefigurative struggle was coming from: 'We started in our own lives, in our own *entorno* (circle), our relationship with our parents and families. We didn't want to be like our mothers, traditional, subordinated. In Spain in the 1960s everything was prohibited. To be free, we had to struggle against Franco. We were up against the whole social order – political relations, personal relations. We wanted everything, the lot! But we discovered the left parties didn't share these aims. They were obsessed with power, but they disdained everyday life. And women always came second! We discovered the parties prohibited everything, just as the state and family did. Did we really have to sacrifice everyday life and personal relationships now to win a revolutionary future? We wanted freedom *now*. There should be no inconsistency between where we wanted to get and the route we would use to get there: "coherencia entre fines y medios". In pacifism we found a more holistic answer. It differed entirely from the left's instrumental approach to peace, peace as a mere tactic for revolution. Peace is betrayed by that!'

SEVEN

Towards coherence: pacifism, nationalism, racism

§ When I first mentioned, on-line, that I hoped to make a study of women's anti-war activism on a worldwide scale, among many supportive emails came a friendly warning from women in Tokyo Women in Black. They urged me to be very careful not to imply, in looking for a worldwide movement, that there's a unified position among women peace activists, or even in WiB as an international network. I should be wary of assuming, and inscribing, they said, a political 'line' where none exists. That indeed was a worry to me at first, but as the work progressed I began to find the opposite danger even more alarming: we might all turn out to have such diverse and contrary views that any notion of allied movements of women spanning many countries would evaporate. That fear is expressed in the title of this book. 'From where we stand', after all, is an incomplete sentence, suggesting that the take any one of us has on war and peace is relative, depending partly on our positionality. But many of us would like to act in concert, for a shared purpose. Are we capable of that? A string of contested words kept coming up in my interviews and discussions. Each word draws another into play, and the meanings intertwine. But for convenience I've thought about them as two clusters, one around 'pacifism', the other around 'nationalism', and that's how I address them in this chapter. They are, it should be noted, not women's issues only. They also entail divergences within the mainstream anti-war movement. But some women and some feminists have their own perspective on them.

Peace, justice and solidarity

It was with the four Women in Black groups in Italy that I pursued the question of pacifism most diligently, and I heard some careful expressions of ambiguity. For a start, some of the women declared themselves pacifist – even if only by contrast with the past. Several referred back to the 1970s saying, 'I wasn't a pacifist *then*' – as though to say, 'I am *today*'. But most quickly qualified the notion.

It's as though the oft-cited phrase 'I'm not a feminist but ... ' can be reversed in this case, so that these feminists may be characterized as typically saying 'I *am* a pacifist but ... '

In fact, whether women said 'I am a pacifist', or (like Mariella Genovese) 'I'm not a pacifist, nor even pacific! I'm just against war and violence', or (like Elisabetta Donini) 'Some of us would like to be pacifists, some have more problems', they all tended to qualify their remark by reference to specific times and places when outright condemnation of violence had not seemed possible. Elisabetta, for instance, went on to say: 'Without weapons in some places you can't survive, or solve problems.' Gabriella Cappellitti similarly felt decisions could be arrived at only case by case: 'In our group in Bologna, we're against all violence. For us all wars are wrong. There are really no humanitarian wars. Violence makes violence ... But there are different kinds of wars and each situation must be considered individually and an answer found on its own merits. In Palestine, in South America – I don't live there! Each person must decide.'

Most of these women, however, seem to have arrived at a belief that violence is not (merely) unethical, it's seldom even *useful*. It doesn't work as a method in the struggle for justice. Either it's defeated, or it leads to the wrong kind of peace, one in which violence remains latent. Thus, for Mariella it's a pragmatic question: 'I'm convinced that in this year of 2005, the military approach, armed conflict, is bound to fail.' You mean, I asked, we can't reach peace through war? 'More than that,' she said, 'it's positively self-destructive.' Palestine was often a test case in this thinking. Gabriella, for instance, could well *understand* Palestinian violence, even suicide bombing; but she could not ascribe it legitimacy. She read something from the fact that in the intifada of 1987, a matter of children and youths throwing stones, a lot of women had felt able to be actively involved, while in this second intifada, in which Palestinians were responding to the massive repression of the Israeli state with more serious armed violence than before, women were scarcely visible. There may be more, as yet untested, nonviolent methods, if you really look for them and are maybe ready to put yourself in danger to try them. 'There's often a possibility of nonviolent resistance. We can develop that space.'

Several of the older women in these Italian Donne in Nero groups were wondering about a change they detected over the last thirty or forty years in their thinking about pacifism, justice and violence.

(I met others in Mujeres de Negro in Spain who were similarly reflective about their past activism.) In the 1970s, as Patrizia Celotto said: 'We feminists weren't involved in any kind of peace movement. Quite the contrary, we had this perspective of international wars of "liberation" – for instance in Latin America. We believed then in the myth of a just war, including the resistance in Vietnam. We didn't see resistance as violence ... Today we don't anymore speak of "liberation".'

Marianita, too, said: 'There was no question in my mind then of nonviolence.' So the question for them was, were the wars of those days, such as the Sandinista revolution against the Nicaraguan dictator Somosa and the Cubans' overthrow of Batista, essentially different from anything being experienced today? Or was it that their own analysis had changed? How is it that then they had expressed solidarity with *liberation* movements, while now they belong to movements for '*peace* and justice'? To help them think this through, the women in Torino had been revisiting the history of the Italian partisans, those who had taken up arms against German Nazism and Italian fascism in the Second World War. They'd explored anew women's role on both sides in that war. They'd looked to forgotten examples of civil, nonviolent resistance. Elisabetta noted: 'To all of us it's very important to be aware that those women and men in the end gave up their weapons and tried to assert the principle that war is not the way to do international relations.' The Second World War had been a testing time for pacifists. We saw in chapter 5 how the rise of Nazi and fascist regimes, undeniably evil, undeniably intent on armed conquest, threw women of the Women's International League for Peace and Freedom and other 'peace women' into disarray and division. It tested the limits of pacifism. At the outbreak of war, the US section of WILPF lost half its membership – equally because it was 'too pacifist' and 'not pacifist enough' (Bussey and Tims 1981).

The wars in the former Yugoslavia in the 1990s were another test of pacifist ethics, presenting different kinds of challenge to those (for instance, Muslims in Bosnia-Herzegovina) suffering the onslaught of ethnic aggression and those (as in Serbia) who were bitterly opposing their 'own' extremist nationalist regimes. Lepa Mladjenović, a member of Žene u Crnom and thus a dissident among the aggressors, wrote about how in Belgrade at the start of the war they had heatedly debated the meaning of a pacifist stance. Were all feminist supposed to be pacifists? Were pacifists always totally against any use of weapons? Can we find examples in history of wars being stopped by peaceful resistance? But then again, can we ever end war by war? Later she wrote about how they had put to each other the notional question, 'If a soldier comes to your door to shoot at you, or at your daughter, what should you do? Shoot back or not?'

> Feminists at that time had little experience with a culture of ethics that would suggest an easy answer. The former Yugoslavia had suppressed religion and, in any case, Yugoslav feminists derived few ideas if any from religious morality. Marxist politics had argued that we should defend our ideas 'even if it came to blood'. However, by 1991, Marxism had lost its popularity in the everyday lives of Yugoslavs. And finally, the former-Yugoslav system had annihilated the notion of human rights. Thus, feminist activists found themselves in a political void with limited knowledge of the history of human rights or international peace politics. (Mladjenović 2003: 160)

In these fraught discussions in Belgrade, as war broke out in the region,

> feminists who declared that they would *not* shoot felt hurt by those who said *yes*, they would shoot. Those who said yes to shooting felt betrayed by those who said *no*; they believed that the pacifists were prepared to let anyone be killed and therefore did not trust them. Feminist pacifists were not sure of the line between shooting to defend and shooting to kill, and therefore did not trust those feminists who said they would shoot. (ibid.)

Lepa made the point that communist Yugoslavia had had no religion to guide such ethical choices. But religion doesn't necessarily help. I looked to the Religious Society of Friends, the Quakers, for guidance on pacifism, since, among Christians, they are of an exceptionally peace-oriented turn of mind. I looked through the compilation of writings, *Quaker Faith and Practice*, that this undogmatic society takes as embodying the Quaker view. It's indicative that I found 'pacifism' dealt with under the heading 'dilemmas'. Isaac Penington in 1661 had written, for instance:

> I speak not against ... peoples defending themselves against foreign invasions; or making use of the sword to suppress the violent

> and evil-doers within their borders – for this the present state of things may and doth require, and a great blessing will attempt the sword where it is borne uprightly to that end and its use will be honourable … but yet there is a better state, which the Lord hath already brought some into, and which nations are to expect and to travel towards. There is to be a time when 'nation shall not lift up sword against nation; neither shall they learn war any more' … this blessed state, which shall be brought forth at large in God's season, must begin in particulars. (Religious Society of Friends 2006)

Subsequent Quakers had edited this passage to clarify that Pennington meant by 'brought forth at large', 'in society as a whole', while 'in particulars' meant 'in individuals'.

Wolf Mendl, whose contribution is dated 1974, noted that the early Quakers hadn't denied the reality of evil. Indeed, he said, those who today identified peace with the absence of conflict, and valued it absolutely 'have given modern pacifism a bad name and have led their critics to refer to them contemptuously as "passivists"'. Recognizing the reality of the dilemma, Quakers have usually instead put their pacifism into practice not by protesting against every war on principle but through an earnest search for alternative ways of resolving conflict, and personal engagement in humanitarian relief, mediation and reconciliation work. They set store by those 'particulars', the contribution and witness each individual can make.

The theory of 'just war' dates back to St Augustine in the fourth century CE and is still an important element in the 'realist' and 'neo-realist' international relations theory that guides most modern diplomacy. To mobilize their people for battle, contemporary governments have to claim their war is just. The notion is in bad repute with peace activists, though, because the grounds for the claim are often insecure. Michael Walzer in *Just and Unjust Wars*, first published in 1977, reviews 'just war' theory, noting that a moral case has traditionally to be made concerning both *jus ad bellum*, the justice of going to war, and *jus in bello*, the means by which a war is fought. In the preface to the 1992 edition, Walzer uses the recently ended war in the Persian Gulf to elucidate the questions that have to be asked. Was Saddam Hussein's invasion of Kuwait an outrage that morally had to be reversed by force? The US-led coalition had oil interests and world leadership at stake. Did that make the cause of liberating Kuwait less 'just'? Were all nonviolent means of freeing Kuwait tried first? There was diplomacy. A blockade was proposed. But are indiscriminate blockades (and indeed lethal economic sanctions, as imposed subsequently) any more moral than military attack? Smart bombs were used to minimize civilian casualties – were they smart enough? Was the destruction of the convoy on the Basra Road justified or excessive? Was the economic infrastructure of Iraq a legitimate target? For Walzer the Gulf War passes the justice test (just!) (Walzer 1992). But many women anti-war activists, including ourselves in London, went on the streets to oppose that war.

All this leaves today's anti-war activists, women and men, feminist and other, with the difficulty of deciding their position *now*, as one war follows fast on another, each presenting its own ethical dilemma. The anti-war movement expands and contracts dramatically from one episode of war to the next, as popular opinion concerning legitimacy and justice responds to each new situation. Where there is a 'pacifist dilemma', it often takes concrete form in choices concerning, on the one hand 'intervention', and on the other, armed movements for 'liberation', 'reform' or 'revolution'. For anti-war or pacifist activists located in Western and/or relatively powerful states, there is sometimes no dilemma. A war can sometimes be seen (despite the propaganda) to be a military adventure in defence of Western interests. It was this aspect of the invasion of Iraq by the US-led coalition in 2003 that convinced so many to join the demonstrations that opposed it. The dilemma more often arises when politicians are invoking human rights to justify 'intervention', when the call is for 'humanitarian' war-fighting. Military 'interference' in the internal affairs of a neighbouring state, breaching sovereignty, has sometimes been condoned because it saved many lives – witness Vietnam's intervention in Cambodia and Tanzania's in Uganda, both in the late 1970s. World opinion was deeply troubled by the failure to intervene to stop the Rwandan genocide in 1994. And what did we feel, after the Gulf War, about the US intervening in Iraqi Kurdistan, and failing to intervene to protect the southern Shia from Saddam's onslaught?

The question often looks different according to the proposed agent of intervention. More trust is placed by the peace movement on inter-state bodies such as the Organization of African Unity or the United Nations than in individual states. But sometimes armed international peacekeeping operations turn out badly, as did that in Sierra Leone by ECOMOG, the small force supplied by the Economic Organization of West African States, and the subsequent

In some circumstances it is easy to say, simply, 'no to war'. Top, women protest unequivocally at RAF Fairford, UK, where bombs were being loaded for Western militarist adventures in the Middle East. In others cases such as the Israeli–Palestinian conflict, the reduction of violence clearly depends on an end to injustice.

intervention by the United Nations. Then the British tried their hand, unilaterally. And while the women of Marwopnet, whom we met in chapter 1, felt nothing but gratitude for this intervention by an ex-colonial power, many anti-war feminists in the UK and elsewhere shuddered at the idea of British ships and helicopters being yet again seen as the answer to conflict. Some anti-war activists have argued for the demilitarization of UN peacekeeping operations and for a greater reliance on unarmed and civilian interventions. But the massacre by Serb extremists of several thousand Bosnian Muslim men permitted by the UN Protection Force at Srebrenica in 1994 left many anti-war activists wishing the Dutch soldiers had used the weapons with which they had been issued.

Lepa Mladjenović and the women in Belgrade, having debated whether it's legitimate to kill to defend yourself and your child, went on to ask each other whether they would support external military intervention if this would stop a war (Mladjenović 2003). The question was posed in acute form first by the siege of Sarajevo by Bosnian Serb nationalist forces and Serb irregulars in 1995 and second by the Milosević regime's aggression in Kosovo/a in 1999. In the choices women made, both positionalities and values came into play. Women were divided in some cases by whether they were situated at the receiving or delivering end of violence, in others by their pro- or antinationalist beliefs and whether or not they were consciously antimilitarist. But outcomes also changed minds. When the three-year agony of Sarajevo was ended by a mere seven days in which NATO neatly 'took out' the surrounding Serb gun emplacements, there were few who continued to oppose NATO's armed intervention.

In 1999, however, NATO acted to counter the Serbian nationalist regime's aggression against Kosovan Albanians, and this was a different matter. The overt humanitarian reason for this action was partly cover for other motives. The USA was keen to have NATO prove its worth in the post-communist world and also wanted to oust Milosević, whom they saw as an obstinate vestigial communist. So NATO planes subjected Belgrade and other sites in Serbia and Kosovo/a to heavy bombing. The outcome was ambiguous. The Serbs intensified their ethnic cleansing of Kosovo/a, profiting from the absence of foreign observers who had fled the bombing. After the bombardment, the flight of Albanians was reversed. Yet the military action led to no permanent solution of the conflict.

Feminists in Serbia and Kosovo/a were therefore divided in their response to the 1999 NATO intervention. Pro-nationalist feminists opposed military intervention, overlooked Serbian nationalist aggression, and blamed NATO alone. But as we saw in chapter 3, anti-fascist feminists including Žene u Crnom took the position that Milosević was responsible for the ethnic aggression and consequently also for the fact that NATO bombs were now raining down on his people's heads. Although at that crucial moment they were prevented by the police from demonstrating against the Serb regime, as we saw in chapter 3 they called on Women in Black in other countries to condemn both Milosević and NATO. This division between women on the question of what stance to take over the NATO intervention was not limited to Serbia – it divided women in the Italian and other women's anti-war movements too. Lepa concluded:

> If we choose at all times to be on the pacifist *no shooting* side, and we meet a friend who was saved in Bosnia or Kosova after the military intervention, we are embarrassed when facing her. She tells us that our position is idealistic and that her reality is something else. We still believe that a world without militarism is possible. Our friend can understand us, she can even believe the same politics herself, for having been in war, she hates war. But her reality is different. We look into her eyes and end up with an ethical problem, because our position has not included her reality. (Mladjenović 2003: 166)

If our dilemma presents itself sometimes as a choice about big power intervention, at others it arises over a choice concerning whether to support local paramilitary liberatory and revolutionary movements. Here it may be useful to consider a situation where armed conflict is in abeyance, where there is a pause to take stock on ethical choices. Guatemala is a case in point, where a decades-long and genocidal conflict ended with a peace agreement in 1996. To the south, in Colombia, as we saw in chapter 1, the guerrilla forces had forfeited their legitimacy, due both to their decades of failure to deliver a reform government and the descent of their methods into barbarity. Colombian women therefore felt they could and must oppose *all* military and paramilitary factions. However, the conflict in Guatemala during the 1970s and '80s posed the question of the justice of 'liberatory' guerrilla warfare in a more complex and ambiguous way (Taylor 1998: Manz 2004). The Guatemalan majority, mainly indigenous Maya, were desperate in their poverty, their mountain lands denuded and exhausted, their exploitation as seasonal labour on the coastal plantations extraordinarily brutal. When they started a co-operative movement to clear farmland for themselves in the uninhabited rain forest, this was seen by the state, the big landowners, the multinational corporations and the US government as dangerously leftist and subversive. The working class was evading the proper capitalist wage relation. The CIA covertly supported questionable elements in the Guatemalan state military, gave training in counter-insurgency technique in the School of the Americas and for many years ensured that no political leadership emerged in Guatemala to curtail the military's operations.

For self-protection and with the longer-term aim of social justice in Guatemala, some peasants and workers took up arms in groups that in 1982 would become the Unidad Revolucionaria Nacional Guatemalteca. How, then, should women have judged the guerrilla campaign? Was it legitimate and indeed necessary self-defence as the Guatemalan poor remain convinced? If so, did this exonerate the guerrillas for resorting to selective assassinations and punishing villagers who did not support them? Was it actually the choice of an armed response that drew down genocide on the heads of the Maya? Had international movements taken quicker and stronger action against poverty and injustice, would this have obviated the need for a violent uprising? Since the peace agreement of 1996, land reform has still not been enacted in Guatemala. The gap between rich and poor is greater than ever. Were there, are there, untried alternative ways that transnational feminist antimilitarism might propose to end such age-old and profound injustices before war breaks out again?

For some women, such questions raise more fundamental ones. What is violence? And what is peace? Most of the women I've interviewed and engaged in conversation speak in a way that indicates an understanding of violence as a continuum, and one with several dimensions. First, it's a continuum in terms of the place it occurs – home, street, community, country, continent (Moser 2001). Second it's a continuum in terms of time. Violence is present in the militarization of societies where open war has yet to break out, in war itself, while peace is negotiated, and in the disorder of post-war conditions. There's a general understanding that, even where there's no direct and overt violence, economic, social and political coercion may exist. There is thus also a continuum of violence running from the physical to the cultural, administrative or juridical. Gender-based and sexualized violence by men against women is a thread linking the points along these continua (Cockburn 2004b).

It is Johann Galtung to whom we mainly owe the concept of structural violence. He named as violent all 'unavoidable insults to basic human needs and, more generally to *life*, lowering the real level of needs satisfaction below what is potentially possible'. The four basic human needs he defined as those of survival, well-being, identity-and-meaning, and freedom (Galtung 1996: 197). In this view violence includes avoidable hunger and misery, lack of care, morbidity, destruction of life-sustaining environment, alienation and exclusion. Our very systems of production and governance that deliver these ills must therefore be recognized as violent. Institutions that generate religion and ideology, science and art engage in cultural violence when they normalize and legitimize this mode of ruling. When violence is seen in this light, those who take up arms to end it (like the Guatemalan guerrillas) could be seen not as initiating violence but as countering it.

The organizations allied in the anti-war movements don't always agree in identifying what Chairman Mao liked to call 'the main contradiction'. Some activists on the left, seeing war as an epiphenomenon of the poverty and inequality inherent in an exploitative mode of production, tend to put their energies into the struggle against capitalist globalization and neo-imperialism. Others (especially those based in the peace movement), seeing militarization and bellicosity as global problems in their own right, mobilize against these. We've seen how the two tendencies ally, often uncomfortably, in large-scale anti-war coalitions and campaigns. Unsurprisingly, a certain schizophrenia is visible at such events in the placards carried by the mass of demonstrators. Women, as we've seen, often criticize the violence of leftist slogans, and criticize the peace movement too when it capitulates to the left's macho style. The movements not only form strategic alliances, they also have overlapping memberships. Women play an active part in both. Nevertheless, differences of priority are an endless source of debate and contestation.

And peace – what is peace? If we believe in a continuum of violence, can we say that a militarized country whose troops remain in the barracks is at peace? If we believe in structural violence, can we say that a country like Guatemala, where a peace accord has been signed but not implemented, where wrongs have not been righted, is really 'at peace'? Then again, peace sometimes seems to require not only the absence of conflict but the obliteration of difference, of 'otherness' however defined. Do we want peace at such a price? If these things are so, is peace necessarily, endlessly, elusive? Jean Bethke Elshtain has described it as an 'ontologically suspicious' concept. Peace, she says, is always used rhetorically as the obverse of war. 'Peace never appears without its violent *doppelgänger*, War, lurking in the shadows. Peace is inside, not outside, a frame with war' (Elshtain 1990: 258). Some now prefer to scale down the quest for 'peace' to one for 'security'. Others prefer to expand the scope of our movement to 'nonviolence', knowing that what we seek is not just the absence of war but an end to the violence that deforms our lives in peacetime too. These semantic manoeuvres are logical, but along the way we lose the beauty of peace. I was going to say the 'glamour', but that would be to deny the special place peace has in our dreams.

National belonging and ethnic otherness

The question 'Is our anti-war movement by definition antinationalist?' has evoked uneasy debate at several Women in Black international encounters. Women are drawn to these encounters from all over the world. They vary greatly in their relation to ethnicity, nation and state, what and how they are officially 'named' and designated. This may in any case be different from the person they subjectively feel themselves to be. They come from countries that are relatively more and relatively less 'nation' states. Some were born into majority, some into minority ethnic groups in those states. They vary too in the wars they've experienced and what part ethnicity and nationalism played in them.

In Serbia, the women who would become Women in Black (Žene u Crnom) were for a while uncertain, as Yugoslavia disintegrated, what they felt about national identity and belonging. As they analysed what was happening around them, they quickly 'came out' as deeply antinationalist. Probably all of them would have agreed with Ksenija Forca when she said, 'If somebody asks me my nationality I say "antinationalist". If I have to write my nationality in some official papers I just put "xxx".' They acknowledged that it was the nationalist extremists claiming to act in 'their' national name, i.e. as 'Serbs', that were principally responsible for the disaster that was engulfing the region. (In Croatia this was not the case. Feminists there were more divided, some claiming, some disclaiming, Croatian national identity.) Because of the key position of Žene u Crnom in the international movement of Women in Black in the 1990s, antinationalism tended to become the latter's default position.

However, when Staša Zajović went on a speaking tour in Spain in the early years of the war, she found women in the anti-war movement in the Basque autonomous region divided on the issue of nationalism. Some, as she was, were deeply opposed to all nationalist sentiment. But she found others who saw Basque nationalist separatism as a progressive and legitimate movement, even if they opposed its violent methods. Žene u Crnom's ideas did not go down well with them. Again, in Cataluña nationalism is a popular movement. It's less militant and violent than Basque nationalism, and the majority of Catalan nationalists do not demand independence from Spain. None the less their claim of autonomy is strongly pressed. It's a powerful cultural movement, and there's passionate support for speaking Catalan as a first language. So some of the women activists in Barcelona too were reluctant to see antinationalism become a Women in Black orthodoxy. Women of Dones per Dones in Barcelona told me that at WiB international encounters: 'We always felt better understood by women of Israel, Palestine and Croatia, women who'd had to fight for the right to existence and the use of their language, than by women (for instance of Serbia) who had only experienced nationalism as something fundamentalist, aggressive and patriarchal.' The issue was one on which they disagreed also with some Spanish feminists who shared the Belgrade women's negative perception of nationalism, and were unsympathetic to the divisive 'sub-nationalisms' threatening Spain with disintegration. They tended (some women of the autonomías felt) to be blind to Spanish nationalism, the nationalism of their own collectivity. With these things in mind, Dones per Dones don't define themselves as antinationalists. Instead, they say: 'We define ourselves as feminists, antimilitarists and *anti-fundamentalists*. We feel these are the words that describe us best. Plus we denounce the militarist and patriarchal postures of our own governments, whether of the Spanish state or the Catalan autonomía.'

Zionism is the national project of worldwide Jewry. And it's the conflict between this Jewish nationalism and the Palestinian national movement that has arisen to protect itself from the Zionist claim to Palestinian land that, of all nationalist wars, evokes most distress today in the women's anti-war movement worldwide. Even among those Jewish activists, in the region and elsewhere, who oppose Israel's occupation of the West Bank, Gaza and the Golan Heights, there's little agreement of interpretation and opinion with regard to Zionism. In the Coalition of Women for Peace, for example, Gila Svirsky recognized that Zionism is often 'equated with nationalism, even imperialism', but she doesn't herself interpret it that way: 'Nationalism is often taken to extremes. But nationalism as an identity is different. I wouldn't call myself a nationalist, but often I say I'm proud of being Israeli and a Jew. The Zionism I grew up with meant the liberation of the Jewish people. A human state was the original vision. But it was at the expense of Palestinians. I'm sorry about that and I'm grateful to those Palestinians who agree now to a compromise on territory.'

Like Gila, Vera Jordan, who is active in Northern Bat Shalom, continues to feel herself Zionist and espouses its nationalism more positively: 'My nationalism's about self-determination. I have to have my country, a Jewish state, which I was denied for so long. I want my own flag, my own anthem. Recognition of the Nakhba [the catastrophe for Palestinians entailed in the creation of the Israeli state] is legitimate, but it shouldn't mean we can't any longer celebrate our Israeli Independence Day. The memories for us are too fresh – memories of the Holocaust and of the pogroms against Jews that occurred in Palestine before the creation of the state of Israel. Half a century isn't enough.'

The question of course remains, 'If not a national Jewish state, what kind of state?' What does democracy mean and is it compatible with Zionism, with nationalism? This is of crucial importance to the one-fifth of the Israeli population that is Palestinian and (as we saw in chapter 4) suffers both interpersonal and institutional racism there. Gila says: 'Israel has to give equal rights to all its citizens. And it has to welcome all immigrants on the same terms.' And women debate tirelessly how to interpret and whether to honour 'rights of return' to Israel – of any Jew, of any Palestinian.

More and more people today, leftists and anti-occupation activists on both sides of the Green Line, discuss the possibility of a solution to the Palestine/Israel problem involving not 'two states for two peoples' but a single state on the land that is now Israel and its Occupied Territories. They envisage a single democratic state in which Palestinians, Jews and others would be equal citizens. The single state-solution is gaining currency mainly because Israel's encroachments into the West Bank (the settlements and the Separation Wall) have caused people to despair of the territorial viability of any future Palestinian state. But it's also a solution favoured by those who deplore nationalism of any kind and feel particular distaste for states that claim to be for one national collectivity above all others. If the one-state idea is anathema to Zionist Jews, it's naturally appealing to the Palestinian minority already living in Israel. Aida Shibli (we met her in chapter 4) feels she has two identities, being both a Palestinian and an Israeli. Every day of her life, she says, she feels this split. The only future that could heal her schizophrenia is a single state uniting people of both names. She said: 'I would give up my Palestinian fantasy, my fantasy of a greater Palestine. In exchange I would ask Jews to give up their fantasy of a greater Zionist state. One state with equal rights. And that's asking no favours!'

Nationalism in practice takes many different forms, and theorists, besides, do not agree on how to evaluate them. It is generally understood that nationalism is an ideology that involves belief in both a social principle, that certain populations can be identified as 'peoples', and a political principle, that such collectivities have a right to live in their 'own' land, to self-governance within their 'own' state. However, the feeling of belonging to a 'people', possessing an ethnic identity, may not always translate into nationalism. Some distinctive cultural or religious groups simply maintain the sense of a common identity without being competitive about it. In the absence of oppression by others they may live happily without autonomy, without their 'own' land. But sometimes people are driven, or are mobilized, to seek more, to defend their rights or even to dominate, expel or kill others (Pieterse 1997). Increasingly, since the late eighteenth century, ethnic activists have tended to define their collectivity as a nation and been satisfied by nothing less than an independent nation state.

A crucial difference, from women's point of view, concerns how the nation is visualized and represented by its nationalist ideologues. Some ethnic groups hark back to the past, stressing either their bloodline or a historic culture – religious tradition, language, mores and taboos, dress and art, the shared experience of certain climacteric moments of triumph or disaster. Atavistic nationalisms of this kind tend to have particularly strongly patriarchal social systems, constructing masculinity and feminity in fixed, reductivist, unequal and complementary mode. Authority is invested in men, among whom the qualities of the leader and warrior are particularly valued. Women are defined as domestic and supportive, and are valued primarily as mothers, the biological and cultural reproducers of the nation (Anthias and Yuval-Davis 1989). In such nationalisms, militarism and bellicosity go hand-in-hand with oppressive gender relations. Nazi Germany is often cited as an example (Koonz 1987). John Horne has shown how both Nazism and Italian fascism made use of a radicalized masculinity, honed in war, to reconstruct a sense of national community (Horne 2004).

Analysts of nationalism differ on how much credence can and should be given to nationalists' origin myths. Is there really an identifiable bloodline surviving here? they may ask. Is the cultural continuity really so great? Or are these notions simply tools some politicians have chosen to use to evoke solidarity with their own project of political power? (For contrasted approaches, see Smith 1995; Gellner 1983.) The question was asked, for instance, about the Yugoslav communist leader Slobodan Milosević. He could clearly be seen to adopt Serb nationalism to strengthen his personal power base when communism began to lose its grip in the USSR, East and Central Europe. Invoking both genealogy and culture, he whipped up Serb sentiment by recalling past glories, and inspired hatred of 'Muslims' by reminding Serbs how the Ottomans had defeated their ancestors on the Field of Blackbirds in 1389 CE. 'Serb land is wherever Serb bones lie buried,' Belgrade intellectuals and the Orthodox Church leaders proclaimed. How much 'truth' is there in this rendering of history, how much is mere invention and manipulation? In a sense it scarcely matters. What matters is that the rhetoric paved the way for the subsequent Serb ethnic cleansing of Croats, Bosnian Muslims and Kosovan Albanians from those lands.

Relegating to 'myth' such nationalist narratives of common origins in the distant past, some academics today favour an understanding of 'nation' as being a rather modern thing, arising in Europe and Latin America only in the late eighteenth and nineteenth century, the fall-out from collapsing empires (Gellner 1983; Hobsbawm 1990). Nations, in this view, are socially constructed realities. Indeed, they may be seen as imagined communities, in which people have come through shared language, a common media and powerful political discourses about both past and future, to conceive of themselves as a united 'people' (Anderson 1983). Some actually existing nation states reflect this 'constructivist' view, dwelling rather little on blood-and-bones or age-old traditions, and representing themselves instead in the mode known as 'civic nationalism', stressing the notion of 'citizenship' (Ignatieff 1999). Such nations are in theory more capable of ethnic inclusiveness, proclaiming equality of rights and responsibilities for all citizens.

Civic nationalisms are seen by feminist theorists as relatively favourable for women. They are patriarchal still, but male power no longer resides in the monarch, the aristocracy, the clerics and the pater familias. Authority is diffused among men in general who continue to dominate public offices and enterprise. Women may be needed not merely as wives and mothers but also as voters and employees (Werbner and Yuval-Davis 1999). Yet, while citizenship opens up areas of freedom, it also imposes laws that normalize, draw borderlines, define the sphere of the public and the private, and police the limits of acceptable 'difference'. Rights can't be assumed to be safe in the hands of any nationalism, even a civic version (Fine 1999). Certainly, even in the civic nation state, an individual's positionality is likely in many ways to determine her or his entitlement. Factors such as age and ability, skin colour and place of birth, may all potentially be a basis for inequities. Gender in particular continues to be a source of oppression; witness the treatment of women in many countries' immigration and nationality laws. Arguing as feminists, Pnina Werbner and Nira Yuval-Davis feel women have to look beyond the boundaries of the nation state, in whatever form, to a future transnational citizenship involving not 'national' identity alone but many different and equally important dimensions of belonging (Werbner and Yuval-Davis 1999). Such a world would certainly be more hospitable to migrants, refugees and asylum-seekers, women among them. Indeed, it might make those categories redundant.

It is exposure to such very different nationalisms that underlies the divergence of opinion among women of the anti-war movements today. Some women have experienced the extremes of Serb nationalism or Hindu communalism. In such cultures the majority of women accept and even rejoice in a complementary, though subordinate, role in the patriarchal family. They sign up to the 'patriarchal bargain', accepting significant limitations on their autonomy, including confinement to the private sphere in exchange for (nominal) protection, respect as mothers and significant power over child-rearing and the inculcation of societal mores (Kandiyoti 1988). They may even urge men into battle against hated others, as we saw in the case of contemporary Hindu nationalist extremism. But gender relations in such societies can also sometimes prompt disloyalty. A minority of women become feminist and antinationalist activists. They resent the double standard whereby women are given high symbolic status, elevated in statues representing the 'motherland' (suckling her babes) or 'justice' (balancing the scales), while in everyday life they remain men's property. If the experience of some feminist women teaches them this is what nation means, it's not surprising if they want nothing at all to do with national identity, for themselves or anyone else.

Virginia Woolf wrote her often-quoted polemic against patriarchal nationalism in the late 1930s. Perceiving the way women were positioned as second-class citizens in an imperialist and war-mongering Britain she opted out of her national identity, proclaiming, 'As a woman I want no country' (Woolf 1977: 125). But other women can't so easily afford to jettison national belonging. Many have experienced nationalism in its moments of heroism and promise, as people have sought independence from some oppressive power. Take the long history of resistance in the Philippines, first against the Spanish, later the USA; the costly struggle to rid Mozambique of Portuguese colonists; or the Indian independence struggle against the British. In such times women have sometimes played an active role, and feminism may for a while have been allowed a smidgin of influence in defining nationalism (Jayawardena 1986). Even though, when victory is achieved, the founders of the new nation frequently put women back in their place, a remembered partnership of nationalism, socialism and feminism, a pledge of ethnic, class and gender equality, may survive as an ideal.

So divergences of opinion on nationalism among today's antimilitarist feminists arise from different positionalities. The convergence of patriarchy and nationhood may be widespread and malign, but there are exceptions. I learned something new from listening to Terri Keko'olani Raymond at the Manila meeting of the East Asia–US–Puerto Rico Network of Women against Militarism. In Hawai'i the struggle against militarism is also a struggle for national rights. But the presence of an ancient feminine principle in the Hawai'an sense of nation makes it very different from the patriarchal nationalisms that prevail elsewhere. Haunani-Kay Trask writes:

> I believe the main reason women lead the nationalist front today is simply that women have not lost sight of *lahui*, that is, of the nation. Caring for the nation is, in Hawaiian belief, an extension of caring for the family that includes both our lands and our people. Our mother is our land, Papahanaumoku, she who births the islands. Hawaiian women leaders, then, are genealogically empowered to lead the nation ...[so] on the front line, in the glare of public disapproval, are our women, articulate, fierce and culturally grounded. A great coming together of women's mana has given birth to a new form of power based on a traditional Hawaiian belief: women asserting their leadership for the sake of the nation. (Trask 1993: 94)

On the related issue of 'racism', the ideas of women I spoke with differed scarcely at all. All saw racism as an evil, and as implicated in war. They were already comfortable with notions it has taken theorists much time and many printed pages to clarify. The first is the understanding that 'race' is itself a racist concept, since there is no scientific basis for categorizing people according to phenotype. Individuals' skin colour, features and physique differ along a gentle gradation. Racism is a mental process in which people grasp at markers, to some extent arbitrary, to distinguish 'us' from 'them', and in so doing define the 'other' not only as different from the 'self', but as inferior or dangerous (Miles 1989). A second shared understanding is that it is appropriate today to use 'racism' to refer to the distinguishing of others not only on the basis of physical appearance (skin colour in particular) but also on the basis of their ethnicity, defined in cultural terms (Balibar 1991). Indeed it may also be applied to the practice of othering someone simply on the basis of being 'not from here', an 'auslander', a stranger, and thus stigmatizing migrants, refugees and asylum-seekers as such. A further hard-won understanding is that racism is not merely an ideology, a set of representations, it's also practices and structures of exclusion. The ideas and practices are often deeply embedded in institutions, such as the military and the immigration system. This point is stressed by Floya Anthias and Nira Yuval-Davis in their careful elaboration of how race invariably intersects with and finds expression in class and gender (Anthias and Yuval-Davis 1992).

Among all the women with whom I discussed anti-racism in the context of our anti-war work, these understandings were current and uncontested. I remember in 2003 Edna Zaretsky, a Jewish woman living in Israel, explaining clearly the function of anti-Palestinian racism for the Jewish state, then well into its fourth decade of occupation of Palestinian lands. 'You *have* to have racism in Israel,' she said. 'The other *must* be inferiorized, stigmatized, if we are to live with ourselves and our actions.' Yet there was a marked difference in the salience each group gave to racism in its work. Some, like Bat Shalom, were actively countering racism in their own society. For some, contesting racist othering was an important part of their work against violence and war, but under another name. For instance, racism in India has expression as 'communalism', the exclusions of caste and the oppression of indigenous tribes.

Organizations vary in how explicitly they tackle racism. Among the international networks, WILPF is notable for the consistent inclusion of anti-racism among its principles. Challenged quite early by African American members on its own institutional racism (Blackwell 2004), today it makes racial justice one of its main missions along with economic justice and peace (WILPF 2006c). For instance, they call for reparation for the Atlantic slave trade, and also campaign for the rights of indigenous peoples. Women in Black, being less institutionalized and structured, and consequently less articulate, have not been this explicit about anti-racism. Yet I found Women in Black groups very alert to the changes in legislation, curtailment of rights and hardening attitudes towards migrants associated with the current phase of international warfare, the US-led 'war on terror' in response to the attacks on the USA and allied countries since 11 September 2001.

The post-9/11 world has reminded us that the wars Western countries wage overseas they also simultaneously wage at home. There are always people of (or presumed to be of) the 'enemy' ethnic group or nation residing in the metropolis. Some have been there for generations, others are the flotsam and jetsam of current or recent wars. Some are economic migrants, some are political refugees with residence rights, others are seeking asylum. Thinking of this, I remembered Aida Shibli, referring to the situation of Palestinians like herself living inside the state of Israel, saying, 'We have to counteract government and official propaganda that represents us as "the other", "the enemy".' Addressing Israeli Jews, she said: 'Your other is living right here inside you and there's no way we can be separated.'

I was particularly struck by a group called Collectif Femmes en

Noir contre les Centres Fermés et les Expulsions (CFEN) in Brussels, Belgium, already mentioned in chapter 6. They are a Women in Black group opposing 'Closed Detention Centres and Expulsions'. These women might well have heard what Aida was saying – 'your other is right here, if you have eyes to see her'. They have chosen to put their whole energy into a feminist campaign to change national immigration policy, fighting politically but also lending support to individual women asylum-seekers. Though this is different from the normal WiB activism involving street demonstrations against war, the Brussels women see the two approaches as compatible. Both are, after all, about the principles of peace and justice, the practice of solidarity with women affected by war and violence, and a critique of their government's racist policies.

CFEN was formed after some high-profile cases of expulsion had hit the media. In one instance a Nigerian woman, Semira Adamu, who had fled to Belgium and claimed asylum because she had been forced into an oppressive marriage in Nigeria, died by suffocation due to the violence of the security officers in their sixth attempt to expel her from the country. In the ensuing political scandal all protest groups expressed their indignation. But the gender aspect of Semira's case was not recognized in the media. Fanny Filosof, a member of CFEN, explained: 'These are acts that are specifically linked to gender. These are things that could only have happened to a woman. Sexual abuse, domestic violence, honour killings, forced marriage, excision, death by stoning … are violent deeds which only affect women. We demand that these violent acts constitute valid criteria for granting asylum and be taken into consideration in the Geneva Convention.'

So CFEN focus their practical work on women asylum-seekers in Belgium. Some are detained in official detention centres, others are outside, either awaiting their papers or living clandestinely. They help them deal with lawyers to obtain asylum rights or 'regularization' and means of living. They help them, when they can, to find a place to stay. They talk to female politicians and NGOs to urge support for them. They encourage women to speak out about their experiences, including sexual abuse, when making a case for asylum. They passionately oppose the 'chilly, egoistic and restrictive asylum policies' of Belgium and of Europe and are 'revolted by a rich Europe that imprisons, expels, and regulates people in a miserly way, creating a host of clandestine women and men, prey to exploiters and other traffickers, while poor countries, adjacent to war zones, take in hundreds of thousands of refugees' (CFEN 2004: 11; my translation). A migrant woman, say CFEN, may be a victim in her country of origin, but when she takes the step of leaving and coming to Belgium, she becomes a resister. She is strong. She has something to tell us about our own society as well as about hers.

Committed to creative argument

Everywhere I went in my journeys of 2004–05 I found women and women's groups deeply committed to a triple project. They were informing and educating the public about the gender realities of militarism and war. They were challenging the militarism and war policies of their own governments, other governments and international institutions. And they were negating othering in many practical ways, working towards alliances across differences exploited by others for war. All these phases of activism led them to aspire to transnational and even global connectedness between their local movements. Increasingly, the technical means for this are in our hands. Most groups, if not all individual woman within groups, have computers and Internet access. An amazing wealth of information, opinion, humour and rage circles the globe and flashes on to the computer monitor of any woman who makes the effort to keep in touch with feminist and anti-war activism. It reaches her in a variety of ways. She's quite likely to be picking up news simply by being in the address book of various individual women who make a practice of circulating information. She may seek out the bulletins of the independent electronic news media such as <zmag.org> and <indymedia.org>. She may add her name to various mailing lists, including those of her local or national Women in Black and Code Pink networks. She may read WILPF's e-newsletter on <peacewomen.org>, or log on to UNIFEM's portal <womenwarpeace.org>, to <feministpeacenetwork.org>, <madre.org> or the World March of Women's website <marchofwomen.org>, and many more.

In earlier chapters we've seen instances of effective cross-border working, in solidarity moves between individual groups in different locations and as transnational networks. Prestigious international peace prizes awarded to individual groups such as Žene u Crnom, La Ruta Pacífica and the Mano River Women's Peace Network have brought those local groups to global prominence. The nomination for the Nobel peace prize in 2005 of 'One Thousand Women for Peace' drew together the names of women from every continent. However, our international reach and effectiveness are impeded by many constraints. Lack of time, when local needs have priority. Lack of funding, especially for foreign travel and computer equipment. Snags in communication. Language is everywhere a problem. English is increasingly a global language, but relatively few of the millions of activist women concerned with war, peace and security read and speak it with ease. Too often those of us who are privileged by speaking English as a native language fail to see translation as *our* problem, rather that of other women. Even a small country like Belgium must continually translate between its two national tongues, Flemish and French. We saw Marwopnet in West Africa struggling to span French and English.

These, though, are mere hindrances to communication that may be overcome with technology, effort and goodwill. A far more important question than the medium is the content of the message. The themes I've singled out for attention in this chapter, clustered around the notions of 'pacifism' and 'nationalism', are only two instances of interesting divergences. In the following chapter we'll see more, on gender issues. Women in Italy, among others, expressed caution about assuming an identity of opinion where this is still untested. There was something exciting, said Elisabetta Donini (Torino), about the 'symbolic contagion' that had disseminated the Women in Black idea around the world so rapidly. 'But there's more to a global social movement than an e-mail network.'

Feminist antimilitarism isn't the only movement that lacks a single unified view on some significant issues. Activists of the World Social Forum movement have been careful to choose a very simple slogan, 'Another world is possible', in order to pin together cleavages on attitudes towards the nation state and reform of the international monetary institutions, and above all to avert a divergence between the current that opposes capitalism and that which only opposes its neo-liberal manifestations (Santos 2004). The mainstream anti-war movement, an alliance between mutually combative leftwing tendencies and a peace movement with many variants, also has internal tensions and differences. Many left groups fiercely criticize the 'war on terror' waged by Bush and his allies and see their enemy's enemy (the so-called terrorists) as necessarily their friend. Most peace organizations discriminate more carefully among potential allies.

In comparison with these movements, the differences within and among feminist anti-war movements are rather slight and there is a justifiable confidence in certain shared values. All the same, there's a danger that for fear of falling apart we may remain less than explicit about our differences, even censor our own thinking. When I was in Bologna, Chiara Gattullo said to me: 'We are a *movement*. We have no rules, and that's good. We don't need a line ... None the less, to be a global movement we have to be conscious of our differences. We need to make clear what each one of us thinks. To do that, we need to discuss more.' What she made me see is that we could visualize a difference between aspiring to a political 'line' and aspiring to political *coherence*. Having a 'line' means that everyone must think alike and speak as one. By contrast, coherence, I suggest, might mean a commitment to argument, within the frame of a broad commonality of values. The argument would be of a particular kind – agonistic rather than antagonistic, creative and dialectical, capable of moving on, uncovering new contradictions and working afresh to transcend them.

I think I've shown that in the case of 'pacifism' and 'nationalism' disagreement doesn't need to be and perhaps can never be definitively resolved. It may appear at the start as a threatening gulf but on closer examination turns out to be a matter of different locations, positionalities and political conjunctures throwing up different perceptions, 'situated' knowledges. Through dialogue or multi-logue we may be able to transform disagreements into a more complex and nuanced understanding of reality. Principled pacifists and those who can tolerate the notion of 'just war' might come together around the concept of 'violence reduction'. Antinationalists and those who feel a need for a national identity might share a commitment to a 'refusal of othering'.

Creating a meaningful and honest discussion of contested issues calls for a particular kind of skilled practice. That practice involves understandings that aren't unique to women's anti-war movements. They're found among theorists of identity and identity politics, and also inform the best versions of conflict reconciliation and transformation work. But they have a certain particularity in our context. In chapter 3 we already saw the concept of 'transversal politics' evolving. The notion emerged as early as 1991 from the interactions of Palestinian/Israeli and Italian women. By the mid-1990s it was being taken up and theorized by them and by others of us who were in contact with them (Yuval-Davis 1997; Cockburn 1998) and towards the end of the decade was being reapplied by me and other women in analysing complex trans-border moves between 'doubly different' women, located in different conflicts and positioned on different sides of them. We described transversal politics then as:

> a democratic practice of a particular kind, a process that can on the one hand look for commonalities without being arrogantly universalist, and on the other affirm difference without being transfixed by it. Transversal politics is the practice of creatively crossing (and re-drawing) the borders that mark significant politicized differences. It means empathy without sameness, shifting without tearing up your roots. (Cockburn and Hunter 1999: 88)

Underlying transversal politics are several valuable insights (see, for instance, Yuval-Davis 1999). First, standpoint epistemology, which recognizes that from each positioning the world is seen differently.[1] There are many truths and their reconciliation, or approximation, can be achieved only through dialogue. Second, respect for each other's realities and the perspectives they generate is essential, and must include acknowledgement of the unequal power inherent in different positions. Third, what you are likely to want cannot be read off from your positionality or 'name', and it's only on the basis of common values (not shared 'identity') that alliance for action becomes possible. Arriving at such an agreed content or message calls for reflexive acknowledgement of one's own positionality or identity; in other words a 'rooting' in one's own ground, and an empathetic 'shifting', by what has been called 'situated imagining', on to the ground of the other (Stoetzler and Yuval-Davis 2002). This is a highly demanding process and there are no short cuts. In our multiple and far-flung movements of women against militarism and war, we don't have many opportunities for frequent, prolonged, intimate face-to-face contact. But many women are aware, this much is clear to me, that we need to find ways of moving beyond hope, commiseration and e-mail to a co-operation that is well-grounded in mutual knowledge.

Note

1 Please see the Introduction for a clarification of what is meant by 'standpoint' and 'positionality'.

EIGHT

Choosing to be 'women': what war says to feminism

§ In the foregoing chapter we looked at some issues on which women, along with the mainstream anti-war movement, have divergent views. In this chapter I turn to some sex/gender issues I heard women debating among themselves. These are specially interesting because they show us more about the kind of feminism we've seen in earlier chapters being generated in anti-war activism. Being located in war, experiencing it at first hand, has contradictory effects on women's thinking. On the one hand it tends to shut down on feminism. Women whose lovers, husbands, fathers and sons are enlisted into the fighting, many of them in mortal danger, can't afford to conceptually separate themselves from men, and are reluctant to envisage any commonalities among men, whom they know both as the lost loved one and the feared enemy. On the other hand, war throws up new challenges for women that many of them have to meet alone. They may have to look after a family single-handed, take on new work or survive displacement. The new self-respect they acquire sometimes leads them towards feminism.

Observing war from a location outside the conflict, too, can lead women in different directions. Some become immobilized and turn away from the cruel reality. Others are appalled by the impact of war and particularly feel for women, whose suffering they can all too easily imagine. Several women in the USA and Europe, for instance, distant from any war-zone, told me how they had been jolted into activism by some sudden awareness, a bolt of pain, when reading a newspaper article or watching TV news about some other country. Empathy however doesn't necessarily lead to activism. It may prompt a humanitarian response, a contribution to the relief of suffering. To intervene *against war* is different. It involves a shift from fatalism to political analysis, and is analagous to the mighty effort women make to transform themselves from war victims to war survivors. Most of the many definitions of feminism I've read emphasize not just an analysis of subordination but also active resistance. For example, feminism is 'an awareness of women's oppression on domestic, social, economic and political levels, accompanied by *a willingness to struggle* against such oppression' (Wieringa 1995: 3; my italics). If this is so, the change of gear from empathy to activism is a defining move. The women of Amargi in Istanbul expressed this clearly. They altogether dissociate themselves, they told me, from the notion that 'women suffer most from war'. 'That's not the point, that isn't why we do it. We're interested in the reasons, the relation between militarism and sexism.' They direct their feminist activism against the military because, 'like nationalism and heterosexism, it's a mechanism through which masculinity is produced'.

First, though, we should ask ourselves whether all the women introduced in this narrative, and all their projects, organizations and networks are in fact 'feminist' at all. Feminism being a term so diversely deployed, the site of so fierce a struggle to fix meaning, it isn't surprising if some women keep a certain distance. Several women, very active in anti-war work, told me, 'I'm not a feminist', even when the work of their organization clearly was so. This may reflect something bell hooks has observed. For many women it's far less problematic to use, even to advocate, feminism as a programme than to adopt it as an identity (hooks 2000). Other women, in specific countries and conflicts, while they may be personally feminist, told me they were unable to label themselves in this way in given political circumstances. This applies particularly where a whole community is experiencing oppression and injustice. Nevertheless the great majority, both of individual women and organizations, I encountered in this study were explicitly feminist. Indeed, most would feel themselves badly misrepresented if I were to suggest they were not.

Even so, anti-war activists do reasonably feel they have to specify rather cautiously what they *don't* mean by the term feminist. There are, after all, many feminisms. There's an individualistic and competitive feminism, widespread in advanced capitalist societies, that has no critique of the system. There's an essentialist and self-righteous feminism that sees women as naturally better than men – though I believe this is less reality than fiction, the invention of anti-feminists. There's a disturbing new development, a raunchy feminism that views soft porn as liberating, and performing 'hot' for the delight of men as an expression of sex equality (Levy 2005). There are Western feminisms that fail to acknowledge the effects of imperialism, and there are inadvertently racist feminisms. None of these has any similarity to the feminisms I encountered in my travels. So what kind of feminism tends to be generated in anti-war activism? We may come nearer to an answer by reviewing certain themes I heard women activists discuss, considering them in the light of recent feminist analyses.

The valorization of everyday life

War brutally destroys 'everyday life', the intricate and delicate systems of sustenance and survival that, with difficulty and courage, people normally inhabit and manage. We saw in Colombia (chapter 1) how women denounce the guerrilla, the paramilitaries and the army for their trashing of the everyday, 'la cotidianidad'. Some months after my visit to Colombia, La Ruta Pacífica let us know they were planning a huge mobilization of women to Choco to express solidarity with communities that were being 'confined' in that region. 'Confinement' was a new kind of attack on daily life. It meant the 'fencing in' of the community by one or other of the armed actors, so that nobody might enter or leave without their authorization. Supply of medicines and food was restricted and there was malnutrition. A few feminists from other countries, including Mujeres de Negro in Madrid, Spain, joined the mobilization in solidarity with the Colombian women. On returning to Madrid, the Spanish women addressed a letter to the Colombian Ambassador to Spain. 'Madam Ambassador,' wrote M. Concepción Martinez Sánchez, 'during the month of November I was in Colombia visiting and sharing daily life with friends in your country. We of the Women in Black like to know how our friends in difficult places are living.' She urged the ambassador to take up a number of specific human rights issues bearing on women's ability to protect everyday life. This is a good example of how, in a double act of solidarity, women's empathy can be translated into feminist action.

The sex- and gender-specific experience of women in war is often neglected, misrepresented or exploited in the media, by politicians and even by the anti-war movement. Many women therefore feel that women, speaking with a firm foothold in 'everyday life', have something fresh to contribute to political processes and peace negotiations. Women activists circulate the information they gather, re-frame it in the light of their analysis, share it with other women and bring it to the notice of the public in street demonstrations and, like Mujeres de Negro above, lobby politicians for action. A good example comes from India. The women of the Women's Initiative for Peace in South Asia, who organized an unprecedented exchange of visits by bus across the border between the 'enemy' states of India and Pakistan, wrote that the prevailing tensions at state level had 'not allowed the collective wisdom of women of the sub-continent to surface. Women activists will mobilize these women's voices so that they are heard in every part of the region making it difficult for the decision-makers to ignore them. They shall become a force in steering the destinies of these two great nations towards peace, progress and prosperity' (WIPSA 2000: 8). It takes a woman to see everyday life as political, to elevate it to the level of the state and international relations – or rather (as Dorothy Smith would say) to require the ruling apparatus to pay attention to the local, the individual, the familial, to 'particular patches of ground' (Smith 1988).

Rita Manchanda, a feminist writer and activist in this South Asian context, pointed out that 'women's perspectives come from the margin or "from below" and therefore may produce better insights into transforming inter-group relations which involve asymmetries of power' (Manchanda et al. 2002: 7). Here's the voice of Donna Haraway again, reminding us that knowledge always comes from *somewhere* and that the perspectives of the subjugated 'promise more adequate, sustained, objective, transforming accounts of the world'. There's good reason, she wrote, 'to believe vision is better from below the brilliant space platforms of the powerful' (Haraway 1991: 191). The view of the world from the windows of WIPSA's cross-border bus may be more reliably informative than that from government offices in New Delhi and Karachi.

The trope of motherhood

I often heard women cite 'motherhood', and more generally 'nurture and care of others', when discussing motivations for women's anti-war activism. Some women feel that to evoke 'motherhood' as a prompt to activism is to exclude the many women who never become mothers and those (though few) who pass their lives without feeling any particular responsibility as women for nurture and care. They don't feel good about women (as at Greenham Common) decorating with babies' clothes the security fences they're picketing, and appealing for peace in the name of their children and grandchildren. Instead of speaking for themselves as autonomous women, they seem to be reducing themselves to nothing-but-mothers, to a biological function and a stereotypical role, thereby reinforcing what society already imposes.

It's true that in the patriarchal family system women are primarily valued as mothers, a function represented as biological and natural, and in nationalistic and militaristic versions of patriarchal ideology the significance of child-bearing and child-rearing is elevated to perverse levels, with women represented as the reproducers of the people and guarantors of its collective culture (Anthias and Yuval-Davis 1989). Women anti-war activists often cite the wars of the former Yugoslavia as a cautionary tale of how motherist thinking can be co-opted for nationalism. As the disintegration of the federation threatened, women of Serbia and Croatia at first came together to protest to the generals against the mobilization of their sons for the impending war. Feminist observers were cheered by this evidence of women uniting across ethnic boundaries on the basis of a common motherhood. But no sooner had war broken out between Serbia and Croatia than patriotism prevailed and the fragile alliance between mothers collapsed. The women ceased protesting against the drafting of their sons when it no longer appeared to be a fratricidal war but a war against the nation's enemy other (Nikolić-Ristanović 1998).

On the other hand, quite a few of the women I spoke with argued that it's not necessarily essentialist to deploy motherhood and the propensity to nurture as a significant factor in women's orientation to peace. Pragmatically and rationally, they say, it reflects an important aspect of most women's lived experience, it can unify women, can be a source of authority and a powerful tool for resistance. Edith Rubinstein, for instance, a woman-in-black in Brussels, told me: 'I *observe* that women act first as mothers and that this tends to pacifism in them. Motherhood is fundamental to women's difference.' She saw nothing 'biologistic' about this stress on motherhood. 'Just as you can be against prostitution either as a puritan or a feminist, so you can value motherhood as a patriarchal nationalist or a feminist antimilitarist,' she said. As to Greenham Common, Rebecca Johnson pointed out that 'motherhood' combined there with quite different expressions of feminism that led to bold and effective actions. For instance, some women criticized the way the 'Embrace the Base' action of 12 December 1982 had been framed. The notion of thousands of women linking arms around the fence to 'embrace' the base may have evoked mothering. But there was no stereotyping in this. 'Don't forget the call we put out was for two days of action. The second day was to *close* the base by blockading the gates.' She reminded me that the emphasis on motherhood had often come, in fact, not from the women campers but from the media. Sympathetic reporters had too often characterized the Greenham protesters as nice 'mothers and grannies' in a misguided wish to counteract the adverse publicity they were receiving as stroppy 'lesbians and feminists'.

However, even rejecting the argument from nature and stressing the argument from social 'roles' when invoking motherhood and family, may be reductive in effect. Reading Catherine E. Marshall's treatise *Women and War*, written during the First World War, you can't help feeling her observation that the 'mother-heart of womanhood has been stirred to its depths' and that 'the experience and habits of mind which women acquire as mothers of families and as heads of households might, if applied to a wider field, throw new light on the problems of the great human family of nations', is both determinist and alarmingly naïve (Kamester and Vellacott 1987: 40). All around her, after all, women were waving the flag and urging men to war. Sara Ruddick is well known for her argument that 'maternal thinking' is key to a politics of peace. She is always at pains to avoid any appeal to nature, stressing that mothering may in principle be practised by women or men. Rather, she says, it is *feminism* that 'actualizes the peacefulness latent in maternal practice', by increasing women's powers not only to care but to *know and act* (Ruddick 1989: 242). All the same, reading Sara Ruddick and other feminist writers on this theme, debating it with each other, women anti-war activists remain divided, and sometimes unsure, as to whether the political activation of motherhood is a help or a hindrance to a project which is, after all, for women's autonomy as well as (and as a step towards) peace.

To my mind the feminist thinker Anna Jónasdóttir takes us further here. Shifting us up a gear from both the appeal to biology/nature and the observation of women's socialization, Jónasdóttir states that the relevant point is *not* that women characteristically engage in a practice of care and of sexual and other kinds of love. The point is that 'the form of the sociosexual relationship that dominates today is the one where women's love power, freely given, is *exploited* by men', much as the worker's labour power is exploited by the owner of the means of production. The conditions of women's existence render their loving the source of men's power over them (Jónasdóttir 1994: 223; my italics).

Male sex/sexual violence

Another important factor prompting women to organize with other women against militarism and war is their alertness to male violence in militarized contexts, particularly male sex/sexual violence.[1] The appalling incidence of rape in the Bosnian and Rwandan genocides of the mid-1990s brought rape into the forefront of protest by women's anti-war groups worldwide. Their outcry, and media interest, brought forcibly to public consciousness something usually repressed: the prevalence of sexual abuse of women by men in *all* wars. Many anti-war activists have worked in the past, or still work today, in projects supporting survivors of violence in normal daily life in their own countries. Feminists who have studied war and post-war situations have helped us to see the strong link between violence against women in the two contexts, 'militarized' and 'civil' situations. Georgette Mulheir and Tracey O'Brien made case studies in Northern Ireland and Croatia in the late 1990s. They affirm the findings of many other researchers that when there's violence in society, during and after armed conflict, male violence against women becomes more frequent and more severe. Men who have weapons will use them to intimidate wives and partners. They theorize that the connection between male violence against women in war and in times called 'peace' is not some natural and enduring feature of manhood but the expression of a structure of power: 'War and community conflict, like alcohol, stress and economic deprivation, can be contributory factors, but the root cause of violence against women remains the need of some men to maintain power and control over women on an individual level, and the collective power imbalance between men and women of a patriarchal system' (Mulheir and O'Brien 2000: 156).

Few if any places are free of male sex/sexual violence against women. Take Britain. It isn't the poorest, most stressed or most militarized of societies, yet in 2004/05 in England and Wales, police recorded 1,035,046 offences of violence against the person, and 60,946 sexual offences. In a typical year, 90 per cent of crimes of the former type are committed by men, and 99 per cent of the latter. On average two women per week are killed in our country by a male partner or former partner (Home Office 2006). The repeated presentation of such facts and figures (I speak here only of Britain, with which I'm most familiar) has curiously little effect on public opinion. The reality of male violence shapes individual women's lives. We think continually how best to protect ourselves and our daughters from violent men. Men of course worry about this too. And men and boys are also vulnerable to rape. But the rapist they fear is a man. Just as, when they fear other kinds of violence, the imagined perpetrator is a man. Women do not fill men's nightmares in the way men fill those of women. On the other hand, at a societal level, male violence is most of the time taken for granted as a fact of life, something that can't be changed and is therefore not worth challenging. Ann Oakley, a feminist sociologist working and publishing in Britain, writes:

> If women killed and damaged ... to the extent that men do, we'd be saying they'd all gone mad (or were caught in the grip of some gigantic plague of hormones). In the past we would have called them evil and burnt them as witches. But what we wouldn't do is accept and justify it as ordinary human behaviour. We may treat individual cases of male crime as news-grabbing pathologies, but still we accept these as a routine part of life, with little attempt to consider why men as a group should behave this way. (Oakley 2002: 46)

The media report and sometimes sensationalize cases of rape and the sexualized murder of women by men. They also express concern about violence per se, as in 'violent youth', 'video games', 'racist attacks' and 'gun crime'. What we don't see is editorials problematizing the phenomenon as male violence, particularly male sexual violence, or questioning as masculine the cultures that generate, exonerate and celebrate it. We see no *policy concern* over masculinity. Given the massive incidence of male violence, its cost to the state, its implications for security and the damage it inflicts on the quality of life, this is an absence like no other. It can be explained only as a political incapacity in those who wield patriarchal power to pathologize one of its age-old means of coercion.

In a city like London, the sex/sexual violence by men against women that is endemic around us might be thought to legitimate public protest in anti-war campaigning against the male violence against women we observe in war. But Women in Black in London, given the customary public avoidance of the theme, are divided on whether to shine a public spotlight on the problem of militarized masculinity and its tendency to sexual violence. We don't lack the analysis. It might even feel possible to draw attention to sexual abuses of the past (let's say the system of military prostitution organized by the Japanese state in the Second World War) or those of 'bad' men far away. On our e-networks for instance we've joined worldwide campaigns for truth and justice in the case of the epidemic of rape, torture, mutilation and murder of women in recent years in northern Mexico and now in Guatemala. It feels less comfortable to point the finger at, for instance, the well-documented abuse of women in war-zones by the 'good' soldiers of contemporary UN peacekeeping operations. It's harder yet to bring the problem right home to the rape and sexual harassment that occur within our 'own' armies, perpetrated by our 'own' soldiers. Hardest of all, within the frame of action against militarism and war, is to draw attention to the weekly and annual toll of rapes and sexual murders in our own city. The fear, and a reasonable one, is that to single out men-and-masculinity for critical attention will needlessly aggravate passers-by, forfeit sympathy and deflect attention from the 'main message': militarism-and-war.

The situation is different in some other countries. I found in India women activists don't hesitate to protest publicly against violence against women in the home, the community and the state's wars. Vimochana is the women's organization, mentioned in chapter 6, that among its many other activities mounts Women in Black vigils in Bangalore. The scale and nature of the violence Vimochana address became clear to me from a reading of the many leaflets produced to accompany their activities and actions in recent years. The violence they problematize ranges from structural violence and war at the level of global society to personal and communal violence at the level of the Indian home and street. They have a powerful critique of the violence of imperialism as it continues in India today in the shape of foreign capital seeking control over the country's resources. They address militarism and war, protesting against the aggressive postures of the Indian and Pakistani states and their nuclear weapons programmes. They've challenged the response of the Indian government to the US-proclaimed 'war on terror'. In the case of the repression of self-determination movements in Kashmir and the North-East states, where rape is widely practised by both the state army and the militants, they call for the total withdrawal of the Indian military. They denounce successive waves of violence against Muslims, Tamils, dalits (untouchables) and adivasis (tribal people).

Visibly running through Vimochana's thinking on state and communal violence is a gender analysis. They represent the pursuit of weapons supremacy by the Indian state as 'macho' posturing. They speak of the fascist Hindutva movement as 'hypermasculinized'. But it's patriarchal violence in family and reproductive relations that most concerns Vimochana and which best explains why, although they share an analysis with the leftwing centre with which they are associated and share premises, they maintain a distinctively women's organization and, under the name Angala, maintain a residential centre for women survivors of male violence. In addition to rape and child marriage, Vimochana and Angala are preoccupied with dowry deaths and honour killings. In one of their leaflets they write of 'an explosion of new and grotesque forms of violence ... in an increasingly consumerist, aggressive, macho, intolerant society'.

So these women in Bangalore see violence as a continuum and look for nonviolent and creative means to address every part of it. Madhu Bhushan, I think it was, said to me: 'We didn't start as women against war, but as women against violence against women. Through that we came to take a stand against violence in the wider society.' One of their slogans is 'Violence-free homes make violence-free communities. Violence-free communities make a violence-free world.'

Organizing as 'women-only'

The title of the international network Women in Black is unambiguous, it proclaims it a *women*'s network. Yet I met a number of WiB groups in different countries in which men were welcome to stand with the women in their public vigils. In December 2004 I invited a discussion on my weblog of the reasoning for and against the inclusion of men in Women in Black vigils. An energetic argument ensued. I draw below on some of the contributions, but also on what I was told in interviews in many different groups.

Those who argued for maintaining a women-only space in the public world (and they included two male contributors to the weblog) reminded us that there are very few such spaces, even now; that they are precious for having been hard won by women over many decades of struggle; that they are not well tolerated by the mainstream and should be defended. Many women in today's women's movements against war have had experience, first in the organizations and parties of the left, and subsequently in the mainstream anti-war movement. They had found them to be 'reproducing the patriarchal model', manifesting a way of addressing and using power very different from that preferred by feminists. Furthermore, it was observed that the mainstream anti-war movement never addressed the gender issues in militarism and war. The men were more interested in being leaders than in solving problems, and were interested not at all in critically examining masculine behaviours and cultures. They tolerated or even incited violence against the opposition or the police.

Learning from these experiences, women had formed women's organizations separate from the men, to evade (as one Spanish Women in Black group told me with good humour) 'patriarchal toxins'. In a women-only group the autonomy of women's thought and their freedom to choose methods and means of action (as we saw in chapter 6) could be guaranteed. Away from men, besides, it was possible to create a safe space for the expression of personal distress. Differences of experience and values between and among women could be more confidently accepted and explored. For such reasons, being a 'women-only' organization should not be seen as discrimination. Remember how María Eugenia Sánchez described the practice of La Ruta Pacífica (chapter 1): 'It's a political choice to be a women's organization, it's not *exclusion*.'

None the less, some women do feel uncomfortable about saying 'no men'. It seems a simple matter of human kindness to say 'welcome'. Many of the men who approached their women's vigils or other actions, women said, were war veterans, sometimes very needy. They were quiet. They caused no trouble. It seemed only right to respond generously to men traumatized by war. It could be a contribution to breaking the cycle of violence. But some women speak about the absence of men, on the one hand from the labour of nurture and love, on the other from the task of active nonviolence, as an evasion of responsibility. In the midst of the jingoist fervour of the First World War, Helena Swanwick wrote that 'men had dropped their end of the burden of living' (Oldfield 2000: 13). This reminded me of the women of *En Pie de Paz* (see chapter 6). They had wanted to work with men in publishing their antimilitarist journal because, they said: 'We don't want to be the only ones to be responsible for peace. We don't want to carry the whole burden, that's why we work with men.' Ironically, as we saw, they had to struggle with the men who, having picked up part of the burden of peace work, simultaneously refused the burden of childcare. Some women today feel similarly that rather than exclude men we should encourage them into peace activism alongside us *and* simultaneously into more equal and less stereotyped gender roles. (Opponents of including men respond to this point by proposing that men might show willing by first working *with each other* on the issue of male dominance and the oppression of women – something they observe very few will do.)

Some of the men joining WiB groups, and some WILPF groups too, are husbands of the women members, and it seems to women churlish to refuse their support and presence. (Observing this, other women charge heterosexual conjugality with fatally undermining women's capacity f›r independent action.) Some husbands were active in Gulf Coast Women in Black along with other male supporters. The women had felt a certain tension around the question of whether or not to include men, but had decided to resolve it positively by accepting them as 'allies', as they termed it. At the same time they reserved decision-making in the organization to women only. (Some women elsewhere, however, feel it would be invidious to have such a disenfranchised category of member. Men should be either fully in or fully out.) In the case of Gulf Coast Women in Black, the men were valued for their active commitment to the group. But there was an additional reason for the women to be proud of them. Everyone had seen those startling photographs of women of Marin County spelling out the word 'peace' with their naked bodies in the anti-war publicity stunt they called 'Baring Witness'. It was Gulf Coast men who took up the challenge (and took off their clothes) to write their mantra with their bodies, vulnerable and pink as those of women, on the bright green grass, under the eye of the camera.

The second reason women give for including men in their groups is entirely different, appealing less to emotion than to logic. It reflects a postmodern understanding of gender and involves a critique of the conventional understanding of both sex and gender as rigidly binary and complementary – sex involving the biological pair male and female, gender involving the cultural pair masculine and feminine. By contrast this analysis represents biological sex as subject to much uncertainty, ambiguity and social influence, and gender not merely as socially constructed but as performance, unfixed and fluid, always varying, often elective (Butler 1992). From this point

At Greenham Common, 1981–94, the decision to exclude men from the peace camp was not unanimous. But the woman-only choice contributed importantly to non violence, mutual confidence and effectiveness. Above and opposite, women lay their bodies in the road to impede the passage of vehicles in and out of the nuclear missile base, July 1983.

of view, variously identified individuals argued on my weblog that Women in Black groups should certainly *not* be defined as women-only, for what does the category 'woman' mean? In opening up our groups, besides, it should not be merely to include 'men', another essentialist category. We should welcome any individual, however defined and self-defined, bearing in mind people who identify as lesbian, gay, bisexual, trans-sexual, trans-gender and inter-sexed. This was cogently argued by Naomi Braine of Union Square Women in Black in New York. Of the twelve women that formed this group, ten had been lesbians, and so too were a good third of the active vigillers when I met them in 2004. Among the male supporters of the vigil, several were gay. This does not mean the group articulates a lesbian politics, Naomi says. 'The majority of us are Jewish. It's our experience as *Jews*, not as lesbians, that motivates us.' And, indeed, some members of the group didn't share Naomi's view of its nature. But she herself valued the group's 'queer sensibility' as guaranteeing a particular politics, one that avoided 'glorifying women as peaceful, all the earth mother stuff' and was capable of generating a more sophisticated gender commentary on war.

The case for gender-inclusiveness was also strongly made by Boban Stojanović whom I interviewed in Belgrade in 2004. He later wrote at length on my weblog about his positive experience in Žene u Crnom (Women in Black). A young gay man, Boban's childhood had been scarred by a violent father and he was deeply afraid of his impending conscription to the Serbian military. Some deserters and conscientious objectors involved with Žene u Crnom had helped him engage in principled 'non-compliance'. He refused everything the military asked of him, including putting his signature to his enlistment. He tells a harrowing story of the verbal and physical violence to which he was subjected until eventually dismissed as 'emotionally immature'. That's how Boban became an activist with WiB. He started to read books. He learned that Women in Black isn't just about women, but is concerned with civil values as a whole. From the start, he says: 'I was accepted here. People would hug me, kiss me, talk to me. It was like another world. I didn't say I was gay. But people knew that, and didn't look at me strangely for it ... I really want to help the group, give support, work in the office. The values here are very, very important for me. My life has totally changed. I learned, for my personal life, I just want to be here. WiB is my first activist group and my last. I don't want to be in any other.'

When the prospect of joining Women in Black first became a possibility Boban said to himself, 'How can I, as a man, be in a women's group?' He terms this now a 'prejudice'. His understanding today is that feminism and antimilitarism are not exclusively women's values.

> Women are for sure the major marginalized group in the world. Right after them are 'different' men ... gay men, sensibilized men, anti-sexists, antinationalists etc. Geographically, the space where Women in Black Belgrade is active has been for more than a decade contaminated by war and militarization, and so the level of non-acceptance of diversity is high ... No matter their sexual orientation or any other allegiance, every activist has felt some aspect of patriarchal oppression ... That is the reason for us all to stay together [in] Women in Black – to resist patriarchy (especially when you feel it yourself), undermine its foundations, constantly destabilize it, pointing to it and transforming our diversity into an element of political action.

Boban does say, 'I feel more secure among women'. But Women in Black in Belgrade is not just a space in which a victimized gay man can feel protected from other men. It presents itself as a space in which women and men alike can live their sexuality in whatever way they choose, as a matter of their own concern, confident that everyone among and around them is *anti-homophobic*, just as they are *antinationalistic*.

What we see in this quiet struggle over women's space, I think, is two readings of gender differentiation based on two different sets of experiences. In other words, as we already know well enough, women do not all have the same positionality and perspective. The lives of some have led to a departure from the complementary identities of masculine and femine. They understand binary gender as non-natural, as the ruler's rules, to be evaded and scorned. Many, after all, have suffered for their identity and struggled for their rights. Meanwhile the sense of self of the great majority of people, worldwide, not excluding many lesbians and gay men, is unequivocally one of being either a woman or a man, among people identifiable and self-identified as women and men. Women experience oppression by men, many experience sexual abuse. It makes sense to them to affirm the identity suggested by that positionality, to build self-respect as a woman and seek the solidarity of other women who feel as they do. Notwithstanding the perils of an 'identity politics' that invokes fixed, exclusive categories, they'd agree with Iris Marion Young that the 'subjective affirmation of affinity' is fair enough in the case of an oppressed collectivity such as 'women' (Young 1990: 179). They're in no doubt that gender is a social construction, they may well understand gender to be lived in a variety of different ways, they may be strongly anti-homophobic, but pragmatically they find women-only organizing to be politically effective and productive (as well as, frankly, more comfortable).

Soldiering: women who want to, men who don't

The nature of our understanding of gender (is it essentialist or social constructionist?) is also tested in the way we deal with soldiering. Some observers, and not only men, seeing women demonstrating on the street or outside a military base, jump to the conclusion, 'They're saying men are the war-makers, women are different.' It's not so simple. Of course, women activists are aware that the armed forces of all countries are predominantly 'manned' by men, and that boys are brought up to think this natural and desirable. More importantly, they observe that the commanding ranks of the military and the political decision-makers who take countries to war are mostly males. I didn't meet any women, though, who represented women as 'naturally' more peace-prone than men. On the contrary, they often observed that some girls and women are personally violent, that women are joining the military in ever-growing numbers and that some bellicose leaders are female. Cynthia Enloe's work has been widely read, so we have come to understand how militarism pervades society, persuading women as well as men of its inevitability, its common sense nature, so that we respond willingly to its many demands of us (Enloe 2000).

Take the enthusiasm of some women for soldiering. The proportion of women in Western militaries is growing (Isaksson 1998). We have accounts of women serving in Russia, China, North Vietnam, Iran and in various revolutionary or resistance militias in periods ranging over centuries (Hacker 1998; De Groot and Bird 2000). As antimilitarists it's instinctive to deplore this, but as feminists we find ourselves understanding the reasons. Women, and especially ethnic minority women, experience unemployment just as men do, and can't afford to turn up their nose at a military wage. Some women long for the adventure, the chance to prove yourself, that military service offers. Besides, in many countries (including Israel, as we saw), serving in the military is, literally or figuratively, a condition of full citizenship. In such circumstances it's understandable if women seek to become soldiers in a bid to overcome their lack of rights, by demonstrating that they fulfil equally their responsibilities as citizens.

This is another contradiction in their lives that women invoke feminist theory to deal with. Ilene Rose Feinman carefully evaluates from a feminist and antimilitarist perspective the meaning of women's militarization, and its probable effect on armies. She concludes that feminism can lead women both towards and away from militarism. We should not ban women from military service, and thereby contribute to the marginalization of women. Rather, we should redefine citizenship (Feinman 2000). Besides, just as feminists observing women joining the military experience it as contradictory, so, too, in a different way, do the soldiering women. Kayla Williams joined US Military Intelligence in Iraq during the invasion of 2003, one of the 15 per cent of the US forces who were female. She wrote, later: 'Always been a girl that catches a guy's eyes. And yet I do fifty-five push-ups in under a minute. Tough, and proud to be tough. I love my M-4, the smell of it, of cleaning fluid, of gunpowder: the smell of strength. Gun in your hands, and you're in a special place.' But she brings you to earth with a jolt. 'Sometimes, even now,' she says, long after returning to civilian life, 'I wake up before dawn and forget that I am not a slut.' Her predominant memory of military service was drowning in a sea of testosterone. She was treated as a sister, mother, bitch or slut, defined only by her sex. 'Sex is key to any woman soldier's experiences in the American military' (Williams 2005: 13, 18). In earlier chapters we've seen several women's organizations helping young women be very clear about the harassment and abuse they will encounter in the armed forces.

While there are many women striving to join the military, there are some men, like Boban, striving not to. Any belief women may harbour in a natural war-proneness in men is disabused by contact with those who won't fight. In most countries with compulsory military service there are movements supporting conscientious objection. Women antimilitarist activists sometimes find themselves involved with male refusers. Sometimes this occurs first within the mixed movements. In some countries women's antimilitarist groups have been active in the mainstream movements of conscientious objection. Sometimes, as in Žene u Crnom, it has meant individual men associating themselves with women activists. Gender issues are often in play. The war resisters' movement in Turkey responds directly to the stress placed in Turkish national culture on forming the proper Turkish man in soldier mode (Altinay 2004). The movement there uses humour, making play on unmanliness, unmilitariness, unpatriotism. They sent me emails about their 'Militourism Festival' in which they visited all the sites favoured by the military and reversed the conventional symbolism. Going in a crowd to the rail station where proud parents customarily see their boys off to the army, the refuseniks spoofed a 'welcome home' ceremony for some mock deserters instead. Outside the military recruitment centre they dumped a heap of old apples, a sour reference to the military's custom of sorting through recruits to identify the 'rotten ones' in the barrel of military manhood.

I spent some time while in Israel talking with Rela Mazali and Tali Lerner of New Profile. As we saw in chapter 5, they describe themselves as 'a feminist organization of women and men' whose focus is on the demilitarization of Israeli society. In particular, they support Israelis refusing to serve in the Defence Forces. They are a mixed organization because the majority of those who refuse to serve are men, and some of these become active in the organization. The men are respectful of women and of feminism; besides, New Profile's women are confident, they have set the frame, established the expectations and lead the analysis. From Rela and Tali, and also from reading Peretz Kidron's book *Refusenik*, I learned about a crucial difference between modes of conscientious objection. The organization Yesh Gvul mainly comprises professional soldiers, adult men, who selectively refuse only one aspect of the expectations the state has of them: service in the Occupied Territories. Peretz Kidron writes:

> 'Selective refusal' is arguably the Israeli peace movement's most original contribution to the 'arsenal' of antimilitary protest … In choosing to challenge the law requiring soldiers to serve where and as ordered, IDF refuseniks do not engage in all-out mutiny: rather, with a *chutzpah* unheard of in other armies, they place themselves on a par with the generals and politicians in judging overall policy, and arrogate to themselves the prerogative of choosing, by their own lights, which orders to obey or disobey. (Kidron 2004: 55)

Such refusers don't see themselves as traitors, whether to the military tradition, the state or masculine virtue. Indeed, Mike Levine, a soldier who contributes to Kidron's book, writes: 'I consider my refusal to be a patriotic act.' This is a far cry from Boban and others in Serbia who see themselves as 'proud traitors' and happily ridicule armed patriarchy and militarized masculinity. New Profile works with young people in their last year at school, numbers of whom today are rejecting not just the occupation but Israeli militarism in its entirety. Facing call-up, they may claim psychological unfitness or a pacifist conscience, but some want out just because they are afraid. While this is fine with feminist New Profile, who are happy to support all refusers whatever their motivation, Yesh Gvul see such youth as 'shirkers', and compare them unfavourably with the military men making their hard choice.

In Israel, women too must perform military service. Recently, for the first time, a young woman made her case for exemption 'for reasons of conscience based on a feminist ideology'. Idan Hilali, age eighteen, school-leaver, wrote in her submission to the military committee:

> I thought that women's participation in the army – and in any other institutions – just like men, was the feminist solution and would bring equality ... [But it] is a patriarchal organization: patriarchy consists of a hierarchic social structure which is underwritten by 'masculine' values such as control, a power orientation, and the repression of emotion ... Army service would impose a way of life on me that is deeply contrary to my values and moral beliefs. I would have to consistently deny and suppress my most fundamental persuasions. I cannot live in such flagrant denial of my conscience and I cannot serve an organization that tramples the values on which my whole moral outlook is built.

Idan would understand Sybil Oldfield who wrote: 'Women are not essentially antimilitary, but militarism is essentially anti-feminist' (Oldfield 2000).

A feminism evoked by militarism and war

The groups I met varied widely in the amount of analysis they engage in, relative to the energy they put into practice. Some groups prefer action to reading and discussion. They feel that keeping a weather-eye on the daily papers and the TV news is the best way to keep up with events and generate appropriate activity in response to them. Some fear the more they discuss and the wider they let their focus range, the more they're likely to disagree, to the detriment of the activism they feel so urgent. Also, there are groups that see the immediate intellectual challenge as getting to grips with the specific system they're up against. The women of the Aldermaston Women's Peace Camp, for instance, need to keep up-to-date on the fine detail of the plans to renew Britain's nuclear warheads.

On the other hand, there are groups and organizations among those presented in earlier chapters that, as we've seen, devote a good deal of time and energy to understanding feminist theory. Many of the Italian and Spanish women had first been active in the left. They had been used to reading, discussion and argument – about trends in capitalism, class relations and strategies of reform and revolution. In the 1970s and '80s they had readily turned to a new feminist literature. New Profile call for the 'civil-ization' of Israel. Through their analysis and writing they've provided other Israeli women with an incisive language in which to think and talk about their heavily militarized state. The women in Belgrade, as we saw in chapter 3, were forced to think and discuss nationalism, militarism and patriarchy when they saw these advancing like a tsunami to overwhelm them. One after another, as they joined that group, women encountered ideas that changed their lives. Ksenija Forca had been a teenager in the Kosovo/a war. She was just twenty-one when she stumbled on the Women's Studies Centre and Žene u Crnom in Belgrade. She told me how 'learning the theory of patriarchy … suddenly the pieces fell together, like a jigsaw. It was like waking up.'

So what kind of feminism did I find in this research to be motivating women's antimilitarist, anti-war activism, evolving within it and flowing from it? In the first half of the twentieth century and again in the 1980s there was considerable tension between the feminism of the anti-war movement and some other feminisms. The 1970s were the heyday of second wave feminism, with demands focused strongly on women's reproductive rights and sexual autonomy, and on opposing male violence. Then, in the 1980s, many women joined the movement against the nuclear arms race. A few months after the 'Embrace the Base' action organized by the Greenham Common Women's Peace Camp had drawn an estimated 35,000 women to the protest against nuclear missiles (see chapter 6), a critical pamphlet was published, the outcome of a radical feminist workshop held at

A Woman's Place in London on 10 April 1983. The authors found nothing in common between women's liberation as they knew it and this women's peace movement. On the contrary, recalling how some suffrage feminists had been diverted into the peace movement at the onset of the First World War, so, after the huge gain in momentum of the 1970s, they now felt in the Greenham phenomenon they were witnessing a 'loss of feminist principles and processes – radical analysis, criticism and consciousness-raising'. Yet again women were being 'co-opted into male struggles'. Attending to a hypothetical threat of future war, they had allowed their attention to be diverted from the all-too-immediate reality of male violence against women. Here were women again taking on the role of 'housekeepers of the world' (Breaching the Peace 1983). A little while later some of the campers put out a response. In their pamphlet they said, 'if feminism is truly relevant to the lives of wymn it will arise where women are'. One contributor added that 'Greenham at the moment is the most vigorous force for lesbian liberation in the world that I know of'. Here we are, the Greenham feminists felt, continually up against anti-feminists in the Campaign for Nuclear Disarmament, now obliged to defend ourselves against some sisters in the women's liberation movement. So, 'Women divided again, and one up for the men!' (Raging Womyn 1984).

Interestingly, I don't detect this rift today. I found contemporary activists to be comfortable both with radical perceptions of patriarchy and radical opposition to militarism, seeing them as interlaced structures. How, then, to characterize the feminism that has evolved these last twenty years in the face of successive wars? Given differences in women's locations and positionalities, it isn't and could never be anything unitary or dogmatic. On the other hand the political standpoint of opposition to war itself delineates certain probabilities. First, this is necessarily a *social constructionist* feminism, not one that sees differences between women and men as applying to all individuals alike and determined by biology. Necessarily – because we have a critique of violent masculinities, yet know from our own lives that not all men practise violence or inhabit a culture of violence. We know some violent women. We see certain masculinities as causally implicated in militarism and war, and at the same time we are activists for peace. If we believed masculinity (and femininity) to be singular, inborn, natural and inescapable, it would make no sense at all to be campaigning for change.

Second, contrary to the fear expressed by the 'Breaching the Peace' pamphleteers, looking through the lens of war has made us acutely conscious of the way women are oppressed and exploited through *their bodies, their sexuality and reproductive capacities*. War deepens already deep sexual divisions, magnifies the contrast between femininity and masculinity, and legitimates male violence. It enhances men's authority in a quantum leap. So this tends to be a 'radical' feminism in the sense that it sees women's oppression as being more than a mere by-product of an exploitative economic system or an unfair system of political representation.

However, antimilitarist and anti-war feminism is by definition multi-dimensional, taking as its scope not just 'body politics' but a far wider range of concerns. For a start it cannot fail to have a *critique of capitalism*, and new forms of imperialism and colonization, class exploitation and the thrust for global markets, since these are visibly implicated among the causes and motors of militarism and war. Next, since many wars involve intra-state and inter-state nationalisms, this feminism also has that cluster *race/culture/religion/ethnicity* in view. In these two significant relational fields of class and race, this feminism perceives the working of gender relations and is alert to how they intersect.

Then again, if 'rights' had not been invented we would surely have needed to invent them. This feminism defends international *human rights and women's rights*, negated in war, and the development of international justice. It has a sense of women's marginalization and *under-representation in political systems*, as we see from women activists' efforts at the UN. Clearly, then, this is a *holistic feminism*. There's no way the thinking of women anti-war activists can be reduced to those limited categories we are used to terming 'radical', 'socialist' and 'liberal' feminism. In the foregoing chapters we've seen women using the insights of all of them without any sense of incompatibility.

Furthermore, the insistence on prefigurative struggle we've seen to be widespread in women's anti-war activism, the notion that our methods must not betray our purposes, implies a *critique of the meanings and operation of power* itself. It is a call for power as domination to give way to power as capacity and capability, 'power to' instead of 'power over'. This is also by definition a *transnational feminism*, in the dual sense of aspiring to cross state borders, and to negate and transcend the system of sovereign nation states. In these movements women tend to ascribe feminist leadership not to women in the white Western world, which none of us can doubt is a significant source of militarization and war, but to women living in conditions of war and, by extension, of colonization and poverty.

Finally, it goes without saying, this feminism also sees *gender power relations as systemic*, not contingent or incidental. Through their analysis of war, women see how masculinities are resistant to change because they are embedded in structures and institutions. As R. W. Connell puts it: 'The *institutionalization* of masculinity is a major problem for peace strategy. Corporations, armed forces, workplaces, voluntary organizations, and the state are important sites of action. Collective struggle, and the re-shaping of institutions, including military and police forces, are as necessary as the reform of individual life' (Connell 2002a: 38; my italics). *Patriarchy* then becomes an inescapable concept in the course of women's anti-war work. I heard many groups naming it, invoking the notion of an enduring, adaptable, surviving structure of male power that generates and sustains the cultures that in turn generate and sustain militarism and war.

A question remains, however. How clearly does *our practice of opposition* reflect this feminist analysis that militarism and war themselves have hammered into shape in our movements? Those that express it boldly are, perhaps surprisingly, often the ones, like Vimochana and La Ruta Pacífica, locally exposed to masculinism, nationalism, militarism and violence in their starkest forms. By contrast some groups have difficulty 'outing' their feminist ideas. It seems to be particularly difficult when addressing an abstract, anonymous and potentially hostile public in Western countries. Partly it's a problem of effective communication. Jennifer Beach, of San Francisco WiB, explained why they don't labour the feminist message in their placards and leaflets: 'It's not that we can't handle being explicit. It's just ... US culture is about short sound-bites. People just scan us to get a sense of what we're saying. Minimal eye-contact time! War: are you for it or against it?' The women of Donne in Nero in Torino told me that concepts such as 'patriarchy' are strange to people and if they are to be understood must be accompanied by impracticably lengthy explanations. Even among themselves these women tend to focus on problems rather than abstractions. 'We refuse "isms",' Margherita Granero said. But, I checked, 'You speak of capitalism, militarism and nationalism?' Yes. 'But you don't use the words socialism or feminism?' No.

No – because circumstances are adverse. These Italian women were 'born' leftwing and feminist in the 1970s. They have a deep and full understanding of class exploitation and women's oppression. But the socialist rug has been pulled from under their feet (our feet) by the neo-liberal turn and by the discrediting of any alternative to the capitalist system. However, it was not about socialism I was questioning them at this point, but feminism. In that respect they feel, as many of us in Western countries do, inhibited by the powerful backlash against feminism today. This explains why in our own group in London and many others in Europe and the USA, you don't often see in leaflets, placards or public statements, any clear indication that an important factor in the perpetuation of militarism and war is patriarchy, systemic male dominance. Likewise, the M-words – men, masculinities, male violence, misogyny – may be common currency between us conversationally, but we find them difficult to use publicly. We're afraid that if we point the finger explicitly against male power as a system and masculine cultures of violence, popular opinion will quite mistakenly see us as blaming all men and exonerating all women, indulging in special pleading for women as an interest group and abstracting from our humanity, our human-beingness. We fear that we will appear to the mainstream anti-war movement in particular as being divisive, at a time when we need all our strength, and deflecting attention from the immediate problem: 'cut defence expenditure', 'end the arms trade', 'stop this war now!' As a result it's less in our public statements than in our communication with each other and in writing that our feminist analysis is explicit.

Note

1 I adopt Lisa Price's formulation here. She suggests we need to be clear that we include in our analysis two aspects of violence directed against women. Some, of which Marc Lepine's shooting of fourteen female engineering students in Montreal in 1989 could be an example, is directed at women as a category, indeed in Lepine's case as feminist women. This is sex violence. Some violence against women involves eroticization, is a sexual practice, as in rape. This is sexual violence. Notwithstanding the distinction, *both* are directed towards the control of women and preservation of male supremacy (Price 2005: 16).

NINE

Gender, violence and war: what feminism says to war studies

> The property of enemy males is confiscated, while the territory itself becomes occupied through the colonization of female bodies ...
>
> The man becomes the owner of the territory/womb as well as the owner of the child she is carrying: 'You have an enemy child in your womb. One day my child will kill you.'
>
> 'She's the feeder of the germ she carries in her; akin to a stranger, she protects the young bud,' said Aeschylus. And she, humiliated in Aeschylus' time, suffers the same humiliation now. 'I have nowhere to go. They are looking at me now as if I were a foreigner, and I have nowhere to return ... '
>
> Aeschylus, Aristotle and the warriors in Bosnia, they are all obsessed with appropriation of the procreative powers of women; they all dream about a male parthenogenesis ...
>
> One thing they all have in common is hate of women, the oldest hate of all.
>
> *Observations by Staša Zajović on rape and ethnic aggression in the Yugoslav wars (ŽuC 1994: 67)*

When feminists make reference to gender, to masculinities, to patriarchy when talking about war, we're often taken to task for 'not looking at the big picture'. The big picture: states and sovereignty, national rivalries, global capitalism. Cynthia Enloe has been one among us brave enough to say 'But suppose this *is* the big picture?' (Enloe 2005). In this chapter I want to argue that gender relations are indeed a significant part of the big picture of militarism and war. This is not to say they are the whole story – far from it. But gender relations are right in there alongside class relations and ethno-national relations, intersecting with them, complicating them, sometimes even prevailing over them, in the origins, development and perpetuation of war. So here I adopt a feminist standpoint derived in chapter 8 from the various kinds of anti-war activism described in some detail in earlier chapters. Standing among the activists, how does war look? Why does war persist? Why, despite all humankind has learned in five thousand years, despite all our social and moral resources, do we step towards the horror time after time? Why is war still thinkable?

War and security: feminists' marginal notes on international relations

There's probably a unique definition of war for every theorist who's tackled the subject, but my reading suggests most agree that, to be deemed 'war', a conflict has to be a collectively organized enterprise; involve weapons and be potentially deadly; be fought for a purpose or with an interest; and most importantly be socially sanctioned, such that the killing is not considered murder. Curiously, then, in spite of appearances, war involves certain understandings shared by the warring groups. It is social, *relational* (see, for instance, Mead 1965; Fogarty 2000). One would have expected for this reason to find war centrally placed among the themes addressed by the social sciences, especially sociology. Yet until relatively recently sociologists left the matter on the one hand to historians and on the other to the discipline of international relations (IR) for which war is, indeed, a key issue. The accident of war's academic location in IR has had a negative effect from women's point of view. The thinking of IR analysts and of statesmen, diplomats and national security specialists has been mutually influential. Up there in the rarefied atmosphere among the political and military elite, white and male, gender theory was hardly likely to thrive.

The hegemonic school of thought among both the academics and practitioners of IR has long been a tough-minded 'realism', well represented in Hans Morgenthau's (1973) respected work *Politics Among Nations*. The classic realist school and today's 'neo-realists' promote what they represent as a rational theory of society and politics, based on the natural sciences, in which 'interests' and 'power' are key concepts. If the striving for domination is an enduring tendency in human society, we must expect each state to look to its own survival. So neo-realists tend to represent war as inevitable. Some even accord it value, believing the pursuit of self-interest by political entities tends to avert moral excess and political folly.

In a particularly creative moment in the early 1990s, feminist political scientists began to mobilize arguments against the neo-realist view of the world (see, for example, Grant and Newland 1991; Peterson 1992; Tickner 1992; Peterson and Runyan 1993; Whitworth 1994; and in particular Tickner 1991 on whose critique of Morgenthau I draw here). The realist understanding of the international system is unduly pessimistic, they've been saying. It's based on assumptions about human nature that are partial, more descriptive of men than women, and it privileges qualities commonly stereotyped as masculine. They have mobilized the work of feminists of the previous decade in support of their case. They've used the arguments of Evelyn Fox Keller, Sandra Harding and other feminist critics of positivist science to invalidate the realists' appeal to a singular 'objectivity'. They've deployed the work of Nancy Hartsock to argue that power need not be defined only and always as domination but may alternatively take the form of capability and mutual enablement. They've drawn on Carol Gilligan and other feminist researchers in psychology and ethics to show that the realist notion of morality is characteristically masculine. Women are socialized into a more relational mode of thinking than men, they say, one that gives grounds for greater optimism about the peaceful resolution of conflict because it suggests that among human beings there does exist a community-building ability that can deal creatively with antagonisms. Ten years on, however, the lack of enthusiasm among the IR mainstream for these thoughts can hardly be overstated. 'Is feminist international relations a contradiction in terms?' asked Gillian Youngs, tackling the IR establishment head-on in the prestigious journal *International Affairs* (Youngs 2004).

Times are changing, these IR feminists were saying, and 'the nation state, the primary constitutive element of the international system for Morgenthau and other realists, is no longer able to deal with an increasingly pluralistic array of problems ranging from economic interdependence to environmental degradation' (Tickner 1991: 32). And, in the ten years that have passed since these feminists first launched their critique of IR, the world has borne out their arguments. Since the Twin Towers were brought down on 11 September 2001, the rigid framework of realist thinking may be in free fall with them. States perpetrate 'terror' not only within but also outside their borders. Those they designate 'terrorists', too, are everywhere and nowhere. Likewise, the Western 'war on terror' is, as we increasingly see to our cost in vamped-up notions of 'homeland security', fought as much at home as abroad (Hardt and Negri 2005). Feminists have argued that not only the realists' theories but those of their mainstream contemporary critics too contain implicit assumptions about gender relations. By suppressing their relevance, they in fact create, sustain and legitimate male domination (Whitworth 1994; Peterson 1992).

The very disciplinary boundaries of IR exclude many relevant realities. Much depends on how you choose to define things, which in turn depends on where you're standing. Shortly before the Second World War, Simone Weil, the French philosopher and pacifist, wrote that the greatest error of war studies 'is to consider war as an episode in foreign policy, when above all it constitutes a fact of *domestic policy*, and the most atrocious one of all' (in Oldfield 2000: 72; my italics). Contemporary feminists continue, like Weil, to haul international relations down to the mundane realities of everyday life, since women otherwise remain below its sight-lines. Spike Peterson and Anne Runyan have shown that women are by no means absent in international politics, it's just that they are in the main a different kind of actor from the statesmen and politicians. Notwithstanding a few who are admitted to those circles, women are typically 'non-state, antistate and transstate actors' (Peterson and Runyan 1993: 113). You see their significance only when 'international relations' is interpreted amply to include such matters as the international exploitation of cheap expendable labour, tourism and migration, and the cross-border trafficking of human beings (Enloe 1989). In recent years, as a corrective to the neo-realist concept of 'security', peace theorists have evolved the notion of 'human security', defined as the satisfaction of 'basic needs' (e.g. Galtung 1996). They are pressing policy-makers to acknowledge that human beings, not states, are the primary agents and objects of security (UNDP 1994). Again, here feminists have been gendering this reinterpretation of security, speaking specifically of 'women's security' and highlighting the gender-specific risk to women in war, in militarized conditions and indeed in 'peace' (Tickner 1992).

It's not, however, just been a question of making women and women's varied needs visible. More important still has been to lodge gender itself on the agenda of IR. Spike Peterson stresses that '*gender is a structural feature* of the terrain we call world politics ... [a] pervasive ordering principle' (Peterson 1998: 42; my italics).

And here we need to turn to sociology, because it's in this context that an understanding of 'gender as a structural feature' has evolved, in feminist theories of patriarchy or systemic male supremacy. It's here that, gradually, over a period of two decades, war studies and gender studies have begun to influence each other.

The sociology of war and militarism: doing gender

It's been suggested that the reason most major sociologists from the Enlightenment to Durkheim failed to address war was that, notwithstanding the military mayhem all around them, they were influenced by the widespread belief that capitalism and modernity, sweeping away feudalism and theocracy, were on the point of making war a thing of the past (Mann 1987). Two world wars put paid to that hope and eventually sociology was obliged to wake up. In 1981 a conference was held at the University of Hull on 'War, State and Society'. The editor of the resulting volume noted that the intellectual revolution of the 1960s and '70s that had produced so much radical and Marxist social theory had somehow 'bypassed this most fundamental of problems' (Shaw 1984: 2). A British Sociological Association conference four years later resulted in a further volume of papers, *The Sociology of War and Peace*, examining the 'culture, ideology and political forces at work in the reproduction of modes of warfare' (Creighton and Shaw 1987: 11). Its editors clearly aimed to establish war and peace firmly within the discipline's problematic. Interestingly, a companion volume arising from the same conference, edited by feminists Jalna Hanmer and Mary Maynard, dealt separately with women and violence (Hanmer and Maynard 1987). There was little cross-referencing between the two sets of concerns. None the less, this was a significant moment for the emergence of a sociology of war with the potential for a gender perspective. Indeed, editors Creighton and Shaw wrote 'there is scope for more substantial work' on the relation between gender and militarism (Creighton and Shaw 1987: 11). The ongoing production in the new field of study didn't immediately fulfil the promise by adopting a gender lens. Nevertheless, interesting new work on militarism and war followed.

In the main, three factors were being singled out as implicated in the perpetuation of war: economics, politics (particularly ethno-national relations) and the military system itself. First, the new war studies looked for the economic mechanisms potentially driving war. With the consolidation of industrial capitalism in Western Europe in the nineteenth century, liberal advocates of enterprise had believed that in conditions of untrammelled free trade, nations would see their common interest as residing in peace. Marxists, on the contrary, saw capitalism's continual need for fresh sources of material and labour and new markets for its products as making colonialism and neo-colonialism, and therefore war, inevitable. As Brian Fogarty put it: 'Capitalists cannot mind their own business, because capitalist economies must continually expand.' Besides, the pursuit of external wars is sometimes a ploy by the ruling class to control the domestic working class (Fogarty 2000: 57). More generally, economic advantage is represented as a motor of war. Business interests can be seen at work beneath the 'security' discourse of states, particularly the USA (Blum 2003). Some analysts suggest that not only are wars fought to secure resources, wars themselves are a fount of riches to local and international profiteers for whom the least desirable condition is peace. They stress the role of the international private sector in civil wars, particularly extractive industries such as oil and mining (Berdal and Malone 2000). The profit-driven arms trade that has left many African countries awash with small arms and light weapons has fuelled armed conflict across the continent (Volman 1998). More generally it's argued that 'economic belligerents ... may use war to control land and commerce, exploit labour, milk charitable agencies, and ensure the continuity of assets and privileges to a group' (Reno 2000: 64).

Secondly, focusing on political and state power, writers have traced the expansion and collapse of empires as an everlasting cause of war. 'Peoples' expand and colonize others, racializing them in the process. The colonized rebel and assert their ethno-national identity. Particular interest has been shown in the spasm of European expansionism across the world from the sixteenth century, at which point the death toll in wars began to increase dramatically (Eckhardt 1992). The period from the late eighteenth century saw the creation of a system of competitive nation states in Europe that kept the continent hostage to war. States, after all, are the sole wielders of legitimate violence. 'The right of "defence" and "law and order" is exchanged for the state monopoly of murder and the duty of military service to murder others in the state's name, internally or externally' (Young 1984: 99). In the age of the nation state war itself changed. Before around 1780 CE in Europe, war-making had been the sphere of the feudal nobility. The stakes had been land and property, heiresses and honour (Mann 1987). But with the French and American revolutions, war began to involve the masses. The new nations were capable of maintaining large standing armies, paid for by taxation. A willing populace became important in sustaining war capability. Wars accompanied the break-up of the Ottoman empire and those of Western European nations. As Asian and African nations achieved independence from colonizers following the Second World War, many succumbed to civil war between internal ethnic interests. But it was disintegration of the political structure of the USSR in the last decade of the millennium that brought ethno-national movements to the forefront of contemporary social analysis as a cause of armed conflict (Horowitz 1985; Gurr and Harff 1994; Hutchinson 2005).

A third approach the social sciences have taken to understanding war has been to consider militarism, militarization, armies and weapons technologies as not only an effect but also a cause of war. Some definitions may be in order here. 'Militarization' is usually considered to refer to the process of preparation and the resulting state of preparedness of society for war (e.g. Regan 1994). 'Militarism' has been defined as a mindset or ideology that accords high value to military qualities (e.g. Berghahn 1981). Today, however, there's considerable slippage between the terms and 'militarism' is often used to describe not just a body of ideas but the practical influence of military organization and values on social structure and national policies (Shaw 1991). Looking at militarization in historical perspective, Charles Tilly has usefully enlisted the concept of 'coercion', by which he means 'all concerted application, threatened or actual, of action that commonly causes loss or damage to the persons or possessions of individuals or groups who are aware of both the action and the potential damage'. He has suggested that, 'Where capital defines a realm of exploitation, coercion defines a realm of domination.' The means of coercion, like the means of production, can be concentrated in certain hands. He shows how capital accumulation and a growing concentration of the means of coercion can be seen acting together to produce states and their influential military institutions (Tilly 1992: 19).

Much has been written about the relationship between the military, politicians and industry, especially that part of industry producing armaments. In the USA and to a lesser extent in other nation states, the connection is understood as a system of obscure economic power and political influence. It has come to be termed the 'military–industrial complex' (MIC), defined as: 'an informal and changing coalition of groups with vested psychological, moral, and material interests in the continuous development and maintenance of high levels of weaponry, in preservation of colonial markets and in military-strategic conceptions of international affairs' (Pursell 1972: ix).

It is argued that the post-1989 period clearly reveals militarization itself as a prompt to war. No longer legitimated by the threat of the 'Soviet empire', the survival reflex of the military–industrial complex has inspired a search for new enemies (Rogers 1994). However, while the MIC with its hidden links to political power may be dangerously influential, even civil society can be seen to be deeply implicated in the military system. Indeed, one measure of militarization is precisely the extent to which ordinary people are enlisted in popularization of military values and in societal preparedness to undertake war (Regan 1994).

Concurrent with, but quite separate from, these mainstream sociological war studies, feminist social scientists have produced a substantial body of work on the theme of militarism and war. While neither denying nor ignoring economic relations, politicized ethno-national relations and militarization itself as factors in the perpetuation of war, they have introduced an entirely fresh and complementary analysis: *gender relations are also at work here*. For a start, some of these writers have furnished empirical evidence of women's gender-specific experiences in a host of different war-zones. They've shown how women live different lives, suffer different kinds of torture and die different deaths in war (e.g. Lentin 1997; Lorentzen and Turpin 1998; Jacobs et al. 2000; Moser and Clark 2001; Giles and Hyndman 2004). Some have had a regional focus on, for instance, Africa (Turshen and Twagiramariya 1998) or compared the place of women in different conflict zones such as Sri Lanka and the former Yugoslavia (Giles et al. 2003). Some have considered a particular moment in the continuum of conflict, showing for instance how women continue to experience violence in the transition from war to uneasy peace (Meintjes et al. 2001; Cockburn and Zarkov 2002). Some have chosen to analyse gender relations in a particular historical moment, such as the partition of India (Butalia 2000) or the end of the Cold War (Enloe 1993).

Some took up the theme of women's enlistment into armies (e.g. De Groot and Peniston-Bird 2000), women's gender-specific interests in peace (e.g. Ruddick 1989) and some women's practice of negotiating across differences deepened by war (e.g. Cockburn 1998). Some invoke psychology and child-rearing practices to account for men's misogyny and the association of masculinity with war (e.g. Reardon 1996). And for some feminist writers, militarization is the focus. Cynthia Enloe, in a series of carefully crafted studies, has shown how ordinary people and countless aspects of their everyday lives are knitted into the fabric of militarization, and how the thinking and behaviour of women – as mothers and wives, girlfriends, sex workers, factory hands – is important to military planners and policy-makers (e.g. Enloe 2000, 2004). Gradually, too, a sub-field of studies of masculinities in relation to militarism and war has emerged, in which the authors include both women and men. I return to their informative insights in the following section.

Theory grounded in women's experience of war

One reason why the academic disciplines have found it difficult to welcome and incorporate the feminist work described above is that feminists draw, explicitly or implicitly, on a theory – that of systemic male domination, or patriarchy – that tends uncomfortably to contradict, interrupt or complicate mainstream understandings of power. What exactly is it that the theory of patriarchy proposes? In the 1960s sociologists had been writing of 'sex differences', 'sex roles' and 'sex discrimination'. In the 1970s, in the flowering of second-wave feminism, the emphasis, language and concepts changed. An important innovation was the notion of systemic power imbalances between the sexes (e.g. Rubin 1975). Some of these feminist thinkers were kicking off from an intellectual grounding in Marxism. They proposed that just as all societies are class systems, stratified as a hierarchy of social groups with different relationships to the means of production, so all societies are sex/gender systems, in which men and women as two socially distinct groups are differently positioned on the basis of their roles in human reproduction (Kuhn and Wolpe 1978; Sargent 1981).[1]

As the mode of production and its class relations (slavery, feudalism and capitalism) developed through successive periods, so the precise forms of sex/gender relations have also varied historically. In all known societies, however, and so far as we can tell in earlier societies too, men have dominated in the sex/gender system. Although there are indications that women had a significance in society and religion in late Palaeolithic and early Neolithic times in the eastern Mediterranean of which they were subsequently deprived, this is still speculative (Eisler 1988). What is quite clear is that from around the beginning of the third millennium before the Christian era all societies have been patriarchal (Lerner 1986). That is to say, men have dominated women, in the family and by extension in all significant social institutions. Some men have also dominated others, in particular older men have held sway over younger men. Other inequalities derive from relative wealth. At every stage of history we can see the economic class system intersecting with that of sex/gender power in such a way that it is men who hold power in the economy, through ownership or control of land and other forms of wealth. Inequalities are also expressed and institutionalized in political power systems: the state and its bureaucratic structures; in organized religion with its influential priesthoods; and, of course, in the military, managing the means of coercion.

To survive, a power system of any kind must be adaptively reproduced from generation to generation. Just as the systems of class and ethno-national power have evolved historically, so has patriarchy (Miller 1998). A particularly significant shift of gear in gender power relations occurred in Europe with the transition from feudalism to capitalism, involving the gradual overthrow of monarchical and aristocratic rule and its replacement by a fully capitalist mode of production and the ascendency of the capitalist bourgeois class. These social changes were reflected in the liberal philosophies of the Enlightenment and eventually in the new political structures of representative democracy. In gender terms this didn't by any means end male dominance. Nor, though it flattened the hierarchies somewhat, did it end status stratification among and between men. It marked, however, something of a shift in Western cultures from a literal 'rule of the father' to, more simply, 'the rule of men' (Pateman 1988). Though some feminists would for this reason prefer to substitute the term 'andrarchy', most continue to use 'patriarchy' to describe the overall gender order and the local male-dominant gender regimes worldwide that flesh it out, in governments and education systems, businesses and militaries, in church, mosque and synagogue, in the housing estate and in the home.

Because the focus of this book is women actively opposing both patriarchal power relations and war, I have not emphasized the active role of women in sustaining and reproducing patriarchy, militarism and war. Fortunately this has not been neglected by other feminist writers, who've shown how and why the majority of women settle for the status and respect, relative though it is, that patriarchy affords women as wives and mothers within the private sphere of the family (Kandiyoti 1988; Yuval-Davis 1997). As Ann Oakley puts it: 'We are lost without it and lost within it' (Oakley 2002: 27). In stressing the social construction of gender difference, however, I have been clear that women are not being represented here as naturally disposed to 'peace', that is to contradicting the patriarchal logic of war. Likewise, as we know all too well, we are not naturally disposed to refuse our subordination either.

One way women are led to active co-operation in patriarchal power relations is very similar to the way, as we'll see below, men are led into war-fighting: an appeal is made to the very best of their human emotions – love and loyalty. When defining the domain of social life in which patriarchal power operates, analysts have differed. Some have stressed that women's subordination rests on their role in human biological reproduction, others that it arises in the exploitation of their labour, inside and outside the home. Neither stands up alone, and both are clearly true. Additionally, I find particularly persuasive the account of Anna Jónasdóttir, already introduced in chapter 8, which shows us how this appeal to 'the best in us' works. It's refreshing for its combination of radical feminist insight with a Marxist-inspired materialist approach in which she extends 'the material' from the economic to include sex and love (Jónasdóttir 1994).[2] Stepping beyond both biological reproduction and women's labour, Jónasdóttir formulates the central dynamic of the sex/gender system as *sexuality*, broadly imagined as a field of social and political power. Within the scope of sexuality she includes care and love, both emotional and erotic. 'Sexual life,' she writes, 'encompasses its own production: the creation and recreation, the formation and empowerment of human beings – children and adults' (ibid.: 13). She elaborates this proposition in a striking passage.

> [P]revailing social norms, accompanying us from birth and constantly in effect around and in us, say that men not only have the right to women's love, care, and devotion but also that they have the right to give vent to their need for women and the freedom

to take for themselves. Women, on the other hand, have the right to give freely of themselves but have a very limited legitimate freedom to take for themselves. Thus men can continually appropriate significantly more of women's life force and capacity than they give back to women ... *if capital is accumulated alienated labor, male authority is accumulated alienated love.* (ibid.: 26; my italics)

In this way Jónasdóttir sees the sex/gender system as a comparatively independent feature of human societies. Of course, it operates in and through other power structures as well as those of heterosexuality, marriage and family life. The social relations of sex and gender intersect continually in influential ways with the unequal relations of class and those of race/ethnicity/nation, so that male supremacy and female subordination are amplified in disadvantaging patterns of ownership and political representation. But there is something specially telling and poignant in Jónasdóttir's tale in which we see women's vulnerability, oppression and exploitation occurring first and foremost in the very aspects of life women value most and to which they devote great creativity: in-loveness and erotic love, devotion and care. This understanding of patriarchy reflects very well the kind of feminism, as described in chapter 8, I've detected among women grounded in war.

Masculinity and policy: an erect posture on the home front

Patriarchy as system, structure and institutions is in continual cyclical interaction with (shaping and shaped by) gender relations as process and praxis. For men as a social group to retain supremacy over women, as they have done extraordinarily well for at least five thousand years, it's necessary not only for women and femininity to be constituted in the way Jónasdóttir describes but *for men and masculinity to acquire a shape that is adequate to power.* Michel Foucault (1981) has helped us see that power is not just 'held', it's exercised relationally in many interpersonal interactions. This relational quality of power is more evident in the case of sex/gender relations than in those of any other power structure. The ruling class has, and indeed is defined by, material wealth and the means to put it to use to create yet more. In this resides its power. The ruling ethno-national group has its institutionalized cultural supremacy. In a breathtaking metaphor, Arnold Toynbee described the penetrating 'beam of light' the ascendant minority of a dominant civilization radiates beyond its frontiers across those lands it dominates, with nothing to restrict its range 'but the inherent limitation of its own carrying-power' (Toynbee 1972: 234). We might prefer not to see Coca-Cola, Nike trainers, Hollywood and Google in such glorious terms, but propelled by economic interests though they may be, they are manifestations of cultural dominance. Like Christian religion and the valorization of whiteness, they travel with a powerful agency from Western into adjacent ethno-national spaces.

By contrast with the ruling economic class and ascendant 'peoples', the ruling sex, as such, has rather few and pitiful resources. Men don't have a larger or more complex brain than women, nor greater manual dexterity. They do have a 20–25 per cent advantage in musculature and a little more height, a sex-specific hormonal energy and a penis. But the latter is a notoriously unreliable resource. To achieve supremacy for men as a social group, it must be culturally transformed into the phallus. The consolidation of the phallus, the symbolic power that extends physical power (like that beam of light) into the social domain, is achieved through the social and cultural process of masculinization. Masculinity must be produced in appropriate forms and activated in social institutions such as economic enterprises and political structures where patriarchy (men as men) can share some of the wealth and authority deriving from the systems of class and racial supremacy. The church and the military are two institutions where, assisted on the one hand by ideology and on the other by hardware, patriarchy has sustained the ascendency of men with striking success.

The cultural process of masculinization not only produces men as different from women, it produces men as different from each other. In certain modes it gives the individual man a good chance not only of dominating women individually and collectively but acceding to some of the resources of the ruling class and, if he is a member of it, the ability to deploy to his own and his descendants' advantage the authority of the ruling ethno-national group. Another version of masculinity fits men well for male dominance in proletarian cultures and contexts but positively unfits them for class rule and can sometimes pit them against ruling-class men and their institutions of law and order. The heterosexual competition for women also sets individual men against each other. So we see, as R. W. Connell (1987) has pointed out, that the effective reproduction of male supremacy, the continual production of men in multiple and hierarchical yet functional masculine forms, is nothing if not riven with tensions and contradictions. Some men are continually vulnerable to humiliation or subversion by others. Some of the contradictions in patriarchal masculinism arise in the context of militarism and war, so that our oppositional movements can, in theory, look to exploit them. This occurs rarely, but when it does it hinges on the perception that not only is patriarchy strengthened by militarism, *militarism needs patriarchy*. Subverting patriarchal relations, therefore, can be an antimilitarist strategy, as we've seen some gay conscientious objectors discovering for themselves.

Let's take as examples two locations among many others where we can see masculinity in play in the maintenance of a war stance. First is the grooming of properly masculine national cultures disposed to war; second, the cultural grooming of actual men for war-fighting.

The notion of 'honour' is something that links men and patriarchy in the family with men and patriarchy in the nation and state. In South-East Turkey, a heavily militarized region, I found women struggling to support each other against the practice of putting to death women whose behaviour is seen as betraying patriarchal honour. I simultaneously learned that across the nearby hillside facing the national frontier are written in massive letters the words 'The Border is Honour'. This isn't just a quaint archaism from a country well known for its manly/militarist construction of the nation (Altinay 2004); the USA too knows that the making of men and nations goes hand-in-hand. If you neglect manhood you imperil the nation, and a national defeat is a disaster for manhood. As already mentioned, a flush of interesting studies of masculinity has appeared recently. I will single out some where the focus is on US political and popular culture. Suzanne Clark, for instance, set out to understand the invisibility of women writers, and indeed of the work of any category of men or women expressing subversion or hybridity, during the forty years of the Cold War. What she reveals in US national policy of that era is 'a male gendering elevated above all questions of marked gender', a 'hypermasculine national mythology that joined manhood, realism and the frontier ethic' (Clark 2000: 3, 5).

Robert Dean is another who has taken a gender lens to observe the US establishment during the Cold War period, looking in close-up at the small fraternity of policy-makers who took the decision to intervene in Vietnam. 'How,' he asks himself, 'did highly educated men, who prided themselves on their hard-headed pragmatism …

Responding to ethnic aggression against Bosnian Muslims (above, 1994) and the attack on the World Trade Center in Manhattan (right, 2001) women's groups mourned deaths while opposing retaliation inspired by masculine or national honour.

lead the United States into a prolonged, futile, and destructive war in Vietnam and Southeast Asia?' His answer is that foreign policy in this period was profoundly shaped by a masculinist conception of the national interest. 'The notion of a brotherhood, of privilege, power, "service", and "sacrifice",' he says, 'was central to the identity narrative of Kennedy's foreign policy elite.' It demanded a relentless defence of boundaries and an utter rejection of appeasement (Dean 2001: 1, 13). Carol Cohn, whom we met in chapter 5, went out of her way to obtain a position in an institution where she could for a while participate in the world of defence intellectuals, mainly men, who 'spend their days matter-of-factly discussing nuclear weapons, nuclear strategy, and nuclear war'. She traces the way masculine bonding between them generates a bland, even humorous and 'sexy', techno-strategic language to describe mass death. It results in an 'astounding chasm between image and reality'. She shows, like Dean, the acute sensitivity of this fraternity to the potentially demasculinizing effect of toying with notions such as suffering, peace or even negotiation (Cohn 1990: 33).

It's widely understood that the defeat of US military power and the loss of 58,000 American lives in Vietnam brought about a crisis in US national self-respect, felt particularly as an issue of masculine honour. Susan Jeffords, analysing novels and films of the period following the withdrawal from Vietnam, shows not only how that war was gendered ('enemies are depicted as feminine, wives and mothers and girlfriends are justifications for fighting, and vocabularies are sexually-motivated') but that the war was retrospectively discussed in terms 'designed primarily to reinforce the interests of masculinity and patriarchy'. Cultural strategies for the re-masculinization of America at this critical time involved creating a masculine bond across class and colour, emphasizing gender difference and marginalizing women (Jeffords 1989: ix; see also Gibson 1994). How to maintain support for endemic militarization and huge military budgets in a country whose culture doesn't favour swaggering militarism? James McBride suggests that's a problem US policy-makers daily address. In his shockingly titled study *War, Battering and Other Sports*, he suggests the answer is boosting masculinism by tacit tolerance for violence against women and overt fetishization of football and other invasive (penetrative) sports that foster moral virtue (vir = man) in the shape of courage and fortitude. '[T]he game of football reinscribes war and the concomitant values of the warrior as a template for the identity of football enthusiasts – the vast majority of men in America' (McBride 1995: 86).

Military needs: enough aggression, not too much

If these careful studies are to be believed, then, masculinity plays a significant part in the US national social policies at home that underpin 'full spectrum dominance' abroad. It no doubt plays a part in the policy thinking of other nation states too (see, for instance, Joanna Liddle and Sachiko Nakajima 2000 on the manipulation of gender relations in Japanese post-war foreign policy). Masculinity also plays an important part in the more practical matter of producing and managing effective armed forces.

There are two apparently conflicting views of masculinity in relation to war-fighting. One view is that men are often excited by soldiering and war because it satisfies and legitimates aggressive impulses they already feel. This view is supported by accounts that show many quite ordinary men to have found pleasure, even ecstasy, in bloodletting. Examples include Joanna Bourke's contemporary study of veterans' recollections of their emotions during battlefield killing (Bourke 1999) and Barbara Ehrenreich's historical review of the exultant feelings war evokes in those who fight (Ehrenreich 1997). The contrary view is that most men are not naturally aggressive – the intense training to which they must be subjected to turn them into effective soldiers would otherwise be superfluous. The facts are probably more complicated than either view suggests. Either way, chiefs of staff and battlefield commanders have a serious human resource management problem, for neither non-aggressive nor over-aggressive men are what they want in their armed services.

How is a functional army to be created out of hundreds of thousands of individual men, shaped heretofore in a variety of cultures, none of which can be assumed to be exactly appropriate to the tasks they are going to be expected to perform in war? Masculinity takes many forms in the civilian world in which fresh young recruits to the military have grown to adulthood. There are different variants in different social classes and ethnic groups, and teenage boys in particular inhabit a range of subcultures – of music, IT, different kinds of sport, the drugs scene, criminality. The system itself, on the other hand, has clear needs and expectations of military men. Each one must be willing at some future moment to kill and to die, but to do so only in a disciplined and approved manner.

Historians and analysts of war routinely make the point that war is not just aggression. A characteristic formulation is that of Colin Creighton and Martin Shaw in their introduction to *The Sociology of War and Peace*: 'Aggression is not force, force is not violence, violence is not killing, killing is not war' (Creighton and Shaw 1987: 3). In one sense, this often-repeated dictum is clearly correct; war is an institution, not fisticuffs. State policy-makers and military planners seldom make war in anger. War is calculated. On the other hand, coming to war as a feminist it is not so easy to set aside 'ordinary' aggression/force/violence as 'not war', since women are saying loud and clear that they experience coercion by men in similar forms in war *and* peace. We see in newspaper and TV accounts and in human rights reports that the gentlemen's agreement concerning the violence acceptable in war is continually broken. Peacekeepers (like the Canadians in Somalia in 1993) beat up and murder local men in the sheer excitement of the hunt. Invading troops (such as the US unit in Iraq's Abu Ghraib prison in 2003) subject male victims to humiliating torture, indulging sadistic fantasies and destroying masculine self-respect in the enemy. In the wars I've described in earlier chapters of this book there is evidence that women have been raped with penises, fists and miscellaneous weapons, their breasts cut off, their foetuses sliced out. They have been impaled. Is the rationality of institutionalized war enough to explain these things?

I suggest that to understand war and its perpetuation through long historical periods we need to break the academic taboo on noticing and analysing the aggression/force/violence that does occur in military preparation and war. We can learn something useful by digging below the cool policy-making surface of war and bringing to view some of the uncomfortable *cultural* realities of training and fighting. Individual and collective emotions and responses do play a part in war-fighting. Some of them are violent, and some of these are positively cultivated. War as institution is made up of, refreshed by and adaptively reproduced by violence as banal practice, in the everyday life of boot camp and battlefield. Masculinity in its various cultural forms is an important content of that cycle: masculinity shapes war and war shapes masculinity. John Horne made a study of masculinity in war and politics over the hundred years from 1850. What he learned from a close look at two world wars led him to adapt Clauswitz's dictum 'war is a continuation of policy by other means' so as to say 'war is masculinity by other means' (Horne 2004: 31).

To understand war, then, we need to explore, as Horne put it, 'the dense associative life of men' (ibid.: 27). It's through hard cultural *work*, the shaping and manipulation of that sociality, that military managers create their armies. And they meet many challenges as they do so. One is the governance of testosterone. While individual men in their lived lives are not necessarily more aggressive than individual women, both social *and* physical factors tend to produce them as such. The presence of the Y-chromosome in the unborn child prompts a surge of male hormones a quarter of the way through pregnancy, again soon after birth and once more at puberty. Without these occurrences male genitalia do not develop – they literally produce men. At the same time, the level of testosterone in any one body at any one moment, and the level of the excitement and aggression associated with its presence, can be stimulated or diminished by social conditions, occurring by chance or intentionally manipulated (Jones 2002).

In certain widespread and influential male subcultures, the masculinity fostered and rewarded is aggressive and violent. We see this in computer games, in certain forms of music, in popular film, in a fascination with knives, in the gun lobby, and in sport. The mindset they produce is a valuable resource for the military, but it calls for cautious handling. I learn from Leo Braudy's massive work on the changing nature of masculinity in war that in the middle ages there were certain groups of warriors whose behaviour on the battlefield was so extremely violent and so plainly out of control that they appalled even their own side. These men were called berserkers. He is uncertain whether they were some kind of bodyguard for the royalty or simply high on drugs. Either way, 'going berserk' came to mean adopting a style of military masculinity that 'went too far, an edge over which the "normal" warrior would not go in war or in peace time' (Braudy 2005: 42). Braudy suggests the film character Rambo is a fictional berserker.

The figure of the berserker reminds us that it's not every form of violent masculinity that will do for the military. Military commanders must take great care to produce men who will be aggressive enough but not too aggressive, and they leave nothing to chance. As Sandra Whitworth puts it, 'the qualities demanded by militaries – the requisite lust for violence (when needed) and a corresponding willingness to subordinate oneself to hierarchy and authority (when needed) – must be selfconsciously cultivated' (Whitworth 2004: 155). While training his men for aggression, the sergeant fosters male bonding by inferiorizing those who are 'not us', using sexist, homophobic and racist allusions. More positively, the military authorities inculcate discipline around notions of community, whose honour each soldier must defend. 'In terms of masculinity, the invocation of personal honour – with its links to family, tribe and nation – gives eternal justification to an act of immediate violence' (Braudy 2005: 49). Barbara Ehrenreich (1997), surveying war in history, points out that, ironically, bloodlust is induced in men less by appeal to aggressive impulses than to positive feelings of community, generosity, righteousness and self-worth. Killing, the warrior feels the ecstasy of submerging his self in the greater social whole.

Given the significance of masculinity in military training and morale, the incorporation of women into the military poses the military managers' problem in an acute form. If they both need and fear men and masculinity, their ambivalence towards women is greater still. They simultaneously need and feel deep contempt for women and femininity. Women by definition spoil the notion of the masculine military community whose raison d'être is the protection of 'their' women and children. On the other hand, when excesses of violent behaviour by militarized men scandalize public opinion, military managers may see a benefit in introducing 'feminine qualities' to the armed services.

It is indeed the case that several factors have made over-aggressive behaviour by soldiers and units more embarrassing than it once was to commanders and politicians. First, there's more media coverage, giving rise at times to tensions around popular concern, military authority and political reputation. Second, wars are often fought on grounds touted as 'humanitarian', for which minimal force is notionally preferable. Third, military interventions today include 'peacekeeping' operations by supposedly neutral international forces. We must none the less recognize that the basic supposition is still a measure of aggressiveness. Major R. W. J. Weneck, in his submission to an inquiry into the excessive violence visited on individual Somali men by those Canadian peacekeepers, wrote: 'The defining role of any military force is the management of violence by violence, so that individual aggressiveness is, or should be, a fundamental characteristic of occupational fitness in combat units.' He admitted that 'it may be extremely difficult to make fine distinctions between those individuals who can be counted on to act in an appropriately aggressive way and those likely at some time to display inappropriate aggression' (Whitworth 2004: 16, 98).

A factor war-managers have to take into account is that violence is widely experienced by men as erotic. The work of Lisa Price is important for helping us see the connection between masculine violence in peace and war. Sexuality itself, she stresses, is gendered, a relationship of power in which men dominate women. What's more, '[t]he socially-organized and organizing practices of gender and sexuality [are such that] violence is experienced as sex, and, too often, sex is experienced as violence'. Women are constituted as socially sanctioned targets against whom men learn it's appropriate to direct violence. Men's violence against women is different from their violence against other men because it's an expression of male supremacist ideology that endows men with 'a sense of entitlement', a right of access to women's bodies. Women may be battered and subdued by men in the absence of an erotic motivation, or the assault may be erotically charged, as in rape. In both cases the act is aggression and is about domination (Price 2005: 110).[3]

The expressions of male violence against women in war suggest a deep misogyny among militarized men, a hatred of women and the feminine. Only this can account for this kind of sexualized violence in which penises, fists and weapons are interchangeable and the purpose of assault is not only the woman's physical destruction but her social annihilation – 'dishonouring', insemination with the aggressor's seed, infection by HIV/AIDS. Misogyny, of course, is not only hatred, but fear. This was compellingly demonstrated by Klaus Theweleit in his analysis of certain novels written in the 1920s by men of the proto-fascist Freikorps, men who refused demilitarization after the First World War and in their volunteer bands contributed to the defeat of communism and rise of fascism in Germany. In a unique move he approaches these warrior males from the point of view not of their attitudes to war but their attitudes to women, women's bodies and sexuality. He shows that the masculine identity of the officers was shaped by their dread of women and that this dread was linked to an acute racism and anti-communism. (Again we see the intersectionality of gender, race and class.) In the novels authored by Freikorps men, when women are not entirely absent they appear in one of two modes: good and pure (as wife or mother);

or evil and terrifying (active women, especially communist women, who not only may but must be destroyed). Masculinity has to dam and hold back the threatening flood, the bloody mass, of the active feminine. Theweleit doesn't suggest all men are like these fascists. But they are, he says, the tip of the iceberg, and 'it's what lies beneath the surface that really makes the water cold' (Theweleit 1987: 171). Two decades on, he would feel chilled anew by the knowledge that Islamic extremist Mohammed Atta, anticipating his suicide in the attacks of 11 September 2001, specified in his will that no woman should be allowed to touch his corpse or approach his grave (Ehrenreich 2003: 79).

It has been suggested, though, that misogyny alone is not enough to explain male violence against women. In a careful study of sexual killers, Deborah Cameron and Elizabeth Frazer point out that while sexualized murder is a crime they find to be committed only by men (women occasionally kill in jealousy or rage but the killing is not eroticized), the victims and objects of desire are not only women but also homosexual men. Of course homosexual men may be killed for their despised femininity. But these authors find a different link. It lies in the socialization of men to aspire to transcendence, 'the struggle to free oneself, by a conscious act of will, from the material constraints which normally determine human destiny' (Cameron and Frazer 1987: 168–9). Transgressive sexual acts, a source of both pleasure and power to men, can be redefined as transcendence, the distinctive project of the masculine and the proof of masculinity. And though these men may act alone, they don't act in isolation; though they are extremists, they belong to their gender. As Simone de Beauvoir understood, in-loveness, devotion, these woman things, are immanence in which men fear drowning. This fear is the impulse to male bonding and to men's 'civilizational' projects. 'It is the existence of other men that tears each man out of his immanence and enables him to fulfil the truth of his being, to complete himself through transcendence, through escape towards some objective', if necessary by destroying 'her' (de Beauvoir 1972: 171).

Three others: the woman, the labourer and the stranger

'So men,' concludes R. W. Connell, 'predominate across the spectrum of violence ... A strategy for demilitarization and peace must include a strategy of change in masculinities' (Connell 2002a: 34, 38). He is right, and our feminist movements against militarism and war are committed to that strategy, but the odds against such change are stacked in a towering edifice of history.

In her much-respected account of the creation of patriarchy in the ancient Near East, the region whence the clearest archaeological evidence and documentation comes, Gerda Lerner reviews many sources for accounts of the historical subordination of women and the establishment of a male-dominant sex/gender system. In the course of the Neolithic agricultural revolution several processes were closely related. One was the subjection of women to men's power in a patriarchal family system. And here we see the first other stepping on to history's stage: *the woman*. In the transformation of human society that came with settled life and larger communities, men as a group acquired rights in women that women as a group did not have in men. Women became property, their value residing in their labour power, reproductive power and sexuality. They were commodified in bride price, sale or exchange price, prostitution and the value of their children. The earlier matrilocal kinship arrangements were superseded, inheritance passed through the male line and powerful social institutions, ideologies and cultures expressed and embodied male supremacy. These changes were not achieved without coercion. Violence and the threat of violence was always inherent in patriarchy (Lerner 1986; see also Engels 1972).[4]

A second process of change in the late Neolithic was economic. As Gerda notes, archaic states, which formed at different times in different parts of the world, are everywhere characterized by the emergence of commodity production and social hierarchies in which propertied classes gain ascendency. The owning and relatively wealthy self needs labour power. And here is the second other, *the labourer*, perceived as different, inferior and exploitable. This othering, too, is violent, because men and women will not build roads, dig canals, mine the earth or erect pyramids and ziggurats unless coerced. (Not incidentally, this was also the moment in human evolution when society began to substitute domination and exploitation for its older symbiosis with the natural world and is thus a turning point of significance also for the current environmental movement.)

To increase the labour power available to a society and to hold it in productive subordination, neighbouring peoples were often raided for slaves. So the third other is also very early on the stage of history: *the stranger*, the one who belongs to another territory, another culture, embodying racialized difference. And the stranger often has a female body. Anthropologists have shown that exogamy, the practice whereby males took 'wives', by force or arrangement, from outside their tribal community, was widely practised from early times as a way of avoiding the negative effects of incestuous relationships among kin (Lévi-Strauss 1969). But, besides, as Gerda Lerner points out, women were highly valued as slaves because they were not only capable of being exploited for their labour power but valuable for their sexual and reproductive capacities too. In women, slavery was self-reproducing, because their children too were property. Nancy Hartsock points out that in Hellenic society 'the realm of freedom and leisure inhabited by citizens depends on the existence of a realm of necessity populated by women, slaves and laborers – but defined in essence by its female nature' (Hartsock 1985: 204). Transcendence and immanence again. In a triple move, men and the masculine principle are empowered, women and the feminine principle disempowered. It is the moment historians like to call the rise of 'civilization' – although I prefer to distance myself with quote marks out of respect for the many alternative cultures it has destroyed.

What has all this to do with war? It's not coincidental that the institution of war, along with state-building, first occurs in human history in the same period as the emergence of class hierarchy and a patriarchal sex/gender system. The first evidence of inter-group conflict, revealed by contemporary excavation, occurs in the fortifications surrounding some larger villages of the later Neolithic period, where some burials show mass deaths also suggestive of violent strife (Dawson 2001). Written evidence begins to be available from around 3000 BCE, and from this it's clear that already by that time sustained warfare had emerged alongside the production of substantial food surpluses, a greater specialization of labour, the growth of sizeable towns, more complex social structures and hierarchical systems of political control.[5] William Eckhardt, reviewing other historians on war, evolves a persuasive 'dialectical evolutionary theory', stating that the more 'civilized' people became the more warlike they became, a correlation he finds to persist in all phases of history. As Eckhardt puts it, 'expanding civilization increased inequalities that, brought about by armed violence, require armed violence to be maintained against revolutionary and rival forces … the more civilized people became, the more warlike they became' (Eckhardt 1992: 4).[6]

As that 'revolutionary and rival forces' suggests, wars have always been fought, and are still fought, not only 'abroad' against foreigners, for their resource-rich lands, but also 'at home' against subordinated classes for control over the means of production and for political power. A good reminder of the economic class dimension of warfare is a roller-coaster account by Arnold Toynbee of the decline of Hellenic civilization. He writes of the bloody wars of the ruling classes over both internal and external proletariats. On the one hand there were uprisings of the disinherited and despised masses of the society itself, sometimes in coalition with slaves imported from colonized regions of the Mediterranean. Externally, there were revolts of those 'others' worked to near death in the distant plantations (Toynbee 1972).

Gender relations are inseparable from those of class and racialized ethnicity in all these violent power moves. They operate, are operationalized, in and through each other. But the three kinds of power relation can never be directly compared. They function in different ways in connection with war. Wealth furnishes the means of coercion, and amassing wealth is often the main purpose and outcome of war (although wars sometimes cost more than they earn). Cultural/'racial' identity may be a political ordering principle within the state, and externally it often defines the warring entities, the 'civilized' versus 'barbarian' forces, the 'people' and 'foreigners'. This dimension of difference is used rhetorically to generate hatred and so legitimize war, and is also an outcome of war. Gender, however, is different again. Women and men as groups are not protagonists in war. There has never been armed struggle by women against men over their collective interests. The heterosexual relation, the fragmentation of women as a collectivity within the family structure, and the grip of men on the means of coercion have always made this unlikely.

There's little need to rehearse here the many ways gender power relations are expressed in war, since the preceding chapters have illustrated them fully. We've seen how militarism and war have gender-specific effects; how patriarchy intersects with the economic and ethno-national systems that drive war; and how gender factors influence international relations and war policy. The means of coercion, mainly in male hands, derive from masculine technological imaginations. Militarism fosters male dominance, and the propensity to violence in masculine cultures perpetuates the war-proneness of societies. Protection of one's 'own' woman or women has been a perennial excuse for men to fight. In addition, patriarchal ambitions have often motivated war and in this light it's interesting to reflect on the contemporary 'war on terror'. Islamic fundamentalism is a reactionary political movement selectively drawing on religious ideology to re-establish strict patriarchal control over women in the family. And not only Islamic fundamentalism. 'Control over sexuality is a central theme of the social programmes promoted by fundamentalist movements everywhere' (WLUML 2004: xii). The particular 'freedom' that Islamic fundamentalists deplore and challenge in Western modernity is not (as often suggested) the notional freedom of 'Western democracy', but rather women's escape from confinement and control by men in the patriarchal family. Their jihad against the USA catches that country, indeed all Western societies, in a profound three-way contradiction. Women's self-respect and autonomy is hated and feared by the conservative Christian political establishment almost as much as it is hated and feared by the Islamist establishment – witness the extreme misogyny and repressiveness of the religious movements influential with the current Republican administration. On the other hand, the licentious and lubricious exploitation of women and sexuality for commercial gain is a vital economic interest for contemporary capitalism. And between the confusingly conflictual interests of these rival contemporary expressions of patriarchy stands a small but persistent feminist movement resisting the repression and exploitation of women in both Islamic and Western worlds – and opposing the war between them.

The gender effect of war is also felt within a society (as an ethnic effect is felt, when racism is heightened against hostage communities of the 'enemy' living within the state). In war the military elite and class elite combine their strength, and in the same move, since these are men and the authority they wield is modelled on and derived from the patriarchal family and kinship system, male supremacy is consolidated in society at large, the feminine principle yet further eclipsed. We see the dominant male self being shaped and tempered in the soldier who fights modern wars, as in the warrior whose sword forged the city states and empires five millennia ago. War violence is often thought of, particularly by peace activists, as the epitome of destructiveness. It is far better understood as productive – though its products are unwelcome to us. It gives birth to new class elites or strengthens existing ones. It produces racialized identities, deepening the differentiation of 'peoples'. It also produces genders. It affirms men and masculinity in a powerfully effective mode. It produces woman as prize and possession, as baggage and as slave.

The word 'intersectionality', that I defined in the Introduction, has appeared at intervals throughout this book. Its main use has been as a reminder of how positioning in relation to the three main systems of power I've identified as most involved in war (class, race and gender) shapes the lives and chances of individuals and groups. But intersectionality functions also at the systemic level. The power system of economic class based on ownership of the means of production; the power system of ethno-nationalism expressed in communities, states and 'civilizations', and the power system that constitutes sex/gender hierarchy *together* shape human social structures, institutions and relational processes. *Together* they establish 'positions' of relative power, thereby laying down the possibilities and probabilities for individuals and groups that variously inhabit them. No one of them produces its effects in the absence of the other two. Militarization and war are caused, shaped, achieved and reproduced over time by all three. The gender drama is never absent: the male as subject, the female as alien, aliens as effeminate. This is why a theory of war is flawed if it lacks a gender analysis.

§

In closing this account of war and women's responses to it, I invite you to imagine one individual who can reveal to us how the coercive power relations of class, of race and gender intersect so as to shape life and chances, and to exemplify what war has to do with this. She's a woman slave. In case you should think this identity improbable, that slavery is a thing of the past, recall that there are thought to be 27 million slaves in the world today (Bales 2005). This woman was enslaved in war. I sometimes imagine her in Africa, a Dinka woman perhaps, carried off by Arabs in the course of the war in Sudan. I see her in Europe too, a woman from Moldova or Ukraine, trafficked into Kosovo/a, sold to a local pimp, confined in a brothel to service international soldiers. Wherever she is, she's a stranger, the stranger. She's also a labourer, though wageless, working for food and shelter. In addition she is woman, sexually enslaved, her body at her owner's disposal. She is, in other words, the paradigm of intersectionality.

Another word that's recurred in this narrative is 'standpoint'. We've seen women observing war from many different positionalities. In this chapter and the preceding one we've put together what I believe is a plausible anti-war feminism and I've reinterpreted 'from where we stand' as a political standpoint, a feminist one. Now, as I come to the end of the story, I want to make a transversal move on my own account. I know at last where I want to stand in order to obtain a perspective on war that has indisputable authority. I'll step into the footprints of this woman war slave.

From where she stands I see something that surprises me. The struggle no longer seems to be against war itself, or rather not against war alone. War is the most violently coercive form taken by othering, the space in which differentiation becomes lethal. Its means, the means of coercion, are fearful in the extreme. But it is othering itself that is the problem. Assuring the self by objectifying, excluding, diminishing, confining, oppressing and exploiting an other – there's not much you can teach the woman slave about these things. Her project, and perhaps our project therefore, doesn't stop at opposition to militarism and war, and goes beyond even the positive search for peace. It's a project of liberation. Liberation from what? From fear. Because the slave fears her ruler. But even more because the rulers too are afraid. I am afraid of whomever I cast out and down.

Notes

1 A fierce debate took place in the 1980s as to whether feminism should be thinking in terms of 'dual systems' (patriarchy plus capitalism, i.e. a sex/gender system plus a mode of production) or whether what we experience is a unitary system: 'patriarchal capitalism' (Sargent 1981). As in the past, I still today find it necessary to use distinct terminologies to describe two distinct bases and processes of power. Indeed, I introduce a third set of power relations that must be taken account of in any discussion of militarism and war, those of ethnicity/race/nation. Maintaining distinctive vocabularies to describe these phenomena precisely enables the valuable insights of 'intersectionality'.

2 Jónasdóttir makes no claim for her theory outside Western economically developed societies. I was introduced to her work by Colombian women, however, and tend to believe her ideas are relevant in many other cultures.

3 See chapter 8, note 1 on sex/sexual violence.

4 The subordination and control of women by men may in fact have begun long before the Neolithic economic revolution, when human

beings first noted the connection between copulation and pregnancy. Mary O'Brien (1981) has suggested that men, becoming aware of their physical part in procreation, seeking to regain possession of the product of their seed, their own offspring, achieved this in the only way they could, by confining, controlling and commodifying women. She extrapolates from this to suggest that men, insecure as procreators, were driven to become creators – of civilization.

5 The earliest Sumerian records show war to be already an accepted part of human existence in Mesopotamia by the beginning of the 3rd millennium before the Christian era. Egypt from 3000 BCE, the Aegean from 2800 BCE, the Indus valley from 2600 BCE and Syria and Palestine from 2400 BCE were all sites of powerful states, founded and defended against external others by warfare. The earliest style of war was static, typically the besieging of cities. After 1700 BCE, with the invention of bronze metallurgy and the introduction of the horse-drawn chariot, it became more mobile. After 1000 BCE, with the dawn of the Iron Age, came the first infantry formations marching huge distances for military conquest. The system is seen full-blown in the Persian Empire of Darius I in 500 BCE (Humble 1980; Dawson 2001).

6 Supporting this theory is the fact that warfare emerged independently in the Americas at a similar stage of economic and cultural development (Dawson 2001).

Bibliography

Abdullah, Ibrahim and Ishmael Rashid (2004) '"Smallest Victims; Youngest Killers": Juvenile Combatants in Sierra Leone's Civil War', in Abdullah, Ibrahim (ed.), *Between Democracy and Terror: The Sierra Leone Civil War*, Council for Development of Social Science Research in Africa, distributed by African Books Collective, Oxford, pp. 238–53.

Abraham, Arthur (2004) 'The Elusive Quest for Peace from Abidjan to Lomé', in Abdullah, Ibrahim (ed.), *Between Democracy and Terror: The Sierra Leone Civil War*, Council for Development of Social Science Research in Africa, distributed by African Books Collective, Oxford, pp. 199–219.

Africa Recovery (2003) February, pp. 17–19.

Alonso, Harriet Hyman (1993) *Peace as a Women's Issue: A History of the US Movement for World Peace and Women's Rights*, Syracuse, NY: Syracuse University Press.

Altinay, Ayse Gul (2004) *The Myth of the Military-Nation: Militarism, Gender, and Education in Turkey*, New York and London: Palgrave Macmillan.

— (2006) 'Feminism and Violence: Where Do We Stand?' Paper to the Sixth European Feminist Research Conference, *Gender and Citizenship in a Multicultural Context*, University of Lodz, Poland, 31 August–3 September.

Amnesty International (1993) 'Bosnia-Herzegovina: Rape and Sexual Abuse by Armed Forces', London: Amnesty International, January.

— (2005) 'Israel and the Occupied Territories: Conflict, Occupation and Patriarchy. Women Carry the Burden'. On line at <web.amnesty.org/library/index/engmde150162005>, accessed 3 April 2006.

Anderlini, Sanam Naraghi (2000) *Women at the Peace Table: Making a Difference*, New York: United Nations Development Fund for Women.

Anderson, Benedict (1983) *Imagined Communities*, London and New York: Verso.

Anthias, Floya (2002) 'Where Do I Belong? Narrating Collective Identity and Translocational Positionality', *Ethnicities*, 2(4), pp. 491–514.

Anthias, Floya and Nira Yuval-Davis (1989) 'Introduction', in Yuval-Davis, Nira and Floya Anthias (eds), *Woman-Nation-State*, Basingstoke: Macmillan, pp. 1–15.

— (1992) *Racialized Boundaries: Race, Nation, Gender, Colour and Class in the Anti-racist Struggle*, London and New York: Routledge.

Bacchetta, Paola (1996) 'Hindu Nationalist Women as

Ideologues', in Jayawardena, Kumari and Malathi De Alwis (eds), *Embodied Violence: Communalising Women's Sexuality in South Asia*, London and New Jersey: Zed Books, pp. 126–67.

Bales, Kevin (2005) *Understanding Global Slavery: A Reader*, Berkeley and London: University of California Press.

Balibar, Etienne (1991) 'Is There a Neo-racism?', in Balibar, Etienne and L. Wallerstein (eds), *Race, Nation and Class*, London: Verso.

Bangura, Yusuf (2004) 'The Political and Cultural Dynamics of the Sierra Leone War: A Critique of Paul Richards', in Abdullah, Ibrahim (ed.), *Between Democracy and Terror: The Sierra Leone Civil War*, Council for Development of Social Science Research in Africa, distributed by African Books Collective, Oxford, pp. 13–14.

Benjamin, Media and Jodie Evans (2005) *Stop the Next War Now: Effective Responses to Violence and Terrorism*, Makawao, Maui, HI: Inner Ocean Publishing.

Berdal, Mats and David M. Malone (2000) *Greed and Grievance: Economic Agendas in Civil Wars*, Boulder, CO and London: Lynne Rienner.

Berghahn, Volker R. (1981) *Militarism: The History of an International Debate 1861–1979*, Leamington Spa: Berg.

Bergner, Daniel (2005) *Soldiers of Light*, London: Penguin Books.

Berkman, Joyce (1990) 'Feminism, War and Peace Politics: The Case of World War I', in Elshtain, Jean Bethke and Sheila Tobias (eds), *Women, Militarism and War: Essays in History, Politics and Social Theory*, Lanham, MD: Rowman and Littlefield, pp. 141–60.

Blackwell, Joyce (2004) *No Peace without Freedom: Race and the Women's International League for Peace and Freedom 1915–1975*, Carbondale: Southern Illinois University Press.

Blum, William (2003) *Killing Hope: US Military and CIA Interventions Since World War II*, London: Zed Books.

Bose, Sumantra (1999) '"Hindu Nationalism" and the Crisis of the Indian State: A Theoretical Perspective', in Bose, Sumantra and Ayesha Jalal (eds), *Nationalism, Democracy and Development: State and Politics in India*, Oxford, New York, New Delhi: Oxford University Press, pp. 104–64.

Bourke, Joanna (1999) *An Intimate History of Killing: Face-to-face Killing in Twentieth Century Warfare*, London: Granta Books.

Bracewell, Wendy (1996) 'Women, Motherhood and Contemporary Serbian Nationalism', *Women's Studies International Forum*, 19(1/2), pp. 25–33.

Braudy, Leo (2005) *From Chivalry to Terrorism: War and the Changing Nature of Masculinity*, New York: Vintage Books, Random House Inc.

Breaching the Peace (1983) anonymously authored collection of radical feminist papers, London: Only Women Press.

Burbach, Roger and Jim Tarbell (2004) *Imperial Overstretch: George W. Bush and the Hubris *of Empire*, London and New York: Zed Books.

Bussey, Gertrude and Margaret Tims (1980) *Pioneers for Peace: Women's International League for Peace and Freedom 1915–1965*, London and Geneva: Women's International League for Peace and Freedom.

Butalia, Urvashi (2000) *The Other Side of Silence: Voices from the Partition of India*, London: Hurst and Co.

Butler, Judith (1992) *Gender Trouble: Feminism and the Subversion of Identity*, New York: Routledge.

Cameron, Deborah and Elizabeth Frazer (1987) *The Lust to Kill*, Cambridge: Polity Press.

Centre for Women's Studies (1997) *Women and the Politics of Peace: Contributions to a Culture of Women's Resistance*, Zagreb: Centre for Women's Studies.

CFEN (Collectif Femmes en Noir) (2004) 'Femmes en Noir Contre les Centres Fermés et Contre les Expulsions', booklet, Brussels: Collectif Femmes en Noir.

Chabal, Patrick and Jean-Pascal Daloz (1999) *Africa Works: Disorder as Political Instrument*, Oxford: International African Institute, James Currey and Indiana University Press.

Clark, Suzanne (2000) *Cold Warriors: Manliness on Trial in the Rhetoric of the West*, Carbondale and Edwardsville: Southern Illinois University Press.

Cockburn, Cynthia (1998) *The Space Between Us: Negotiating Gender and National Identities in Conflict*, London and New York: Zed Books.

— (2002) 'Women's Organization in the Rebuilding of Postwar Bosnia-Herzegovina', in Cockburn, Cynthia and Dubravka Žarkov (eds), *The Postwar Moment: Militaries, Masculinities and International Peacekeeping*, London: Lawrence and Wishart.

— (2004a) *The Line: Women, Partition and the Gender Order in Cyprus*, London and New York: Zed Books.

— (2004b) 'The Continuum of Violence: A Gender Perspective on War and Peace', in Giles, Wenona and Jennifer Hyndman (eds), *Sites of Violence: Gender and Conflict Zones*, Berkeley and London: University of California Press, pp. 24–44.

Cockburn, Cynthia and Dubravka Žarkov (eds) (2002) *The Postwar Moment: Militaries, Masculinities and International Peacekeeping*, London: Lawrence and Wishart.

Cockburn, Cynthia and Lynette Hunter (eds) (1999) 'Transversal Politics', thematic issue of *Soundings: Journal of Politics and Culture*, 12, summer.

Cockburn, Cynthia with Rada Stakić-Domuz and Meliha Hubić (2001) *Živjeti Zajedno ili Živjeti Odvojeno* (To Live Together or to Live Apart), Zenica, Bosnia-Herzegovina: Medica Women's Association with the Open Society Institute.

Code Pink (2006) 'Global Women Launch Campaign to End Iraq War', press release, 5 January. On line at <www.codepink4peace.org>, accessed 6 January 2006.

Cohn, Carol (1987) 'Sex and Death

in the Rational World of Defense Intellectuals', *Signs: Journal of Women in Culture and Society*, 12(4), summer, pp. 687–718.
— (1990) '"Clean Bombs" and Clean Language', in Elshtain, Jean Bethke and Sheila Tobias (eds), *Women, Militarism and War: Essays in History, Politics and Social Theory*, Lanham, MD: Rowman and Littlefield, pp. 33–55.
— (forthcoming) 'Mainstreaming Gender in UN Security Policy: A Path to Political Transformation', in Rai, Shirin M. and Georgina Waylen (eds), *Analysing and Transforming Global Governance: Feminist Perspectives*, Cambridge: Cambridge University Press.
Cohn, Carol with Felicity Hill and Sara Ruddick (2005) 'The Relevance of Gender for Eliminating Weapons of Mass Destruction', adaptation of a presentation to the Commission on 12 June 2005, Paper No. 38, Stockholm: Commission on Weapons of Mass Destruction.
Cohn, Carol, Helen Kinsella and Sheri Gibbings (2004) 'Women, Peace and Security', *International Feminist Journal of Politics*, 6(1), March, pp. 130–40.
Communalism Combat (2002) 'Genocide Gujarat 2002', *Communalism Combat Journal*, 77–8, Year 8, March–April.
Connell, R. W. (1995) *Masculinities*, Cambridge: Polity Press.
— (2002a) *Gender*, Cambridge: Polity Press.
— (2002b) 'Masculinities, the Reduction of Violence and the Pursuit of Peace', in Cockburn, Cynthia and Dubravka Žarkov (eds) (2002), *The Postwar Moment: Militaries, Masculinities and International Peacekeeping – Bosnia and the Netherlands*, London: Lawrence and Wishart.
Connolly, William E. (1991) *Identity/Difference: Democratic Negotiations of Political Paradox*, Ithaca, NY and London: Cornell University Press.
Creighton, Colin and Martin Shaw (eds) (1987) *The Sociology of War and Peace*, London: Macmillan.
Davis, Uri (1987) *Israel: An Apartheid State*, London and New Jersey: Zed Books.
Dawson, Doyne (2001) *The First Armies*, London: Cassell.
Dean, Robert D. (2001) *Imperial Brotherhood: Gender and the Making of Cold War Foreign Policy*, Amherst: University of Massachusetts Press.
De Beauvoir, Simone (1972) *The Second Sex*, Harmondsworth: Penguin Books.
De Groot, Gerard J. and Corinna Peniston-Bird (eds) (2000) *A Soldier and a Woman: Sexual Integration in the Military*, London: Longman/Pearson Education.
Diamond, Louise and John McDonald (1996) *Multi-track Diplomacy: A Systems Approach to Peace*, West Hartford, CT: Kumarian Press.
DiN (Donne in Nero) (1991) letter exchanged December between *Donne in Nero* women in Torino and Bologna planning the conference of 1992, unpublished typescript.
— (1992) 'Gender and Nation: A

Paradox', preparatory paper prior to conference, Bologna, unpublished typescript.

Drakulić, Slavenka (1993) 'Women and the New Democracy in the Former Yugoslavia', in Funk, Nanette and Magda Mueller (eds), *Gender Politics and Post-Communism*, New York and London: Routledge, pp. 123–30.

Duhaček, Daša (1994) 'Travel on, Europe', in Center for Women's Studies, Research and Communication (eds), *What Can We Do for Ourselves?*, Belgrade: Center for Women's Studies, June.

Eckhardt, William (1992) *Civilizations, Empires and Wars: A Quantitative History of War*, Jefferson, NC and London: MacFarland & Company Inc.

Ehrenreich, Barbara (1997) *Blood Rites: The Origins and History of the Passions of War*, London: Virago.

— (2003) 'Veiled Threat', in Joseph, Ammu and Kalpana Sharma (eds), *Terror Counter-Terror: Women Speak Out*, London and New York: Zed Books, pp. 77–80.

Eisler, Riane (1988) *The Chalice and the Blade*, San Francisco, CA: HarperCollins.

El-Bushra, Judy (2003) *Women Building Peace: Sharing Know-how*, London: International Alert.

Elshtain, Jean Bethke (1985) 'Reflections on War and Political Discourse: Realism, Just War and Feminism in a Nuclear Age', *Political Theory*, 13(1), pp. 39–57.

— (1990) 'The Problem with Peace', in Elshtain, Jean Bethke and Sheila Tobias (eds), *Women, Militarism and War: Essays in History, Politics and Social Theory*, Lanham, MD: Rowman and Littlefield, pp. 255–66.

Engels, Frederick (1972) *The Origin of the Family, Private Property and the State*, New York: Pathfinder Press.

Enloe, Cynthia (1989) *Bananas, Beaches and Bases: Making Feminist Sense of International Politics*, London, Sydney and Wellington: Pandora.

— (1993) *The Morning After: Sexual Politics at the End of the Cold War*, Berkeley and London: University of California Press.

— (2000) *Maneuvers: The International Politics of Militarizing Women's Lives*, Berkeley and London: University of California Press.

— (2004) *The Curious Feminist: Searching for Women in a New Age of Empire*, Berkeley and London: University of California Press.

— (2005) 'What if Patriarchy is "The Big Picture"? An Afterword', in Mazurana, Dyan, Angela Raven-Roberts and Jane Parpart (eds), *Gender, Conflict and Peacekeeping*, Lanham, MD, Boulder, CO, New York, Toronto and Oxford: Rowman and Littlefield, pp. 280–4.

Equality Now (2002) 'Israeli and Palestinian Women Call on the "Quartet" to Create an International Commission of Women Peace Activists', press release, 22 August 2002. On line at <www.equalitynow.org/english/pressroom/press_releases>, accessed 27 August 2002.

Feinman, Ilene Rose (2000) *Citizenship Rites: Feminist Soldiers and Feminist Antimilitarists*, New York and London: New York University Press.

Fine, Robert (1999) 'Benign Nationalism? The Limits of the Civic Ideal', in Mortimer, Edward with Robert Fine (eds), *People, Nation and State: The Meanings of Ethnicity and Nationalism*, London and New York: I.B. Tauris, pp. 149–61.

Fogarty, Brian E. (2000) *War, Peace and the Social Order*, Boulder, CO and Oxford: Westview Press.

Foucault, Michel (1981) *The History of Sexuality, Volume 1, an Introduction*, Harmondsworth: Pelican.

Gallego Zapata, Esther Marina (2003) 'Queremos los barrios de Medellin libres de miedo, guerra y violencia', in La Ruta Pacífica (ed.), *La Ruta Pacífica de las Mujeres: No parimos hijos ni hijas para la guerra*, booklet of essays in English documenting the history and philosophy of La Ruta Pacífica, June, Medellín: Colombia, pp. 107–15.

Galtung, Johann (1996) *Peace by Peaceful Means*, Oslo: International Peace Research Institute and London, Thousand Oaks, CA and New Delhi: Sage Publications.

Gareau, Frederick H. (2003) *State Terrorism and the United States: From Counterinsurgency to the War on Terrorism*, London: Zed Books and Atlanta: Clarity Press.

Gberie, Lansana (2004) 'The 25 May Coup d'état in Sierra Leone: A Lumpen Revolt?', in Abdullah, Ibrahim (ed.), *Between Democracy and Terror: The Sierra Leone Civil War*, Council for Development of Social Science Research in Africa, distributed by African Books Collective, Oxford, pp. 144–63.

Gellner, Ernest (1983) *Nations and Nationalism*, Oxford, UK and Cambridge, USA: Blackwell.

Gerson, Joseph (1991) 'Introduction', in Gerson, Joseph and Bruce Birchard (eds), *The Sun Never Sets: Confronting the Network of Foreign US Military Bases*, Boston, MA: South End Press, pp. 3–28.

Gibbings, Sheri (2004) 'Governing Women, Governing Security: Governmentality, Gender Mainstreaming and Women's Activism at the United Nations', masters thesis, September, Toronto: York University.

Gibson, James William (1994) *Warrior Dreams: Paramilitary Culture in Post-Vietnam America*, New York: Hill and Wang.

Giles, Wenona and Jennifer Hyndman (eds) (2004) *Sites of Violence: Gender and Conflict Zones*, Berkeley and London: University of California Press.

Giles, Wenona, Malathi de Alwis, Edith Klein and Neluka Silva (eds) (2003) *Feminists Under Fire: Exchanges Across War Zones*, Toronto: Between the Lines.

González, Fernán E. (2004) 'The Colombian Conflict in Historical Perspective', in García-Durán, Mauricio (ed.), *Alternatives to War: Colombia's Peace Processes*, issue no. 14 of *Accord: International Review of Peace*

Initiatives, London: Conciliation Resources, pp. 10–17.

Grant, Rebecca and Kathleen Newland (eds) (1991) *Gender and International Relations*, Milton Keynes: Open University Press.

Gurr, Ted Robert and Barbara Harff (1994) *Ethnic Conflict in World Politics*, Boulder, CO, San Francisco, CA and Oxford: Westview Press.

Hacker, Barton (1998) 'From Military Revolution to Industrial Revolution: Armies, Women and Political Economy in Early Modern Europe', in Isaksson, Eva (ed.), *Women and the Military System*, New York, London, Toronto, Sydney and Tokyo: Harvester, Wheatsheaf.

Hanmer, Jalna and Mary Maynard (eds) (1987) *Women, Violence and Social Control*, Basingstoke: Macmillan.

Haraway, Donna J. (1991) *Simians, Cyborgs, and Women: The Reinvention of Nature*, London: Free Association Books.

Harding, Sandra (1986) *The Science Question in Feminism*, Milton Keynes: Open University Press.

Hardt, Michael and Antonio Negri (2005) *Multitude*, London: Penguin Books.

Harford, Barbara and Sarah Hopkins (eds) (1984) *Greenham Common: Women at the Wire*, London: Women's Press.

Hartsock, Nancy C. M. (1985) *Money, Sex and Power: Toward a Feminist Historical Materialism*, Boston, MA: Northeastern University Press.

— (1998) *The Feminist Standpoint Revisited and Other Essays*, Boulder, CO: Westview Press.

Hill, Felicity (2005) '*How* and *When* Has Security Council Resolution 1325 (2000) on Women, Peace and Security Impacted Negotiations Outside the Security Council?', masters thesis, Uppsala: Uppsala University.

Hill, Felicity, Mikele Aboitiz and Sara Poehlman-Doumbouya (2003) 'Non-governmental Organizations' Role in the Build-up and Implementation of Security Council Resolution 1325', *Signs: Journal of Women in Culture and Society*, 28, summer, pp. 1255–69.

Hobsbawm, E. J. (1990) *Nations and Nationalism Since 1780: Programme, Myth, Reality*, Cambridge: Cambridge University Press.

Home Office (2006) *Crime Statistics for England and Wales*. On line at <www.crimestatistics.org.uk>, accessed 1 June 2006.

hooks, bell (2000) *Feminist Theory: From Margin to Center*, London: Pluto Press.

Horne, John (2004) 'Masculinity in Politics and War in the Age of Nation-states and World Wars, 1850–1950', in Dudink, Stefan, Karen Hagemann and John Tosh (eds), *Masculinities in Politics and War: Gender in Modern History*, Manchester and New York: Manchester University Press, pp. 22–40.

Horowitz, Donald L. (1985) *Ethnic Groups in Conflict*, Berkeley and London: University of California Press.

Human Rights Watch (2004a) 'Colombia: Briefing to the 60th Session of the UN Commission on Human Rights'. On line at

<www.hrw.org>, accessed 28 July 2004.
— (2004b) 'Colombia and the "War" on Terror: Rhetoric and Reality'. On line at <www.hrw.org>, accessed 28 July 2004.
— (2006) 'Displaced and Discarded: The Plight of Internally Displaced Persons in Bogotá and Cartagena'. On line at <www.hrw.org>, accessed 3 January 2006.
Humble, Richard (1980) *Warfare in the Ancient World*, London: Cassell.
Hutchinson, John (2005) *Nations as Zones of Conflict*, London, Thousand Oaks, CA and New Delhi: Sage Publications.
Ignatieff, Michael (1999) 'Benign Nationalism? The Possibilities of the Civic Ideal', in Mortimer, Edward with Robert Fine (eds), *People, Nation and State: The Meanings of Ethnicity and Nationalism*, London and New York: I.B. Tauris, pp. 141–8.
International Alert (2002) *Gender Mainstreaming in Peace Support Operations: Moving Beyond Rhetoric to Practice* (Dyan Mazurana and Eugenia Piza Lopez), July, London: International Alert.
International Initiative for Justice in Gujarat (2003) *Threatened Existence: A Feminist Analysis of the Genocide in Gujarat*, Mumbai: Forum Against Oppression of Women.
Iraq Coalition (2003) 'Coalition Provisional Authority Order No. 39: Foreign Investment'. On line at <www.iraqcoalition.org/regulations>, accessed 13 January 2006.
Isaksson, Eva (ed.) (1998) *Women and the Military System*, New York, London, Toronto, Sydney and Tokyo: Harvester, Wheatsheaf.
Jacobs, Susie, Ruth Jacobson and Jennifer Marchbank (eds) (2000) *States of Conflict: Gender, Violence and Resistance*, London and New York: Zed Books.
Jarrett-Macauley, Delia (2005) *Moses, Citizen and Me*, London: Granta Books.
Jayawardena, Kumari (1986) *Feminism and Nationalism in the Third World*, London and New Jersey: Zed Books.
JCW (Jerusalem Center for Women) (2005) 'The Jerusalem Link: A Women's Joint Venture for Peace'. On line at <www.j-c-w.org/principles.htm>, accessed 29 November 2005.
Jeffords, Susan (1989) *The Remasculinization of America: Gender and the Vietnam War*, Bloomington and Indianapolis: Indiana University Press.
Johnson, Rebecca (2005) 'Gender, Race, Class and Sexual Orientation: Theorizing the Intersections', in MacDonald, Gayle, Rachel L. Osborne and Charles C. Smith (eds), *Feminism, Law and Inclusion: Intersectionality in Action*, Toronto: Sumach Press, pp. 21–37.
Jónasdóttir, Anna G. (1994) *Why Women are Oppressed*, Philadelphia, PA: Temple University Press.
Jones, Steve (2002) *Y: The Descent of Man*, London: Abacus.
Kajahiro, Kyle (2003) 'Aloha'Aina vs. Militarism', *The File: News Journal of the Native Hawai'ian Multi-media Network*, 1(6), pp. 1–2.

Kamester, Margaret and Jo Vellacott (eds) (1987) *Militarism Versus Feminism: Writings on Women and War*, London: Virago Press.

Kandeh, Jimmy D. (2004a) 'In Search of Legitimacy: The 1996 Elections', in Abdullah, Ibrahim (ed.), *Between Democracy and Terror: The Sierra Leone Civil War*, Council for Development of Social Science Research in Africa, distributed by African Books Collective, Oxford, pp. 123–43.

— (2004b) 'Unmaking the Second Republic: Democracy on Trial', in Abdullah, Ibrahim (ed.), *Between Democracy and Terror: The Sierra Leone Civil War*, Council for Development of Social Science Research in Africa, distributed by African Books Collective, Oxford, pp. 164–79.

Kandiyoti, Deniz (1988) 'Bargaining with Patriarchy', in *Gender and Society*, 2(3), pp. 274–90.

Kapuściński, Ryszard (2002) *The Shadow of the Sun: My African Life*, London: Penguin Books.

Keck, Margaret E. and Kathryn Sikkink (1998) *Activists Beyond Borders: Advocacy Networks in International Politics*, Ithaca, NY: Cornell University Press.

Kidron, Peretz (ed.) (2004) *Refusenik! Israel's Soldiers of Conscience*, London and New York: Zed Books.

Kirk, Gwyn and Margo Okazawa-Rey (1998) 'Making Connections: Building an East Asia–US Women's Network Against US Militarism', in Lorentzen, Lois Ann and Jennifer Turpin (eds), *The Women and War Reader*, New York and London: New York University Press, pp. 308–22.

Koonz, Claudia (1987) *Mothers in the Fatherland: Women, the Family and Nazi Politics*, London: Methuen.

Korac, Maja (1998) *Linking Arms: Women and War in Post-Yugoslav States*, Uppsala: Life and Peace Institute.

Koroma, Abdul Karim (2004) *Crisis and Intervention in Sierra Leone 1997–2003*, Freetown and London: Andromeda Publications.

Kpundeh, Sahr (2004) 'Corruption and Political Insurgency in Sierra Leone', in Abdullah, Ibrahim (ed.), *Between Democracy and Terror: The Sierra Leone Civil War*, Council for Development of Social Science Research in Africa, distributed by African Books Collective, Oxford, pp. 90–103.

Kuhn, Annette and AnnMarie Wolpe (eds) (1978) *Feminism and Materialism: Women and Modes of Production*, London, Henley and Boston: Routledge and Kegan Paul.

La Ruta Pacífica (2003) *La Ruta Pacífica de las Mujeres: No Parimos Hijos ni Hijas para la Guerra*, Medellin, Colombia.

— (undated) basic leaflet descriptive of the organization.

Lentin, Ronit (ed.) (1997) *Gender and Catastrophe*, London and New York: Zed Books.

Lerner, Gerda (1986) *The Creation of Patriarchy*, Oxford: Oxford University Press.

Lévi-Strauss, Claude (1969) *The Elementary Structures of Kinship*, Boston, MA: Beacon Press.

Levy, Ariel (2005) *Female Chauvinist Pigs: Women and the Rise of Raunch Culture*, New York, London, Toronto and Sydney: Free Press.

Liddington, Jill (1989) *The Road to Greenham Common: Feminism and Anti-militarism in Britain Since 1820*, New York: Syracuse University Press and London: Virago Press.

Liddle, Joanna and Sachiko Nakajima (2000) *Rising Suns, Rising Daughters: Gender, Class and Power in Japan*, London: Zed Books.

Lorentzen, Lois Ann and Jennifer Turpin (eds) (1998) *The Women and War Reader*, New York and London: New York University Press.

McBride, James (1995) *War, Battering and Other Sports: The Gulf Between American Men and Women*, New Jersey: Humanities Press.

McGreal, Chris (2005) 'Israel Redraws the Roadmap, Building Quietly and Quickly', *Guardian*, 18 October, p. 17.

Malcolm, Noel (1994) *Bosnia: A Short History*, London: Macmillan.

Manchanda, Rita, Bandita Sijapati and Rebecca Gang (2002) *Women Making Peace: Strengthening Women's Role in Peace Processes*, booklet, Kathmandu: South Asia Forum for Human Rights.

Mann, Michael (1984) 'Capitalism and Militarism', in Shaw, Martin (ed.), *War, State and Society*, London: Macmillan.

— (1987) 'War and Social Theory: Into Battle with Classes, Nations and States', in Creighton, Colin and Martin Shaw (eds), *The Sociology of War and Peace*, London: Macmillan, pp. 54–72.

Manz, Beatriz (2004) *Paradise in Ashes: A Guatemalan Journey of Courage, Terror and Hope*, Berkeley and London: University of California Press.

Mazurana, Dyan, Angela Raven-Roberts and Jane Parpart (eds) (2005) *Gender, Conflict and Peacekeeping*, Lanham, MD: Rowman and Littlefield.

Mead, Margaret (1965) 'The Anthropology of Human Conflict', in McNeil, Elton B. (ed.), *The Nature of Human Conflict*, Englewood Cliffs, NJ: Prentice-Hall, pp. 65–9.

Meertens, Donny (2001) 'The Nostalgic Future: Terror, Displacement and Gender in Colombia', in Moser, Caroline O. N. and Fiona C. Clark (eds), *Victims, Perpetrators or Actors? Gender, Armed Conflict and Political Violence*, London and New York: Zed Books.

Meintjes, Sheila, Anu Pillay and Meredeth Turshen (eds) (2001) *The Aftermath: Women in Post-conflict Transformation*, London and New York: Zed Books

Miles, Robert (1989) *Racism*, London and New York: Routledge.

Miller, Pavla (1998) *Transformations of Patriarchy in the West, 1500–1900*, Bloomington: Indiana University Press.

Mladjenović, Lepa (1993) 'Universal Soldier: Rape in War', *Peace News*, no. 2364, March, p. 6.

— (2003) 'Feminist Politics in the Anti-war Movement in Belgrade: To Shoot or not to Shoot?', in Giles, Wenona, Malathi de

Alwis, Edith Klein and Neluka Silva (eds), *Feminists Under Fire: Exchanges Across War Zones*, Toronto: Between the Lines, pp. 157–66.

Moghadam, Valentine M. (2005) *Globalizing Women: Transnational Feminist Networks*, Baltimore, MD and London: Johns Hopkins University Press.

Moon, Seungsook (1998) 'Gender, Militarization and Universal Male Conscription in South Korea', in Lorentzen, Lois Ann and Jennifer Turpin (eds), *The Women and War Reader*, New York and London: New York University Press, pp. 90–100.

Morgenthau, Hans (1973) *Politics Among Nations: The Struggle for Power and Peace* (5th rev. edn), New York: Alfred Knopf.

Morokvasić, Mirjana (1986) 'Being a Woman in Yugoslavia: Past, Present and Institutional Equality', in Godantt, Monique (ed.), *Women of the Mediterranean*, London: Zed Books.

Moser, Caroline O. N. (2001) 'The Gendered Continuum of Violence and Conflict: An Operational Framework', in Moser, Caroline O. N. and Fiona C. Clark (eds), *Victims, Perpetrators or Actors? Gender, Armed Conflict and Political Violence*, London and New York: Zed Books, pp. 30–52.

Moser, Caroline O. N. and Fiona C. Clark (eds) (2001) *Victims, Perpetrators or Actors? Gender, Armed Conflict and Political Violence*, London and New York: Zed Books.

Mulheir, Georgette and Tracey O'Brien (2000) *Private Pain, Public Action: Violence Against Women in War and Peace*, Limerick: University of Limerick, and Centre for Peace and Development Studies.

Nashashibi, Rana (2003) 'Violence Against Women: The Analogy of Occupation and Rape. The Case of the Palestinian People', Palestinian Counseling Center. On line at <www.pcc-jer.org/Articles>, accessed 5 January 2006.

Network: East Asia–US–Puerto Rico Women against Militarism Network (2002a) one-page descriptive leaflet.

(2002b) Final statement, network 4th international meeting, Seoul, S. Korea.

— (2004) one-page descriptive leaflet.

New Profile (2005) 'Request for General Support 2005–6', unpublished paper, 16 October.

Nikolić-Ristanović, Vesna (1998) 'War, Nationalism, and Mothers in the Former Yugoslavia', in Lorentzen, Lois Ann and Jennifer Turpin (eds), *The Women and War Reader*, New York and London: New York University Press, pp. 234–9.

Oakley, Ann (2002) *Gender on Planet Earth*, Cambridge: Polity Press.

O'Brien, Mary (1981) *The Politics of Reproduction*, Boston, MA, London and Henley: Routledge and Kegan Paul.

O'Hanlon, Michael E. (2005) *US Defense Strategy after Saddam*, monograph, the Letort Papers, July. On line at <www.strategicstudiesinstitute.army.mil>, accessed 12 January 2006.

Oldfield, Sybil (2000) *Alternatives to Militarism 1900–1989*, Wales: Edwin Mellen Press.

Pateman, Carole (1988) *The Sexual Contract*, Cambridge: Polity Press.

Peterson, V. Spike (ed.) (1992) *Gendered States: Feminist (Re)visions of International Relations Theory*, Boulder, CO and London: Lynne Rienner.

— (1998) 'Gendered Nationalism: Reproducing "Us" Versus "Them"', in Lorentzen, Lois Ann and Jennifer Turpin (eds), *The Women and War Reader*, New York and London: New York University Press, pp. 41–9.

Peterson, V. Spike and Anne Sisson Runyan (1993) *Global Gender Issues*, Boulder, CO, San Francisco, CA and Oxford: Westview Press.

Petrović, Ruza (1985) *Etnicki mesoviti brakovi u Jugoslaviji* (Ethnically Mixed Marriages in Yugoslavia), Belgrade: University of Belgrade, Institute for Sociological Research.

Pieterse, Jan Nederveen (1997) 'Deconstructing/reconstructing Ethnicity', *Nations and* Nationalism, 3(3), November, pp. 365–96.

Pineda, Rocío (2003) 'Lisístratas colombianas a las puertas del nuevo milenio', in La Ruta Pacífica (ed.), *La Ruta Pacífica de las Mujeres: No parimos hijos ni hijas para la guerra*, booklet of essays in English documenting the history and philosophy of La Ruta Pacífica, June, Medellín: Colombia, pp. 64–72.

PNAC (Project for the New American Century) (1997) 'Statement of Principles', 3 June. On line at <www.newamericancentury.org>, accessed 12 January 2006.

— (1998) 'Letter to President Clinton on Iraq', 26 January. On line at <www.newamericancentury.org>, accessed 12 January 2006.

Price, Lisa S. (2005) *Feminist Frameworks: Building Theory on Violence against Women*, Halifax, Canada: Fernwood Publishing.

Pursell, Carroll W. Jr (ed) (1972) *The Military–Industrial Complex*, New York and London: Harper & Row.

Raging Womyn (1984) pamphlet in reply to *Breaching the Peace* (1983), no publisher.

Rashid, Ismail (2004) 'Student Radicals, Lumpen Youth and the Origins of Revolutionary Groups in Sierra Leone', in Abdullah, Ibrahim (ed.), *Between Democracy and Terror: The Sierra Leone Civil War*, Council for Development of Social Science Research in Africa, distributed by African Books Collective, Oxford, pp. 66–89.

Reader, John (1998) *Africa: A Biography of the Continent*, London: Penguin.

Reardon, Betty (1996) *Sexism and the War System*, New York: Syracuse University Press.

Regan, Patrick M. (1994) *Organising Societies for War: The Processes and Consequences of Societal Militarisation*, Westport, CT and London: Praeger.

Rehn, Elisabeth and Ellen Johnson Sirleaf (2002) *Women, War, Peace: The Independent Experts'*

Assessment on the Impact of Armed Conflict on Women and Women's Role in Peace-building, New York: United Nations Development Fund for Women.

Religious Society of Friends (2006) *Quaker Faith and Practice*. On line at <http://quakersfp.live.poptech.coop/qfp>, accessed 15 May 2006.

Reno, William (2000) 'Shadow States and the Political Economy of Civil Wars', in Berdal, Mats and David M. Malone (eds), *Greed and Grievance: Economic Agendas in Civil Wars*, Boulder, CO and London: Lynne Rienner, pp. 43–68.

Rodriguez, Jorge Rojas (2004) 'Political Peacebuilding: A Challenge for Civil Society', in García-Durán, Mauricio (ed.), *Alternatives to War: Colombia's Peace Processes*, no. 14, *Accord: International Review of Peace Initiatives*, London: Conciliation Resources, pp. 34–7.

Rogers, Paul (1994) 'A Jungle Full of Snakes? Power, Poverty and International Security', in Tansey, Geoff, Kath Tansey and Paul Rogers (eds), *A World Divided: Militarism and Development After the Cold War*, London: Earthscan Publications, pp. 1–25.

Roseneil, Sasha (1995) *Disarming Patriarchy: Feminism and Political Action at Greenham*, Buckingham and Philadelphia: Open University Press.

Rubin, Gayle (1975) 'The Traffic in Women', in Reiter, Rayna (ed.), *Towards an Anthropology of Women*, New York: Monthly Review Press.

Ruddick, Sara (1989) *Maternal Thinking: Towards a Politics of Peace*, London: Women's Press.

Sachar, Howard M. (1996) *A History of Israel: From the Rise of Zionism to Our Time*, New York: Alfred A. Knopf.

Said, Edward W. (1995) *The Politics of Dispossession: The Struggle for Palestinian Self-determination 1969–1994*, London: Vintage.

Sánchez, Gonzalo and Donny Meertens (2001) *Bandits, Peasants and Politics: The Case of 'La Violencia' in Colombia*, Austin: University of Texas Press.

Santos, Boaventura de Sousa (2004) 'The World Social Forum: Towards a Counter-hegemonic Globalization', in Polet, François and CETRI (eds), *Globalizing Resistance: The State of Struggle*, London and Ann Arbor, MI: Pluto Press.

Sargent, Lydia (ed.) (1981) *The Unhappy Marriage of Marxism and Feminism: A Debate on Class and Patriarchy*, London: Pluto Press.

Seifert, Ruth (1995) 'War and Rape: A Preliminary Analysis', in Stiglmayer, Alexandra (ed.), *Mass Rape: The War against Women in Bosnia-Herzegovina*, Lincoln and London: University of Nebraska Press, pp. 54–72.

Setalvad, Teesta (2002) 'When Guardians Betray: The Role of Police', in Varadarajan, Siddarth (ed.), *Gujerat: The Making of a Tragedy*, New Delhi: Penguin Books, pp. 177–211.

Shah, Anup (2005) 'High Military Expenditure in Some Places', 1 June. On line at <www.globalissues.org>, accessed 12 January 2006.

Shaw, Martin (1984) 'Introduction', in Shaw, Martin (ed.), *War, State and Society*, London: Macmillan, pp. 1–22.
— (1987) 'The Rise and Fall of the Military-democratic State', in Creighton, Colin and Martin Shaw (eds), *The Sociology of War and Peace*, London: Macmillan.
— (1991) *Post-military Society: Militarism, Demilitarization and War at the End of the Twentieth Century*, Cambridge: Polity Press.
Shlaim, Avi (2005) 'Sharon's Iron Wall', *New Statesman*, 31 October.
Silber, Laura and Allan Little (1995) *The Death of Yugoslavia*, London: Penguin Books, BBC Books.
SIPRI (Stockholm International Peace Research Institute) (2006) *Yearbook 2006*. On line at <http://www.sipri.org/contents/milap/milex/mex_trends.html.>, accessed 18 August 2006.
Smillie, Ian, Lansana Gberie and Ralph Hazleton (2000) *The Heart of the Matter: Sierra Leone, Diamonds and Human Security*, Ottawa: Partnership Africa Canada.
Smith, Anthony D. (1995) *Nations and Nationalism in a Global Era*, Cambridge: Polity Press.
Smith, Dorothy E. (1988) *The Everyday World as Problematic: A Feminist Sociology*, Milton Keynes: Open University Press.
Stasiulis, Daiva, and Nira Yuval-Davis (eds) (1995) *Unsettling Settler Societies: Articulations of Gender, Race, Ethnicity and Class*, London, Thousand Oaks, CA and New Delhi: Sage Publications.
Stiglmayer, Alexandra (ed.) (1995) *Mass Rape: The War against Women in Bosnia-Herzegovina*, Lincoln and London: University of Nebraska Press.
Stoetzler, Marcel and Nira Yuval-Davis (2002) 'Standpoint Theory, Situated Knowledge and the Situated Imagination', *Feminist Theory*, 3(3), pp. 315–33.
Swerdlow, Amy (1990) 'Motherhood and the Subversion of the Military State: Women Strike for Peace Confronts the House Committee on Un-American Activities', in Elshtain, Jean Bethke and Sheila Tobias (eds), *Women, Militarism and War: Essays in History, Politics and Social Theory*, Lanham, MD: Rowman and Littlefield, pp. 7–28.
Tate, Winifred (2004) 'No Room for Peace? United States' Policy in Colombia', in García-Durán, Mauricio (ed.), *Alternatives to War: Colombia's Peace Processes*, no. 14 of *Accord: International Review of Peace Initiatives*, London: Conciliation Resources, pp. 70–3.
Taylor, Clark (1998) *Return of Guatemala's Refugees: Re-weaving the Torn*, Philadelphia, PA: Temple University Press.
Tešanović, Jasmina (1994) 'Women's Writing in War', in Center for Women's Studies, Research and Communication (eds), *What Can We Do for Ourselves?*, Belgrade, June.
Theweleit, Klaus (1987) *Male Fantasies*, Cambridge: Polity Press.
Tickner, J. Ann (1991) 'Hans Morgenthau's Principles of Political Realism: a Feminist Reformulation', in Grant,

Rebecca and Kathleen Newland (eds), *Gender and International Relations*, Milton Keynes: Open University Press, pp. 27–40.
— (1992) *Gender in International Relations: Feminist Perspectives on Achieving Global Security*, New York and Oxford: Columbia University Press.
Tilly, Charles (1992) *Coercion, Capital and European States AD 990–1992*, Cambridge, MA and Oxford: Blackwell.
Toynbee, Arnold (1972) *A Study of History*, Oxford and London: Oxford University Press and Thames and Hudson.
Trask, Haunani-Kay (1993) *From a Native Daughter: Colonialism and Sovereignty in Hawai'i*, Honolulu: University of Hawai'i Press.
Turshen, Meredeth and Clotilde Twagiramariya (eds) (1998) *What Women Do in Wartime: Gender and Conflict in Africa*, London and New York: Zed Books.
UNDP (United Nations Development Programme) (1994) *New Dimensions of Human Security*, Human Development Report 1994. On line at <http://hdr.undp.org/reports/global/1994/en/pdf/hdr_1994>, accessed 3 April 2006.
— (2004) Human Development Index. On line at <http://hdr.undp.org/reports/global/2004/pdf/hdr04_HDI.pdf>, accessed 3 April 2006.
United Nations (2002) *Women, Peace and Security: Study of the United Nations Secretary General as Pursuant Security Council Resolution 1325*, 16 October, S/2002/1154, New York: United Nations.
US Federal Government (2002) 'The National Security Strategy of the United States'. On line at <www.state.gov/documents>, accessed 13 January 2006.
Vagts, Alfred (1959) *A History of Militarism*, Westport, CT: Greenwood Press.
Varadarajan, Siddharth (ed.) (2002) *Gujerat: The Making of a Tragedy*, New Delhi: Penguin Books.
Volman, David (1998) 'The Militarization of Africa', in Turshen, Meredeth and Clotilde Twagiramariya (eds), *What Women Do in Wartime: Gender and Conflict in Africa*, London and New York: Zed Books, pp. 150–62.
Walzer, Michael (1977, revised 1992) *Just and Unjust Wars: A Moral Argument with Historical Illustrations*, New York: HarperCollins/Basic Books.
Werbner, Pnina and Nira Yuval-Davis (1999) 'Women and the New Discourse of Citizenship', in Yuval-Davis, Nira and Pnina Werbner (eds), *Women, Citizenship and Difference*, London and New York: Zed Books, pp. 1–38.
Whitworth, Sandra (1994) *Feminism and International Relations*, New York: St Martin's Press.
— (2004) *Men, Militarism and Peacekeeping: A Gendered Analysis*, Boulder, CO and London: Lynne Rienner.
Wieringa, Saskia (1995) 'Introduction: Sub-versive Women and Their Movements', in Wieringa, Saskia (ed.), *Sub-versive Women: Women's Movements in Africa, Asia, Latin America and the*

Caribbean, London and New Jersey: Zed Books, pp. 1–22.

Williams, Kayla (2005) *Love My Rifle More than You: Young and Female in the US Army*, London: Weidenfeld and Nicolson.

WILPF (Women's International League for Peace and Freedom) (2001a). On line at <www.wilpf.int.ch/racialjustice/durban.htm>, accessed 17 January 2006.

— (2001b). On line at <ww.wilpf.int.ch/programme/program01-04> accessed 17 January 2006.

— (2006a). On line at <www.wilpf.int.ch/unitednations>, accessed 18 January 2006.

— (2006b). On line at <www.wilpf.org>, accessed 17 January 2006.

— (2006c). On line at <www.wilpf.int.ch/programme>, accessed 17 January 2006.

WIPSA (Women's Initiative for Peace in South Asia) (2000) 'Journey for Peace: Women's Bus of Peace from Delhi to Lahore', booklet, New Delhi: WIPSA.

WIPSA and South Asian Network of Gender Activists and Trainers (2003) *Shanti Parasmoni: South Asian Women's Journey for Friendship and Peace*, New Delhi: WIPSA and SANGAT.

WLUML (Women Living Under Muslim Laws) (2004) *Warning Signs of Fundamentalisms*, London: Women Living Under Muslim Laws.

Women's Panel (2002) *The Survivors Speak: How Has the Gujarat Massacre Affected Minority Women?* (Syeda Hameed, Ruth Manorama, Malini Ghose, Sheba George, Farah Naqvi and Mari Thekaekara), sponsored by Citizens Initiative, Ahmedabad, 16 April.

Woodward, Susan L. (1995) *Balkan Tragedy: Chaos and Dissolution After the Cold War*, Washington, DC: Brookings Institution.

Woolf, Virginia (1977) *Three Guineas*, Harmondsworth: Penguin Books.

Young, Iris Marion (1990) *Justice and the Politics of Difference*, Princeton, NJ: Princeton University Press.

Young, Nigel (1984) 'War Resistance, State and Society', in Shaw, Martin (ed.), *War, State and Society*, London: Macmillan, pp. 95–116.

Youngs, Gillian (2004) 'Feminist International Relations: A Contradiction in Terms? Or: Why Women and Gender are Essential to Understanding the World "We" Live in', *International Affairs*, 80(1), pp. 75–87.

Yuval-Davis, Nira (1997) *Gender and Nation*, London, Thousand Oaks, CA and New Delhi: Sage Publications.

— (1999) 'What is Transversal Politics?', in Cockburn, Cynthia and Lynette Hunter (eds), 'Transversal Politics', thematic issue of *Soundings: Journal of Politics and Culture*, 12, summer, pp. 94–8.

Zajović, Staša (1994) 'I am Disloyal: Nationalism, War, Personal Experience', in Center for Women's Studies, Research and Communication (eds), *What Can We Do for Ourselves?*, Belgrade, June.

ŽuC: Žene u Crnom (1994, 1997, 1998, 1999, 2001, 2002 and 2005) successive issues of *Women and Peace*, Belgrade: Žene u Crnom, 11 Jug Bogdanova.

Index

Aawaaz e-Niswaan organization (India), 26–30
Abu Husein, Mariam Yusuf, 124, 125–30
Adamu, Samira, 201
Afghanistan, 95; visit by Code Pink, 64–5; war in, 13, 50, 53
Africa Women's Committee for Peace and Development (AWCPD), 37–8
Ahmetaj, Nora, 93
Akeela, an activist, 27
Albanian women, 92–3
Aldermaston, Women's Peace Camp, 166, 177, 226
Alianza Iniciativa de Mujeres Colombianas por la Paz (IMP), 46, 153, 155
alienation, concept of, 6; alienated love, 242
All People's Congress Party (APC) (Sierra Leone), 33
Alonso, Harriet, 134
Amargi Kadın Akademisi (Istanbul), 159, 207
Aman (Peace) organization (Delhi), 169
American Friends Service Committee, 61
Amnesty International, 108, 140, 147
Anarchistim neged Hagader (Anarchists against the Wall) (Israel), 110
Andjaba, Martin, 141–2
andrarchy, concept of, 240
Angala organization (India), 215
de Angelis, Pat, 56–7
ANSWER organisation (USA), 61
Anthias, Floya, 100, 199
anti-militarism, 130, 147, 190, 221, 228; feminist, 203–4
anti-nationalism, 192–3, 195, 198
anti-racism, 199, 200
anti-war movement (mainstream), 4, 9–12, 61, 110, 156, 181, 186, 191, 203, 208, 216, 230; masculinity of, 61, 94–5, 110, 216, 224 *see also* Movimiento de Objeción de Conciencia
Aristophanes, *Lysistrata*, 20–1
Arria formula meetings, 142, 145
Asian Women's Human Rights Council (AWHRC), 52, 160, 168
assassination, 18, 190; in Palestine, 116; of women leaders, 17
Associazione per la Pace (Italy), 94
asylum-seeking women, 157, 201
Atta, Mohammed, 252
Augustine, St, 185
Autodefensas Unidas de Colombia (AUC), 14–15, 153
Autonomous Women's Centre Against Sexual Violence (Belgrade), 86, 89–90, 93

Babri Masjid mosque, demolition of, 24, 27
Badawi, Khulood, 113, 119–20, 123, 124
Bala, Nazlie, 93
Ballantyne, Edith, 140–1
Bangura, Zainab, 36, 37
Barghouti, Amal Kreishe, 114, 116
'Baring Witness' protest, Marin County, 217
Basque nationalism, 179, 193
Bat Shalom (Israel), 106, 112–14, 115, 119, 121–2, 123, 200; Northern, 124, 125–30, 194
Beach, Jennifer, 164, 229
de Beauvoir, Simone, 252
Benjamin, Medea, 62–3, 64
Berkman, Joyce, 132–3
berserkers, 249
Bharatiya Janata Party (BJP) (India), 24, 32
Bhushan, Madhu, 215
Bin Laden, Osama, 50
Black Sash Movement (South Africa), 51
Blanc, Judy, 51
body, female, 254, 257; agency of, 6; as booty of war, 20; as site of violence, 31; colonization of, 231; political use of, 176–8, 176
Bosnia-Herzegovina, 2, 52, 81, 82, 95, 102, 103, 183

Boston Consortium on Gender, Security and Human Rights, 145
Bourke, Joanna, 247
Bozinović, Neda, 94
Braine, Lila, 59
Braine, Naomi, 59, 60, 220
Bratunac, 103; massacre in, 104
Bremer, Frederika, 132
British Peace Society, 132
Brownell, Mary, 40
Broz, Josip ('Tito'), 80–1
Bryant, Gyude, 41
Bush, George W., 49–50, 63, 65
Butler, Sandy, 157–8, 165, 171

Cameron, Deborah, 252
Camp David negotiations, 107
Campaign for Nuclear Disarmament (CND), 227
Canadian troops, violence of, in Somalia, 250
Cappellitti, Gabriella, 182
Casa de la Mujer (Bogotá), 18
Casas, María Isabel, 23
Catalan nationalism, 193
Celotto, Patrizia, 183
Central Intelligence Agency (CIA) (USA), 190
Centre for Anti-War Action (Belgrade), 84
Centre for Women War Victims (Zagreb), 91, 95
Centre of Women's Studies and Gender Research (Belgrade), 86
Centro di Documentazione delle Donne (Bologna), 100
Chakravarty, Uma, 24
Chazan, Naomi, 154
Chechnya, 95
Cheney, Dick, 49
child combatants, 15, 34–5, 42, 58, 182
Chowdhury, Anwarul, 140
Cinato, Ada, 157
Citizens for Peace in Space, 176
Citizens' Initiative (Ahmedabad, India), 26
citizenship, 20, 122–3, 194, 197, 198, 223, 254
Civil Society Assembly for Peace, 18
Clark, Suzanne, 244
class, analysis in women's anti-war activism, 28, 30, 65, 68–9, 84, 226, 228, 230–1; in Guatemala, 190; of Palestinians in Israel, 122; relations, 1, 6–8, 239–43, 246–7, 251, 253; as motivation in war, 8, 11, 13, 18, 236, 255–7
Coalition of Women for Peace (Israel), 59, 111, 194
Code Pink: Women for Peace, 9, 48, 50, 62–6, 158, 164, 170, 202
coercion, 17, 190, 237, 248, 253; means of, 213, 237, 240, 255, 258
coherence, between ends and means, 178, 180 *see also* prefigurative struggle; of analysis/dialogue, 11, 204.
Cohn, Carol, 145, 148, 149, 246
Collectif Femmes en Noir contre les Centres Fermés et les Expulsions (CFEN) (Brussels), 157, 169, 201
Colombia, 8, 95, 153, 155, 171–2; warfare in, 13–23, 189, 208
Commission on Weapons of Mass Destruction, 149–52
Committee for the Search for Peace (Colombia), 17
Community Alliance Lane County (CALC), 166
Connell, R.W., 243, 252
conscientious objection, 225 *see also* Movimiento de Objecion de Conciencia, refusal to serve *and* war resisters
Conscientious Objection Network (Belgrade), 85–6
Conté, Lansana, 39, 40
Copelon, Rhonda, 45, 140
Courts of Women, 168–9
Cox, Mabell, 37, 42
Creighton, Colin, 248
Croatia, 95, 100, 192–3, 210, 212
Cruisewatch, 176
Cultural Centre Damad (Serbia), 102
Cyprus, 2

De Ambrogio, Marianita, 183
Dean, Robert, 244–6
DeLargy, Pam, 146
demilitarization, 19, 23, 68, 76, 188, 224, 251–2
democracy, 36; principles of, 167
Dhanapala, Jayantha, 144
Diallo, Cellou Dalein, 41
Diamond, Lucy, 39
diamond trade, in wartime, 36, 38

Djindjić, Zoran, 103
Dolev, Sharon, 124
Dones per Dones (Barcelona), 44, 95, 164, 193
Donini, Elisabetta, 93–4, 100, 182, 203
Donne in Nero (Italy), 52, 85, 93, 94, 157, 158, 203, 229
dowry deaths, 215
drugs, smuggling of, 41
Duhaček, Daša, 86, 87
Durebang organization (South Korea), 74, 75
Durrant, Patricia, 142
Dyfan, Isha, 142

e-mail: mailing lists, 66, 111, 158, 159, 214; use of, 68, 102
East Asia-US-Puerto Rico Women's Network against Militarism, 9, 48, 67–78, 170
Eckhardt, William, 254
Economic Organization of West African States (ECOWAS), 188; Monitoring Group (ECOMOG), 186
Ehrenreich, Barbara, 247, 250
El Taller International, 52, 160, 168
ELENA Priština centre, 93
Elshtain, Jean Bethke, 192
En Pie de Paz journal, 179, 216–17
English language, use of, 27, 203
enlistment in the military, 77 *see also* soldiering
Enloe, Cynthia, 100, 145, 222, 231, 239
Equality Now organization, 154
ethnic cleansing, 196
ethnic otherness, 192–202
ethnicity: and intersectionality 101, 149, 242, 255; and nation, 192; and race, 7, 199; as a factor in war, 88, 258; in feminism, 228
ethno-nationalism, 7, 257
Evans, Julie, 63
everyday life: effects of war on, 15–17; valorization of, 208–9

fascism, 135, 183; and masculinity, 196, 215, 251–2; in India, 26, 215; in Yugoslavia, 80, 189
Feinman, Ilene Rose, 223
Female Auxiliary Peace Societies, 132
feminism, 11, 20, 22, 30–33, 46, 57, 121–2, 86–87, 130, 198, 207, 221–3, 225–30, 258; and war studies, 231–59; backlash against, 230; in India, 156; in Yugoslavia, 83–6; liberal, 61, 228; materialist, 6, 241; radical, 6, 226, 228, 241; second-wave, 135; socialist, 156, 228
Feministička 94 publishing house (Belgrade), 86–7
Femmes Africa Solidarité (FAS), 37–8, 43
Field of Blackbirds, battle of, 196
Fifty-Fifty campaign (Sierra Leone), 37
Filosof, Fanny, 201
Fogarty, Brian, 236
Food and Agricultural Organization (FAO), 137
football, fetishization of, 246–7
Forca, Ksenija, 226
Ford Foundation, 145
foreigner, as other, 7, 231, 255 *see* also stranger
Forum against the Oppression of Women (India), 26, 27–30
Forum for African Women Educationalists, 37
Foucault, Michel, 242
Fox Keller, Evelyn, 233
Frazer, Elizabeth, 252
Freikorps, 251–2
Friends of UNSC Resolution 1325, 144
Fuerzas Armadas Revolucionarias Colombianas (FARC), 14, 15

Gabriela organization (Philippines), 164
Gadhafi, Muammer, 35
Gaitán, Jorge Eliécer, 14
Galtung, Johann, 191
Gattullo, Chiara, 161, 204
gay men: experience of, 220–1; killing of, 252
gender: analysis of militarism and war, 8, 12, 18, 20, 35, 37–8, 86–7, 111, 143, 145, 147, 149, 169, 202, 215, 231, 234, 238, 246, 255–7; and anti-war movement, 9, 61, 216, 224; and intersectionality, 7–8, 68, 88, 149, 199, 228, 242, 251, 255, 257; and militarism, 100, 196; and nationalism, 45, 96, 197–8; and nuclear weapons, 152; and sexuality, 251; and violence, 31, 139, 191, 201; as relation of power, 6–8, 229, 240,

255; as social construction, 222, 241, 257; difference, in attitudes to war, 1; in experience of war, 120, 139, 208, 234, 238; post-modern understanding of, 217, 220; hierarchy 6, 257; identity, 100; in International Relations discipline, 234; in national policy, 242–7; in UN activity 141, 144–5; in UNSC 1325, 148–9, 152; issues in armed conflict 141, 142; mainstreaming, 142, 145, 147; perspective, 7, 154, 166 (in UN peacekeeping operations) 139; processes, 6, 242; structures, 26; studies (and women's studies), 86–7, 90, 145, 159, 226, 235; theory, 5, 232, 235
gender order, 6, 11, 147, 240
Genovese, Mariella, 182
Gerson, Joseph, 67
Gibbings, Sheri, 146
Global Fund for Women, 43
Global Network against Weapons and Nuclear Power in Space, 176
Godinho-Adams, Natercia, 145
Gorelick, Sherry, 173
Granero, Margherita, 161, 229
Grau, Elena, 178
Greenblatt, Terry, 61, 154
Greenham Common Women's Peace Camp, 63, 135–6, 165, 167, 174–6, 179, 209, 210–11; *Breaching the Peace*, 227–8; 'Embrace the Base' action, 170, 175, 210–11, 226; use of witch symbolism, 170
Grupo Mujer y Sociedad (Colombia), 18
Guandalini, Mariarosa, 94
Guatemala, 214; peace agreement in, 189, 191
Guinea, 38, 39
Gujarat, genocide in, 13, 23–33
Gulf War, 136
gun culture: link with masculine identity, 152; opposition to, 149
Gush Shalom (Peace Bloc) (Israel), 110

Hague Appeal for Peace, 140, 147
Hameed, Syeda, 164
Hanmer, Jalna, 235
Haraway, Donna, 209
Harding, Sandra, 233
Hartsock, Nancy, 233, 254
Hawai'i, 68, 76; anti-militarism in, 198–9
Hazeley, Florella, 37
Heinrich-Böll Stiftung, 102
Helie, Anissa, 45, 46
Heyzer, Noeleen, 141
Hilali, Idan, 225
Hill, Felicity, 141, 143, 146; address to Blix Commission, 149–52; master's thesis, 146, 148
Hindu nationalism, 8, 23–33 *passim*, 197–8, 215
HIV/AIDS, 37, 251
honour, concept of, 244
honour killings, 215, 244
hooks, bell, 207
Horne, John, 248–9
van Houten, Carol, 166
human rights, 184, 228; of women, 19–20
humanitarian war, 182, 188, 250
Husain, Sahba, 169
Hussein, Saddam, 49, 50, 65

identity, 205; construction of, 100–1; issue of, 88–93; manipulation of, 80–3
Iiyambo, Aina, 146
India, 8, 13, 172; independence struggle in, 198; violence against women in, 214
Inter-agency Task Force on Women, Peace and Security (United Nations), 144
International Action Network on Small Arms (IANSA), 149
International Alert organization, 43, 146, 147
International Congress of Women, 133
International Convention on the Prevention and Punishment of the Crime of Genocide, 167
International Criminal Court, 109
International Criminal Tribunal on the Former Yugoslavia, 45
International Initiative for Justice in Gujarat (IIJG), 26, 30–3, 45, 167
International Institution of Exhumation and Identification, 104
International Peace Research Association, 140, 145
International Peace Update, 137
International relations, 11–2, 49, 133,

183, 209, 255; discipline (IR), 145, 185, 232–4; and feminism, 209, 232–4.
International Women's Commission (IWC), 154
International Women's Committee for Permanent Peace, 134
Internet, use of, 59, 111, 202
intersectionality, 7–8, 68, 88, 101, 140, 149, 199, 251, 255, 257–8; concept of, 7–8; of power structures, 8, 257–8
Intifada: first, 51, 107, 119; second, 58, 108, 110, 117, 119
Iraq: visit by Code Pink, 65; war against, 50, 53, 136, 186
Iraqi Women's Will, 66
Isha l'Isha (Haifa), 154
Islam, 37, 80; subordination of women within, 46
Ispahani, Mahnaz, 143
Israel, 2, 49, 50, 95, 224–5, 226; disengagement from Gaza Strip, 110; establishment of, 106–9; law on Equal Rights for Women, 154–5; military service in, 223 (refusal of, 224); occupation of Palestinian land, 194; peace movement in, 117–18; two-state solution, 194–5; Women in Black visits to, 93; women in, 106–31 *see also* Palestinian issue
Italy, 9
Izquierdo, Almudena, 94

Jameson, Melissa, 60
Jamila, an activist, 145
Japan, 77
Jeffords, Susan, 246
Jerusalem, 94; status of, 117, 120
Jerusalem Center for Women (JCW) (Marcaz al-Quds la I-Nissah), 106, 112, 114
Jerusalem, East, 113
Jerusalem Link, 106, 112, 114–15, 120–1, 129, 154
Jews Against the Occupation (JATO) (USA), 59
Jews for Racial and Economic Justice (JFRE) (USA), 59
John, Helen, 167–8, 173, 174–6
Johnson, Rebecca, 174–6, 210
Jónasdóttir, Anna, 21, 211, 241–2
Jones, Sian, 174–6, 177
Jordan, Vera, 194
jus ad bellum/jus in bello, 185
justice: for Palestinians, 50, 52, 114, 118, 126, 157; in Guatemala, 189–90, 214; in Gujerat, 23–33 *passim*; post 9/11, 57; post-war, 19, 28, 45, 79; tension with peace, 10, 134–5, 181–191 *passim*
Justicia para Nuestras Hijas (Justice for our Daughters) (USA), 57
Jusu-Sheriff, Yasmin, 41

Kabbah, Ahmad Tejan, 34, 39, 41
Kadima Party (Israel), 110
Kajosević, Indira, 53–6
Kanaka Maoli people, 76
Kashmir: armed conflict in, 169; rape in, 214–15
Keck, Margaret, 146
Keshet, Yehudit, 118, 123
Khalidi, Natasha, 114, 115, 116, 120–1
Khan, Sabah, 30
Khoury, Samira, 125–30
Kidron, Peretz, 224–5
King, Angela, 141
King, Martin Luther, 58
Kingston, Maxine Hong, 64
Kirk, Gwyn, 77–8
Klein, Naomi, 65
Klot, Jennifer, 141, 146
Korac, Maja, 90
Korea, South, 68–9, 75, 77; military prostitution in, 74
Kosovo/a, 83, 92, 93, 103
Koštunica, Vojislav, 103
Kumar, Corinne, 52, 160, 168–9
Kurdish and Turkish women, connections between, 159
Kurdistan, 186
Kuwait, Iraqi invasion of, 185
Kyoto Protocol, 137

labourer, as other, 12, 252–3, 257
Lamberti, Raffaella, 100
Lamperer, Linda, 75
Lamptey, Comfort, 144
land, women's relationship with, 128
land laws, discrimination against Palestinians, 122
land reform, 75; in Guatemala, 190
law, uses of, in anti-war activism, 166–9
League of Communists (Yugoslavia), 81, 83, 84

League of Nations, 134
Lee, Anne, 176
Left movements, 12, 14–5, 49, 51, 60–1, 110, 122, 125, 128, 176, 178, 180, 190–1, 194; and peace movement, 9, 12, 44, 61, 203; women and, 122, 135, 156–7, 180, 215–6, 226, 230 *see also* Movimiento de Objeción de Conciencia
Lerner, Gerda, 253, 254
Lerner, Tali, 224
lesbians, 26, 46, 60, 84, 158, 211, 220–1, 227
Liberia, 33, 39
Liddington, Jill, 132
Liddle, Joanna, 247
Ligue Internationale de la Paix et de la Liberté, 132
Lilit organization (Yugoslavia), 84
lobbying campaigns, 4, 57, 165
location, use of term, 7
love, 21, 23, 42, 76, 179, 206, 211, 216, 241–2, 252

M'Bayo, Mabel, 39, 40, 42
M'Carthy, Rosaline, 38, 39
Machsom-Watch (Israel), 111, 123
Madres of the Plaza de Mayo (Argentina), 51
Magallón, Carmen, 179
Maillé, Béatrice, 144
Makua Valley (Hawai'i), land issue in, 76
Malekar, Molly, 113–14, 119, 122
mainstream, definition of, 12
Manchanda, Rita, 209
Manipur (India), naked protest in, 177–8
Mano River Union, 44
Mano River Women's Peace Network (Marwopnet), 37, 38–9, 40–1, 43, 165, 188, 202, 203; 'border work', 41; UN Prize for Human Rights, 44
Manorama, Thangiam, killing of, 177–8
Marin County, naked protest in, 217
Marshall, Catherine E., 211
Martin, Florence, 140
Martín Sanchéz, Concepción (Concha), 95, 100, 208
Marxism, 6, 184, 239
masculinity/ies, 36, 61, 69, 196, 231, 246; and honour, 250; and nationalism, 195–6; and transcendence, 252; and war, 6, 231, 239, 247–9, 257, (in Sierra Leone war) 35–6, 42; and weapons, 149, 152; as cultural, 11, 227–8, 243–4, 249; as policy issue, 213, 242–6; change in, 252; difficulty of addressing, 149, 214, 230; fascist, 251–2; in military training, 247–252; institutionalisation of 229, 243; militarized, 68, 88, 148–9, 171, 207, 214, 225, 249; of anti-war movement, 61, 95, 110, 216, 224; propensity to violence, 212–15, 255; studies of, 239, 244
Massalha, Manal, 123
Maynard, Mary, 235
Mazali, Rela, 224
Mazurana, Dyan, 146
Mazzawi, Nizreen, 125
Mbikusita-Lewanika, Inonge, 142
McBride, James, 246
Medica Women's Therapy Centre (Zenica), 91–2
Meertens, Donny, 16
Meira Paibi women's movement (India), 177
Mendez, Luz, 142
Mendl, Wolf, 185
Menwith Hill military base, 176
La Mesa Mujer y Conflicto Armado (Colombia), 23
Mexico, 214
Miličević, Jadranka, 88–9, 91
militarism: and feminism, 222–3, 225, 227, 238; and masculinity, 61, 149, 171, 227, 229–30, 239, 244; and nationalism, 24, 61, 196, (in Yugoslavia) 86–8, 93, 95, 100, 103, 226, (in Israel) 111, 130, 225, (in Turkey) 159, 207 (of USA) 68, 77; and patriarchy, 24, 61, 85–7, 171, 196, 226, 241, 244, 255; and sport, 246–7; as system, 62; definition of, 237; sociology of, 235–7
militarization, 9, 57, 67, 69, 74, 77, 100, 103, 130, 137, 149, 156, 165, 168, 190–1, 221, 223, 229, 257; definitions of 237–9
military expenditure, global, 77
military recruitment in schools, 166
military-industrial complex (MIC), 238
Million Women marches, 61

Milosević, Slobodan, 82–3, 93, 103, 188–9, 196
Mindanao, 69, 76
Mischkowski, Gabriela, 45
misogyny, 230, 239, 251–2, 256
Mladjenović, Lepa, 84, 88–9, 94, 183–4, 188
modalità, 157, 164
Mohamed, Faiza Jama, 142
Mohammed, Yanar, 66
Montenegro, 102
Morgenthau, Hans, 232–3
motherhood, 11, 209–12
Movement of Democratic Women for Israel (TANDI), 112
Movimiento de Objeción de Conciencia (MOC) (Spain), 44, 94–5
Movement for the Restoration of Democracy (MRD) (Sierra Leone), 36
Mozambique, 198
Mujeres de Negro (Women in Black): (Colombia), 44; (Spain) 45, 95, 164, 166, 183, 208, 209
Mujeres que Crean (Medellín), 19
Mulheir, Georgette, 212
Muna, Maha, 140
Muslims, 23–33 *passim*, 81, 103–4, 169, 183, 188; 'demographic threat' of, 84

Nagka organization (Philippines), 75
Nainar, Vahida, 32–3, 45
Nakajima, Sachiko, 247
Nakaya, Sumie, 146
naked protests, 177–8, 217
Nakhba, 106–9, 119
Naser-Najjab, Nadia, 117–8, 121–2
National Abortion Rights Action League (NARAL), 61
National Conciliation Commission (Colombia), 17
National Patriotic Front of Liberia, 34
National Provisional Ruling Council (NPRC) (Sierra Leone), 34
nationalism, 181–205; as racism, 126; civic, 197; feminist response to, 83–6; masculinity of, 244; ideology of, 195–9; Serbian, 196, 197; use of term, 10–11
Nazism, 183; and masculinity, 196, 251–2 *see also* fascism
New Profile organization (Israel), 59, 111, 130, 224–5, 226
NGO Working Group on Women and Armed Conflict, 140, 143, 144–5
Niboyet, Eugenie, 132
Nicaragua, 183
nonviolent direct action, 4, 109–10, 174–7
nonviolent resistance, 83, 92, 107, 182–3, 215
North Atlantic Treaty Organization (NATO), 48, 188–9; bombing of Belgrade, 93
Northern Ireland, 2, 212
Nuclear Non-Proliferation Treaty, 152
nuclear weapons, 167, 177, 178; British protests against, 174

Oakley, Ann, 213, 241
objeción fiscal, 164
O'Brien, Tracey, 212
Okazawa-Rey, Margo, 77
Oldfield, Sybil, 225
Olive Leaf Circles, 132
One Thousand Women for Peace, 203
Organización Feminina Popular (Colombia), 44
Organization of Women's Freedom in Iraq, 66
organizational structures of women activists, 10, 59, 66
Oslo Accords, 107, 124
othering, 258; legitimation of, 130; refusal of, 79, 106–31, 202; use of term, 7–8 *see also* ethnic otherness
Ottoman Empire, 80

pacifism, 19–20, 180, 181–205; dilemma of, 186; use of term, 10–11
Palestine: expropriation of land, 128; Jewish settlements in, 109, 110, 113, 120; Women in Black visits to, 93; women in, 106–31
Palestine Liberation Organization (PLO), 107
Palestinian issue, 50, 53, 58, 59, 60, 61, 79, 157, 193–4; important for Women in Black, 52
Palestinians, 182; citizens of Israel, 9, 106, 112, 113, 119, 122–5, 194, 200; in Occupied Territories, 9, 106; vanished villages of, 127
Papahanaumoku, 76
patriarchy: and class structures, 243, 255; and nationalism, militarism,

24, 61, 68, 85–8 *passim*, 100, 193, 195, 197–8, 225–6, 244; and peace/left/anti-war movements, 84, 216, 221, 225; as factor in war, 230–1, 252; as intersectional with other power structures, 8, 254–5; concept of, 6, 229, 240; creation of, 253; feminist theory of, 11, 226, 235, 239–42 *passim*, 258; historical evolution of, 240; in women activists' analyses, 11, 20–1, 24, 26–7, 41, 46, 61, 68, 85–90 *passim*, 100, 108, 121, 129, 131, 157, 171, 198, 221, 225–9 *passim*, 242; interaction with gender processes, 242, 246; interests in contemporary war, 256; structures of, 242–3; theory of, 11, 239–242; violence of, 89, 156, 159, 212–5, 253; women's active role in, 6, 32, 102, 197, 241
peace: concept of, 191, 192; women's interests in, 239
peace camps, women's, 173–6
peacekeeping operations, 44, 139, 141, 144, 186, 188, 214, 250
PeaceWomen portal, 138, 143
Penington, Isaac, 184–5
Perez, Carmen Valencia, 76
Peters, Rebecca, 149
Peterson, V. Spike, 234
phallus, symbolic power of, 243
Philippines, 68–9, 75; resistance in, 198
Philippines Working Group (PWG), 69, 75
Pine Gap peace camp, 174
Pineda, Rocío, 21
politica trasversale, concept of *see* transversal politics
Poole, Maureen, 37
positionality, 7–8, 11, 30, 69, 92, 101, 127, 181, 197, 205, 221, 258; concept of 7–8
Pratt, Memunata, 37, 41
Pratt, Nana, 38, 39
prefigurative struggle, 178–80
Prieto, Patricia, 18
prison sentences for activism, 167–8
Project for the New American Century (PNAC), 49
prostituted women, rights of, 74
prostitution, military, 69, 74–5, 149, 214
Puerto Rico, 68, 75
Putumayo (Colombia), mobilization in, 22–3

Al-Qaeda, 49, 50
Quakers *see* Religious Society of Friends

race, concept of, 7, 12 *see also* ethnicity
racism, 11, 137, 181–205; construction of enmity, 129; in Israel, 123, 124, 126, 194, 200
Rantisi, Raja, 117–18, 121–2
rape, 18, 22, 31, 35, 139, 167, 212, 213, 248; as aspect of genocide, 45; as tool for ethnic cleansing, 82; as war crime, 149; failure to prosecute, 45; in Kashmir, 214–15; in war, 89–90, 92; Israeli occupation as, 121; marital, 27; murder of women, 32; policing of women, 17; politically motivated, 16; sensationalization of, 213
Rashtriya Swayamsevak Sangh (RSS) (India), 24
Raymond, Terri Keko'olani, 170, 198
Reality Tours, 111
Reardon, Betty, 140
Reclusa, Montse, 179–80
Redepaz network (Colombia), 17–18
refugee camps: Palestinian, 107, 111; visiting of, 40
refugees, 90; Palestinian, rights of, 117
Rehn, Elizabeth, 146
Reid, Frances, 165
Religious Society of Friends, 56, 132, 184–5
Republika Srpska, 103
research approach, 3–5
responsibility and guilt, relationship between, 104
Revolutionary United Front (RUF), Sierra Leone, 33–7, 38
Ribera, Isabel, 179
right of return, of Palestinians, 115, 118, 120, 194
rights of women, 83, 84, 139, 228
ritual, women's use of, 170–2
Rodríguez Gimena, María del Mar, 94
rooting, concept of, 101
Rosenwasser, Penny, 171
Rubinstein, Edith, 210
Ruddick, Sara, 211
Rumsfeld, Donald, 49, 64
Runyan, Anne, 234

Russia, 95
La Ruta Pacifica de las Mujeres, 18–23, 43, 153, 164, 171–2, 202, 208, 216, 229; awarded Millennium Peace Prize, 43
Rwanda, 52; genocide in, 186

Sabarmati express incident (India), 25
SAFE Korea organization, 69, 74
San Francisco Women in Black, 160, 164, 229
Sánchez, María Eugenia, 20, 43, 216
Sánchez, Olga Amparo, 18
Sangh Parivar movement (India), 24, 25
Sankoh, Foday, 34, 35, 36, 37, 38
'sans papiers' women, 157
Sarajevo, 91; siege of, 188
Šarenkapić, Žibija, 102
School of the Americas, 190
Second World War, 183
security, 192; of women, 234 (concept of, 78)
Selek, Pinar, 159
self, concept of, 7–8
Seneca Falls peace camp, 136, 174
separation wall in Israel, 109, 195; demonstrations against, 110; opposition to, 113, 171
September 11 attacks, 49, 57, 60, 233
Serbia, 9, 100, 102, 192, 210; women's antimilitarism in, 79–105
Setalvad, Teesta, 25
sex workers, rights of, 27
sex/gender system, 6, 12, 239–242, 253–4, 258 *see also* gender order
sexual servitude, 16, 35, 257–8 *see also* slavery
sexuality, 27, 60, 221, 228, 241–2, 251–3, 256
Shalom Achshav (Peace Now) (Israel), 110
Shamas, Maha Abu-Dayyeh, 154–5
Sharon, Ariel, 58, 60, 107, 109–10
Shaw, Martin, 248
Sheehan, Cindy, 65
Shibli, Aida, 113, 119, 123, 124, 130, 195, 200
shifting, concept of, 101
Siegrist, Saudamini, 146
Sierra Leone, 8, 13, 33–43, 165, 186
Sikkink, Kathryn, 146
silence: of vigils, 51, 56; political use of, 172–3
Sirleaf, Ellen Johnson, 146
situated knowledge/imagination, 7, 204–5, 209
slavery, 19, 20, 33, 200, 239, 253–8 *see also* sexual servitude
Slovenia, 94
small arms and light weapons: association with masculinity, 152; gathering of, 37; monitoring of, 41
Smith, Dorothy, 209
Snellings, Lieve, 158
sociology of war, 232, 235–9
soldiering, women's involvement in, 222–5, 239
Solomon, Judy, 59
Spain, 9; women activists in, 94–100
Srebrenica, 103–4; massacre in, 104, 188
standpoint: epistemology, 6–7, 11, 205; feminist, 11, 30, 227, 232, 258
Stojanović, Boban, 220–1
Stojanović, Slavica, 86, 89
stranger, as other, 12, 199, 231, 253–4, 257 *see also* foreigner
street activism, 160–4
Sudan, 52
Sugana, Celine, 158, 172
suicide bombing, 108, 117
SUIPPCOL programme, 43
Sukkot festival, celebration of, 126–7
Svirsky, Gila, 111, 194
Swanwick, Helena, 216
symbolism, women activists' use of, 22, 170–2

Ta'ayush (Life in Common) (Israel), 110
Tanzania, intervention in Uganda, 186
Taylor, Charles, 34, 36, 39, 40
Taylor-Lewis, Agnes, 39
Tešanović, Jasmina, 86, 87, 161
Terrell, Mary Church, 138
Thatcher, Margaret, 174
theory: use of, 5; grounded in women's experience, 239–42
Theweleit, Klaus, 251–2
Thorpe, Christiana, 37
Tickner, Ann, 145
Tilly, Charles, 237
torture, 92; of women, 16
Toynbee, Arnold, 242, 255
Track-2 diplomacy, 39
transnational networks against war, 48–78, 132

transversal politics, 9, 101, 204–5
Trask, Haunani-Kay, 198–9
Traubmann, Lily, 113, 115, 125–30
Trident missile system, 166
Turkey, 159, 224, 244

Umm el Fahm, 127
Unidad Revolucionaria Nacional Guatemalteca (URNG), 190
Union of Soviet Socialist Republics (USSR), 136; collapse of, 237; threat of, 238
United for Peace and Justice, 61
United Kingdom (UK): violence against women in, 212–3; women's camps in, 173–6
United Nations (UN), 132–55 *passim*; Decade for Women, 135 *see also* peacekeeping operations
UN Children's Fund (UNICEF), 137
UN Commission on the Status of Women (CSW), 139
UN Department for the Advancement of Women (DAW), 141
UN Department of Peacekeeping Operations, 144
UN Development Fund for Women (UNIFEM), 43, 141, 142, 146, 154, 202; Women, War and Peace portal, 143
UN Economic and Social Council (ECOSOC), 137, 139–40
UN General Assembly: Resolution 181, 106–7; Resolution 194, 115; Resolution 242, 109
UN Mission in East Timor (UNTAET), 144
UN Mission in Sierra Leone (UNAMSIL), 43
UN Security Council, 140; Resolution 1325 (on Women, Peace and Security), 10, 38, 134, 138–43, 148, 152 (in Israel and Palestine, 154)
UN World Conferences on Women 139; Fourth (Beijing), 36, 52, 140, 160
United States of America (USA): agenda in Colombia, 15; Cold War-period establishment, 244–6; defeat in Vietnam, 246; military aid to Israel, 109; military domination by, 48–9, 77; military expenditure of, 67–8, 77; re-masculinization of, 246; women's soldiering in, 223
United States' Women's Peace Party, 133
Urgent Action Fund (UAF), 43
Uribe, Álvaro, 15
Urubá (Colombia), massacres in, 22

Vamos Mujer (Medellín), 19
Veseli, Haxhere, 145
Vieques, Puerto Rico, health effect of militarization, 75–6
Vieques Women's Alliance, 76
Vietnam, intervention in Cambodia, 186
vigilling, 51, 160–4, 170, 177; methodology of, 161
Vimochana organization (Bangalore), 156, 158, 160, 214–15, 229
violence: as method of resistance, 182; domestic, 89, 121, 137, 214; experienced as erotic, 251; in Indian society, 156; in individuals, 58; in war, 248 (productive, 256); of militarism, 249; of Palestinians, 182; of police, campaigns against, 27; opposition to, 165; reduction of, 204; seen as continuum, 190; male sexual, 6, 16, 30, 31, 191, 212–15; structural, 191
La Violencia (Colombia), 14
Vishwa Hindu Parishad (VHP), 24
Visitare Luoghi Difficili organization, 94, 100
Visiting Forces Agreements, 69, 75
Vrowen in 'T Zwart (Leuven), 158

Walker, Alice, 64
Walzer, Michael, 185–6
war: as institution, 248; as masculinity, 249; concept of, 232; effects on everyday life, 15–17; factors of perpetuation of, 235; gender effects of, 255, 256; gender issues in, 238; just war, 183, 185; lack of study of, 235; origins of, 254; protecting women in, 148; role of private sector in, 236; sociology of, 235–9; women's responses to, 13–47
'war on terror', 9, 15, 49, 60, 62, 69, 200, 214, 233, 256; criticism of, 203
war resisters, 94, 224, *see also* conscientious objection, Movimiento de Objeción de Conciencia *and* New Profile
War Resisters' League, 56, 61
war studies, 231–59

warwomenpeace.org, 202
websites, 4–5, 56, 111, 143; as research tool, 4–5
Weil, Simone, 234
Weiss, Cora, 140
Weneck, R.W.J., 250–1
Werbner, Pnina, 197
West African Association of Women (WAWA), 37
Whittington, Sherrill, 144
Whitworth, Sandra, 146, 149, 249
Williams, Kayla, 223
Wilson, Diane, 63
women: as other, 12, 252–8; as perpetrators of violence, 43; as slaves, 257; autonomy of, feared, 256; commodification of, 253; experience of oppression, 120; hatred of, 231; role of, 196; sanctioned as targets of violence, 251; symbolic status of, 198; transformation to war survivors, 206; valued as slaves, 254
Women Act Against Military Violence (Okinawa), 75, 165
Women Against Fundamentalisms, 46
Women and Armed Conflict workshop, 139–40
Women for Life on Earth, 165
Women for Peace, 9
Women for Peace (Serbia), 102
Women in Black, 2–3, 9, 44, 48, 50, 51–3, 66, 94, 102, 159, 160, 189, 192, 193, 202–3, 215, 220; in US context, 60–2; international encounters of, 91–2; origins of, in Israel, 48, 51, 62; relation to anti-racism, 200
Women in Black groups: Bay Area, 61, 157, 165, 170–1; Belgrade, 95, 102 *see also* Žene u Crnom protiv Rata; Berkeley, 160; Gulf Coast, 160, 172–3, 217; India, 214; Israel, 85, 111; Italy, 181–3 *see also* Donne in Nero; Jerusalem, 58; London, 2, 213–14; Madrid, 94; Public Library, New York, 53–8, 173; Spain, 216 *see also* Mujeres de Negro; Tokyo, 181; Union Square, New York, 58–60, 173, 220; Washington DC, 63
Women Visiting Difficult Places, 94, 100
Women's Caucus for Gender Justice, 140, 147
Women's Commission for Refugee Women and Children, 140, 147
Women's Forum (Sierra Leone), 36
Women's Initiative for Peace in Greece and Turkey (Winpeace), 159–60, 166
Women's Initiative for Peace in South Asia, 164–5, 209
Women's International League for Peace and Freedom (WILPF), 10, 56, 63, 133–8, 158, 183, 200, 217; and the United Nations, 132–55; anti-racism of, 137–8; Interracial Committee, 137; organization and scope of, 136–8
Women's Peace and Arbitration Auxiliary, 132
Women's Peace Party (USA), 137, 138
Women's Peace Politics seminar (Belgrade), 101
Women's Pentagon Action (1980), 135
Women's Strike for Peace (WSP), 135
Women's Studies Centre (Belgrade), 86–7, 89
Women's Summits to Redefine Security, 68
women-only organizing, 1, 174, 215–22
Woolf, Virginia, 198
World March of Women, 202
World Social Forum, 52, 203

Yesh Gvul (Israel), 224–5
Yom al Ard (Land Day), 128
Young, Iris Marion, 145, 222
Youngs, Gillian, 233
Yugoslavia, former, 95, 210; national identity of, 80–3
Yuval-Davis, Nira, 45–6, 100, 101, 197, 199

Zaidenberg, Yehudit, 125–30
Zainab, a market vendor, 42
Zajović, Staša, 84, 94, 102, 103, 193, 231
Zamir internet server, 90
Zaretsky, Edna, 200
Žene u Crnom protiv Rata, Belgrade, 52, 53, 83–97 *passim*, 100, 101–5, 158, 161, 183, 189, 192, 193, 202, 220–1, 224, 226; international encounter, 56; Millennium Peace Prize, 56
Ziferblat-Knopova, Yana, 111
Zionism, 126, 193–4